ZEO
HEAD WITHOUT A BODY

CIRCUS

Cinders to Sawdust

TOM JONES
TOM JONES
TOM JONES

CIRCUS

Cinders to Sawdust

By ESSE FORRESTER O'BRIEN

Illustrations and Jacket Design by JAMES T. JONES

The Naylor Company
Publishers of the Southwest
San Antonio, Texas

By The Same Author

ELEPHANT TALES
OUR BABIES
BOTTLE BABIES
ADOPTED BABIES
CLOWNS OF THE FOREST
BARNEY
BAYLOR BEAR MASCOTS
ANIMAL TOTS
REINDEER ROUNDUP
ART AND ARTISTS OF TEXAS

LIBRARY OF CONGRESS CATALOG CARD NUMBER 59-9291

PRINTED IN THE UNITED STATES OF AMERICA

THIS BOOK

IS

AFFECTIONATELY DEDICATED

TO

MY GRANDCHILDREN

MARJORIE ESSE O'BRIEN

AND

WILLIAM FORRESTER O'BRIEN, JR.

Author's Note

In the early days, the cinders from the coal-burning locamotives and cooking and heating stoves were used on the circus lot and in the tent, as well as along the road to the circus grounds. It is a long way from cinders to the colored sawdust used today.

– ESSE FORRESTER O'BRIEN

Acknowledgments

Special thanks is given to the editors of *White Tops,* the well-known circus magazine, for their generous permission to use material from forty-seven articles; and to Brandt & Brandt, New York, N. Y., for permission to reprint lines from *Circus Day,* by Courtney Ryley Cooper, Copyright 1931 by Courtney Ryley Cooper, reprinted by permission of Brandt & Brandt, New York, N. Y. Appreciation is extended also to Simon and Schuster, publishers, and to the authors, for permission to quote from the *The Big Top,* by Hartzell Spence and Fred Bradna, copyright 1952; to *Bandwagon,* for permission to reprint from numerous articles; to Wyatt Blassingame, for permission to reprint from articles in *The Family Circle* and other publications; to *Life* magazine and to *Reader's Digest,* for permission to use material from "Chang-Eng's American Heritage," by Archie Robertson; to *Etude* Magazine, for permission to reproduce lines by James Francis Cooke; to Little, Brown and Company, publishers, for permission to use material from *Circus Doctor,* by Dr. J. Y. Henderson; to *Billboard* magazine, for permission to reprint from numerous articles; to Bobbs-Merrill, publishers, for permission to reprint "The Circus Day Parade," by James Whitcomb Riley, from *Rhymes of Childhood,* copyright 1953 by Bobbs-Merrill; to Harper and Brothers, publishers, and the estate of J. D. Morrison, for permission to reprint lines from "A Bag of Tools," by R. L. Sharpe, from *Masterpieces of Religious Verse,* edited by James Dalton Morrison; and to *The Diners Club News,* for permission to reprint material from several articles.

To the following individuals and publications for their invaluable assistance in supplying pictures and information, the author is deeply indebted:

Fred Allen: for "The Last Laugh," R.B.B.&B. Program.

O. K. Armstrong: for "The Hagenbecks and Their Animal Friends," Reader's Digest.

Harlon Babcock: for his poem, "The Circus," *White Tops,* Jan., Feb., 1951.

G. Lineaus Banks: for *Blondin, His Life and Performances,* 1862.

P. T. Barnum: for *My Struggles and Triumphs* (autobiography); also *History of Animals* by P. T. Barnum and London Shows Combined.

Tom Bartlett

Billy Barton: for "The Hunt Story," *White Tops,* Mar., Apr., 1952.

Clyde Beatty — Personal letters and circus program.

Harry P. Bowman

Suerre O. Braathen

Joe Bradbury

Frank Braden: for "It's in the Blood" and "Gilding the Lily," 1945; "The Circus and The Armies," 1942; and "Struttin' Big," 1949, Circus Talent Search; R.B.B.&B. Program, 1951.

Fred Bradna: for *The Big Top,* by Fred Bradna and Hartzell Spence, Simon & Schuster.

George Bria

Bridgeport Public Library, Bridgeport, Connecticut.

James Brooks

J. Bryan, III: for "Gargantua and Toto."

Mr. and Mrs. Benjamin J. Bump: for History of Mr. and Mrs. Tom Thumb.

Roland Butler: for R.B.B.&B. Program, 1950; "Winter Quarters," also R.B.B.&B. Program, 1952; "The Big Show's Winter Home," also R.B.B.&B., 1953; "Monsters to Mistin," also "The Big Show Marches On," R.B.B.&B. Program, 1951; "Magazines Cover the Circus," 1949; and many other articles. Numerous conversations, letters, great help in many ways.

Herbert A. Calkins: for "Old Time Circus Day," "Buffalo Bill" (letter), *White Tops,* July, Aug., 1951.

Canon City *Daily Record,* Canon City, Colorado.

Canon City Museum, Canon City, Colorado.

Russell Carpenter

George L. Chindahl: for "The Whitney Show," *White Tops,* Christmas, 1941.

Bill Chipman: *New York Daily Times.*

Bobby Clark: for R.B.B.&B. Program, 1947.

Mabel Clark

Patricia Coffin

Harry W. Cole: for "A Circus Author's Errors," *White Tops,* Jan., Feb., 1952.

Antoinette and Arthur Concello, famed aerialists: for conversations and letters.

George S. Conklin

Richard C. Conover: for "John Robinson Show."

James Francis Cooke

Courtney Ryley Cooper: for Book, *Circus Day,* Farrar and Rinehart, publishers, copyright 1931 by Courtney Ryley Cooper.

Cosmopolite: for "Alfredo Codona and the Art of the Aerial Acrobat," *White Tops* (loose leaf).

Anthony D. Hippisley Coxe: for "The Circus," *White Tops,* July, Aug., 1951.

Bing Crosby

The Dallas News

Elsie N. Danenburg: for book on Bridgeport, Connecticut.

Cecil B. DeMille: for "Soul of the Circus," "The Greatest Show on Earth," R.B.B.&B. Programs, 1950, 1951.

Charles E. Duble: for "Mighty Haag Shows," *Bandwagon,* Sept., 1952.

Ken Dunshee: for "Horses in Short Prance," also "Funny Business," 1944, *News from Home Magazine,* (Editor).

George (Papa) Denman, Mr. and Mrs. Walter Huff; Mr. and Mrs. Cheerful Gardner; Walter McClain; Larry Davis. Elephant trainers.

The Elkhart Truth, Elkhart, Indiana.

Family Circle: for articles by Wyatt Blassingame.

Leonard B. Farley, Museum Librarian, Hertzberg Circus Collection, San Antonio, Texas: for inestimable assistance in collecting material and photographs.

William Fields: for "Northward, Ho!", R.B.B.&B. Program, 1950.

Charles P. Fox: for "American Calliope," *Bandwagon.*

Floree Galt: for "The Real Music of the Circus," *White Tops,* Mar., Apr., 1952.

Leo Gaudreau: for "Alfred Court," *White Tops.*

Blevens Miller Gibbs

M. G. Gorrow: for "Coming and Going," *White Tops,* May, June, 1950.

Edward Graves

Captain Anthony Greenhaw

J. R. Griffin

Samuel Gumpertz: for R.B.B.&B. Program.

Bernard Head: for "Come and Get it," R.B.B.&B. Program, 1945.

Dr. J. Y. Henderson: for Book, *Circus Doctor,* Little, Brown and Company; and conversations.

Henry A. B. Bishop Historical Room, Bridgeport Public Library, Bridgeport, Connecticut.

Hertzberg Circus Collection: for "Ballyhoo Born of Barnum," "Tom Thumb," "Jenny Lind," "Posters Odd and Old," all from booklet, *Circusana,* and research work there, San Antonio, Texas.

Melvin D. Hildreth

Edwin C. Hill: for "The Human Side of the Circus," R.B.B.&B. Program.

W. H. Hohenadel, Editor of *White Tops*: for permission to quote from numerous articles, and for inestimable assistance in every respect.

Joe Holling

Edward Howe: for "Con Colleano," Cole Bros. Circus Program, 1950.

Dr. Chester Hoyt — Museum of the American Circus — narrator.

Marvin Hunter: for "Mollie Bailey," *Dallas News.*

Tom Inabinette: for "Gufoyle and Manuel King," "Lions," *White Tops,* July, Aug., 1953.

Harry James

Van Johnson

Mrs. Paul Jung: for "I am the Wife of a Clown," R.B.B.&B. Program, 1947.

Arthur Kanter: for "Prima Donnas of the Circus," R.B.B.&B. Program, 1946; "Fast and Forte," R.B.B.&B. Program, 1945; "Six High in the Wind," (Letter), 1947.

Emmett Kelly: for "Weary Woeful Willie," R.B.B.&B. Program, 1951.

F. Beverly Kelley: for permission to quote from numerous articles.

James W. Kelly: on Arturo.

John B. Kennedy, commentator.

F. C. Kessler: Curator, Canon City Museum Association, Canon City, Colorado.

Marshall L. King

Jannie and Karl Kae Knecht: for "How the C.F.A. Was Organized," *White Tops,* Mar., Apr., 1951; "Another Story of the Brothers Ringling," *White Tops,* July, Aug., 1953; many other articles. Material on Houdini as well as personal recollections. Conversations and letters; untold help in every way on every subject.

John C. Kunzog: for "Ezra Stephens," "Barnum of Maine," "Originator of the Bannerline," *Bandwagon,* June, 1953.

Bette Leonard, Circus Historical Society.

Allen Lester, R.B.B.&B. Circus press department: for "Adventures in Dollars and Sense," R.B.B.&B., 1945.

Life magazine: for "The Strange Stories of Gargantua and Toto" by J. Bryan, III.

Little, Brown and Company: for *Circus Doctor,* by Dr. J. Y. Henderson.

Daniel P. Mannix: for "The Big Cats Walk Alone," *White Tops.*

Vivienne Mars, Custodian, Hertzberg Circus Collection, San Antonio, Texas: for invaluable aid in actual help, letters, conversations, research.

Clem McCarthy: for "William Hyer and Starless Night," R.B.B.&B. Program, 1946.

Walter McClain

Richard J. McGarrity

Bill McKendrick

Henry McLemore: for clipping, "Chimpanzee Act at Danish Circus," "Schumann Circus," *White Tops,* Aug., Sept., 1940.

Don McNeill: for "Cookhouse Magic," R.B.B.&B. Program, 1950.

The Milwaukee Journal

Bill Montague: for "Flying High," *White Tops,* Jan., Feb., 1951; and "The Greatest Show on Earth," *White Tops,* Mar., Apr., 1952.

Steve Morris, Louisville *Times*: for "Cole Bros. Circus," *White Tops,* Sept., 1940.

Frank Morrissey: for "Spring in the Garden," and "Circus Clock Ticks All Year Round," 1945.

Museum of the American Circus: for Satyr and Astley Circus and much information, letter, pictures from John L. Sullivan, curator.

Mrs. William Nelson

Sylvester Nemes

The New York Times

David Niven: for "Life Gets Too Tame," *White Tops,* Jan., Feb., 1953.

Clyde V. Noble: for "The Home of the Man on the Flying Trapeze," also "Art Concello and Other Flyers," *White Tops,* Sept., Oct., 1950.

John and Henry Ringling North: for conversations, letters, privilege of visiting the circus in winter quarters, Sarasota, Florida, and their many fine articles.

Arline Osman: for "California, the Happy Hunting Ground for Circus Fans," *White Tops.*

Col. B. J. Palmer

C. E. Perigo

William Lyons Phelps: for quote, "I would advise everyone . . . ," (letter), R.B.B.&B. Program, 1951.

Fred H. Phillips: for "The Riding Rudynoffs," *White Tops,* Mar., Apr., 1953.

Photographers: Harry A. Atwell, W. Earl Burnell, Dick Miller, Reggie Bogart, Dick Butler, Chester Photo Service, Jean Davis, Robert D. Good, Richard Hawkins, Bernard Kobel, Bill McKendrick, Thomas O. Mueller, Vittus Nielson, Louis Nethersole, Carl Okerbloom, Carl Rasmussen, G. C. Ratliff, Herman L. Rick, Star Photo Service, Harry Quillen, Earl W. Varney.

Jake Posey

Princeton University Circus Collection

Harry Quillen: for "Cheerful Gardner," *White Tops,* Mar., April.

G. E. Ratliff: for "Kentucky Giants," *White Tops,* July, Aug., 1951; Ratliff is author of column, "Big Sandy Past and Present," *Daily Independent,* Ashland, Kentucky.

Bill Richards: on Mel Koontz.

Vivian Richardson: for "Mollie Bailey," *Dallas News.*

Ringling Bros. and Barnum & Bailey Circus Programs, Press Sheets and Press Department.

Archie Robertson: for permission to use material from "Chang-Eng's American Heritage," *Life, Reader's Digest;* also letters and information.

Dorothy Roe: for "Elsie and Paul Jung," "Sew and Tinker as Big Show Travels," *White Tops.*

Jack Rogers: for "Winifred Colleano," *White Tops,* Christmas, 1938.

Rex de Roselli: for "Clowning a Serious Business," *White Tops.*

John Rosenfield — Column — The Passing Show — *Dallas News.*

Dr. Hugh Grant Rowell: for "Washington Irving and the Circus," R.B.B.&B. Program, 1949.

Eugene Russell

The San Francisco Chronicle

Sarasota Herald-Tribune, Sarasota, Florida.

M. S. Scaperlanda: for conversations, letters, much information.

James W. Shettel: for "Welsh Circus," "Rope Walking," "Sells Bros." "Memories of the Circus and Its People," *White Tops,* Aug., Sept., 1940, Jan., Feb., 1946.

Joe Siegrist — "The Voice from the Big Top," *White Tops,* June-July, 1935.

A. Morton Smith: for conversations and letters on Gainesville Circus.

Bob Smith: for "Howdy Doody Joins the Circus," R.B.B.&B. Program, 1950.

Hartzell Spence: for Book, *The Big Top* (as told by Fred Bradna), Simon and Schuster, 1952.

Fred Stafford: *White Tops.*

Mabel Stark: personal letters.

Goldie Steele, assistant to Vivienne Mars, Curator of Hertzberg Circus Collection, San Antonio, Texas: for letters and help in research.

Janet Sterling: for "The Shoe that Danced Around the World," *White Tops,* Spring, 1941.

Bill Stearn, commentator.

James Strook

Studebaker Wheel

Col. C. G. Sturtevant, (Circus Historian): for numerous conversations, letters, etc. "The Cradle of the American Circus," Nov., Dec., 1948: "Biographies of Famous Circusmen," Mar., Apr., 1951; "The Clark Family," Christmas, 1938; "The American Circus Parade," "Richard Sands," Mar., Apr., 1948; "Sands and Lent," Mar., Apr., 1948; "The Circus in New Orleans," "Side Show People," June, July, 1936; "The Flying Act and its Technique," May, 1932; *White Tops;* and in almost every issue over a period of many years. "Great Show Celebrities," Aug., Sept., 1940; "The Circus in America During the Civil War," Christmas, 1950; "P. T. Barnum of Connecticut," May, June, 1934; *White Tops.*

Ed Sullivan, columnist: "Little Old New York," *New York Daily News.*

John Sullivan, Curator of Museum of the American Circus, Sarasota, Florida: for conversations, letters, much help in research.

Lowell Thomas: for "He Fell to Fame," R.B.B.&B. Program, 1945.

Fred Bailey Thompson: for "Origin of the Term, Strawhouse," *Bandwagon,* Christmas, 1952.

Roland Tiebor

James B. Thompson

James B. Tomlinson

Tom Thumb Museum, Lakesville, Massachusetts.

Tufts College Museum, Medford, Massachusetts.

The Waco News-Tribune

Jacob A. Wagner

Mack Williams

Charles Wirth

Clyde Wixom

Fred de Wolfe and Bertha de Wolfe

A. Uleland: for *Life of Barnum.*

Picture Credits

From the *Museum of the American Circus,* Sarasota, Florida:

The Celebrated Miss Wilkinson, the Female Wire Dancer; "Prodigy 'Twixt Brute and Man"; Astley's Bill; Frank "Slivers" Oakley

From *Kobel:*

Barnum and Bailey Snake Wagon; Annie Oakley; Buffalo Bill Cody; The Hartford Fire; Lillian Leitzel as she appeared in Chicago; Monument to Lillian Leitzel; Ada Mae Salo and her Reptilian Friend; "Giraffe-neck" Women

From *Robert D. Good:*

The Two Jesters' Calliope; Merry-go-round, Buchanan's Yankee Robinson Circus; Jenny Lind; Irene Woodward, the Tattooed Lady

From *Dick Miller:*

Five Graces Band Wagon; John Ringling North II and Lou Jacobs; George Escalana, Boss Painter of Ringling Bros., Barnum and Bailey Circus; Rene and Madeleine Geraldo; Dieter Tasso; La Norma, the Flying Temptress; Mary Jane Miller; Kareff Manus; The Chaludis, "Daredevil Cyclists"; Pinito del Oro; The Loyal Repinsky Family; Ernie Burch; Paul Jung; Charlie Bell and Peanuts; Fred and Will Hanlon; Colonel Nile; Portrait Study of Toto; Albert Rix and Tommy; The Doll Family

From *White Tops:*

Richard Sands Poster (1843)

From *Vittus Nielsen:*

Horses' Basketball Game

Horses' Basketball Game No. 2

From the *Hertzberg Circus Collection:*

Mollie Bailey; A Family or "Mud" Show; Famous Forepaugh Poster; General Tom Thumb; Little Lillian Leitzel; Lillian Leitzel on the Roman Rings; Nio Nialto, Forward Somersault on the Tightwire; Poodles Hanneford; The Great Blondin; George L. Fox; Joey Grimaldi; Jules Tounour; Bird Millman

From the *Barnum Museum:*

Barnum's Poster Reply

From *H. A. Atwell:*

Jake Posey's Hands — The 40-Horse Team; Alfredo Codona; The Inimitable Lillian Leitzel; Leitzel and Codona; Ella and Fred Bradna; May Wirth and One of Her Famous Horses; Emmett Kelly; Big Ruth

From *W. Earl Burnell:*

First Ringling Circus Tent; Ringling Bros. First New Grandstand Truck; Famous Mustache Cup Poster; Otto, Charles, and Alf T. Ringling, P. T. Barnum, James A. Bailey; Circus Ground; 1000 Pounds of Chicken; Brunn, The Juggling King; Edie and Shortie; Joe Barbetti and Cliff Chapman with Big Ruth; Portrait Study of Joe; Fixing a Flat; Rope-walking Tiger; Mlle. Toto and Gargantua II; Portrait Study of Gargantua; Alfred Court and Satan; Jack LeClair and Emmett Kelly

From *Roland Butler:*

John Ringling; Merle Evans; Traveling "Hotel Ringling"; The Flying Concellos; Unus; Mr. Mistin, Jr.; Lucio Cristiani; Lou Jacobs — Bells in His Belfry; Paul Jerome and His Neon Nose; Adam the Orangutang; Emir the Leopard; Cucciola, the Midget, atop Zoppe, famous Bareback Rider

From *John Ringling:*

John Ringling; Mabel Ringling; Ca'D'Zan, John Ringling Residence in Sarasota

From *Herman L. Rick:*

A Budding Equestrian

From *Concello:*

John Ringling North; Henry Ringling North

From *Earl W. Varney:*

The Great Wallendas

From the *Canon City Museum:*

"The Shoe that Danced Around the World"

From *Helen Baldwin:*

Felix Adler; Emmett Kelly — Circus Immortal; Arthur Beason; That's All, Folks

From *Mabel Stark:*

Mabel Stark and Her Famous Rope-walking Tiger

From *G. C. Ratliff:*

The Kentucky Giants — Capt. and Mrs. Martin Van Buren Bates

From *Thomas O. Mueller:*

Karl Kae Knecht

From *Cecil B. DeMille:*

Cecil B. DeMille and Paul Horompo on Set of "The Greatest Show on Earth"

FRONT END SHEET

From *W. Earl Burnell:*

Portrait of a Tiger; The Gorilla Babies, Gargantua II and Mlle. Toto; Two Tigers; Gargantua Shows His Arm Stretch

From *Robert Mickle:*
Dan Rice from *White Tops*

From the *Barnum Museum,* Bridgeport, Connecticut:
Poster, Zeo

From *Richard Hawkins:*
Soup Pots

From *Roland Tiebor:*
Seal Picture

From the *Gainesville Circus:*
Evelyn Kaps

From *Kobel:*
George Augur and Tom Sodrie

From *Dick Miller:*
Luciana; Giraffes — Edi and Her Baby, Boston; Man Shearing Elephant with Blowtorch; Old Big Top; Fred and Will Hanlon

From *Canon City Museum,* Canon City, Colorado:
Bird Millman

From *Roland Butler:*
Joe, the Lion; Clown with Giraffe and Moon (Poster); The Alanzas

From *Harry Quillen:*
Clyde Beatty and Cats

From *Fort Worth, Texas, Zoo:*
Elephant with Birthday Cake

BACK END SHEET

From *Dick Miller:*
The Six Frelanis; Con Colleano; Elephant with Trunk Up; Con Colleano with Charlie Bell and John Tripp; The Behees; Tommy, the Bear; Otto Griebling; Frankie Saluto

From *W. Earl Burnell:*
Tiger on Ball; Lou Jacobs (foot up); Lou Jacobs; Lou Jacobs and Paul Jerome; The Rope Walking Chimpanzee

From *Roland Butler:*
Jack Bostock; Seal; Rudolph Mathias

From *Robert Mickle* (Rephotographed by him):
Col. Zack Miller; Paul Nelson; Ernest and Charles Clark

From *Walter Nielson,* Copenhagen, Denmark:
Katcha and the White Horse, Schumann Circus

Contents

WELCOME TO CLOWN ALLEY

MENAGERIE

List of Illustrations

56. Rene and Madeleine Geraldo – Dick Miller
57. The Great Wallendas – Earl W. Varney
58. Dieter Tasso – Dick Miller
59. La Norma, The Flying Temptress – Dick Miller
60. Mary Jane Miller, Daring and Decorative Young Aerialist – Dick Miller
61. "The Shoe That Danced Around the World" – Canon City Museum
62. Ella and Fred Bradna – H. A. Atwell
63. Kareff Manus – Dick Miller
64. Vittorio Zacchini, "The Human Cannonball" – given by V. Zacchini
65. The Chaludis, "Daredevil Cyclists" – Dick Miller
66. Nio Nailto. Forward Somersault on Tightwire – Hertzberg Circus Collection
67. Pinito Del Oro – Dick Miller
68. Brunn, The Juggling King – Burnell
69. Unus – Butler
70. Mr. Mistin, Jr., The World's Youngest and Greatest Xylophone Virtuoso – Butler
71. Poodles Hanneford – Hertzberg Circus Collection
72. May Wirth and One of Her Famous Horses (1923) – H. A. Atwell
73. Lucio Cristiani – Butler
74. The Loyal Repinsky Family – Dick Miller
75. The Great Blondin – Hertzberg Circus Collection.

Section III between pp. 184-85

76. Jack LeClair and Emmett Kelly – Burnell
77. Ernie Burch – Dick Miller
78. Felix Adler – Helen Baldwin
79. George L. Fox – Hertzberg Circus Collection
80. Joey Grimaldi – Hertzberg Circus Collection
81. Jules Tounour – Hertzberg Circus Collection
82. Frank "Slivers" Oakley – John L. Sullivan, Curator, Ringling Museum of the American Circus, Sarasota, Fla.
83. Emmett Kelly, Circus Immortal – Helen Baldwin
84. Emmett Kelly – H. A. Atwell
85. Lou Jacobs – Bells in His Belfry – Butler
86. Paul Jung – Dick Miller
87. Felix Adler and His Goose – Roland Butler
88. Charlie Bell and Peanuts – Dick Miller

Section IV between pp. 224-25

121. Jack Earle and Major Mite – Kobel
122. Famous Handbill Advertising the United Brothers, Chang and Eng – from Archie Robinson
123. Karl Kae Knecht, Organizer, Circus Fans of America, and Founder of *White Tops* – Thomas O. Mueller Studio, Evansville, Ind.
124. Cecil B. DeMille and Paul Horompo on Set of "The Greatest Show on Earth" – Cecil B. DeMille
125. That's All, Folks – Helen Baldwin

Introduction

This book is a compilation of historical facts and incidents with touches of glamor and tinsel sprinkled on the sawdust. No history of America would be complete without relating the contribution made to American life by the circus. In it you find the birth of new customs, new literature, and new music and art. In the circus are found clues to the development of real American genius for efficiency, advertising, publicity, and inventiveness.

The circus is the most truly international of all forms of entertainment. And be it said, to its everlasting glory, the one entertainment that has never needed a censor. The true circus act needs no interpreting, nor does it interpret anything. It is a studied demonstration of skill — skill that has been perfected through the centuries. The circus is a colossal humanitarian and an international benefactor of man where hundreds of people of different nationalities are banded together with but one consuming desire: — to entertain, to please, to lift man out of the doldrums of life by sheer magic, by perfection of training of body and limb, and by the art of clowning. The circus is a priceless gem, yet its setting is such that it can be enjoyed by the rank and file of men, the rich and the poor, the good and the bad — even a bad man is a better man after seeing a circus, because he has been drawn back into the orbit of clean fellowship with other men.

Of all five senses, it is said that smell has the first call on memory. The sawdust, that smell of tanbark; that peculiar sour odor of the elephants; that wild animal odor; and that gnawing circus hunger that strikes immediately with the first whiff of parching peanuts; these are not fantasies but realities. We may like to dream of the circus as a village on the border line between real and make-believe — a will-o'-the-wisp village, here today, gone tomorrow, but we enjoy the reality.

To the children, the circus is their world, blown into a huge balloon of tingling excitement, awe-inspiring animals, and fantasies of fairyland.

There are the bands, the rumble of the sun-burst wheels, lions, elephants, horses, clowns — the whole circus spangle-land plays tricks with memory. Or, as Harlan Babcock expressed it in his *White Tops* poem:

WHEN THE CIRCUS COMES TO TOWN

and

Though I'm borderin' on fifty,
An' to work a willin' slave,
When the circus hanker leaves me
Then I'll know I'm near the grave

I Origin of the Circus

EARLY PERFORMERS

CIRCUS DAY PARADE

THE FAMILY SHOWS

ADAM FOREPAUGH

PHINEAS T. BARNUM

GENERAL TOM THUMB

JENNY LIND

THE BARNUM & BAILEY CIRCUS

THE RINGLINGS

BUFFALO BILL'S WILD WEST SHOW

ANNIE OAKLEY

CLYDE BEATTY CIRCUS

ALFREDO CODONA AND LILLIAN LEITZEL

ROPE WALKERS

BLONDIN

and many, many others ☞

Origin of the Circus and Early Performers

The circus is not American in origin, although its gigantic size and growth are the result of American ingenuity, foresight, and courage. The beginning of the circus dates back to the days of the Roman gladiator and the Greek amphitheater exhibitions. The word "circus" is Latin, meaning "circle." It was used in reference to a circular arena in which games, races, and gladiatorial combats were presented. Tiers of seats for spectators rose all around the arena. Such a circus was built in Rome from about 616 to 578 B.C., and was called *Circus Maximus*. Julius Caesar rebuilt and enlarged this circus building to a seating capacity of 350,000.

The circus has come a long way and has undergone

many changes since those Roman days of 2000 years ago. The modern circus has been developed from four different types of amusement: (1) The Roman races and athletic contests, and the celebration of the return of heroes; (2) The itinerant players and jugglers of the Middle Ages; (3) The Italian Comedy, with its incomparable art of improvisation; (4) The country fairs and festivals of the European and English countryside.

The modern circus was born in England in 1768. The well-known English writer, Anthony D. Hippisley Coxe, tells us of Philip Astley, known as the "Father of the Circus," giving his first ring performance in Half Penny Hatch, Lambeth (London). Astley, as an ex-sergeant major and a trick rider, found that if he galloped in a circle, while standing on his horse, that the centrifugal force helped him to keep his balance. So the circus ring came into being as a performing ground, and Astley's forty-two-foot circle was the very first of the sawdust rings, according to Mr. Coxe.

In America there was a permanent theater in Philadelphia, as early as 1766; however, in 1744 the first exhibition of tightrope walking had been held in an open space in Philadelphia, called Society Hill. Other single acts or performances were given through the year 1773. Then came a blow to the amusement world. By an act of Congress, 1774, any amusement performance was forbidden, and it was not until 1780 that another exposition appeared.

The first circus building in Philadelphia was erected in August of 1785, in Center Square. An American, Mr. Poole, was the adventurer. In his advertising he "beseeches the ladies and gentlemen, who honor him with their presence, to bring no dogs with them."

The year 1792 is very important in American circus history, for, in that year, John B. Ricketts, a famous equestrian, came to Philadelphia from Scotland and brought his royal circus. Although very small, Ricketts was the first in this country to have a "Circus Company." However, it was not until April 3, 1793, that the Ricketts Company gave the first complete circus performance in America. He drew large crowds, partly because his buildings were heated with stoves.

General George Washington attended the Ricketts Circus on April 22, 1793, and also on later dates. He gave "the benefit of his presence as guarantee of respectability." General George Washington is known as our country's first distinguished circus fan, just as Queen Victoria was England's first.

In 1799, Ricketts was completely bankrupted by fire. At this time, Jailson's Circus was playing a short engagement in Philadelphia and Mr. Philip Jailson gave a benefit performance for Mr. Ricketts and raised funds for the latter's return to England. The vessel on which he embarked in 1800 foundered at sea and all aboard were lost.

It is significant to note that one part of the early circus originated in America — the idea of the wagon show, moving from town to town for exhibitions. In America the circus has enjoyed the most colorful, dramatic, thrilling, and magnificent periods of frontier and pioneer development of any organization. It knows the bloodstream of the American people as surely as a Western ranchman knows his cattle. The circus has been a barometer of life in America from the big, brave years of our pioneer living and our swashbuckling days of plunging, onward to the mechanized age of atomic power and space exploration.

THE CRADLE OF THE AMERICAN CIRCUS

THE CRADLE of the American circus is located around the city of Philadelphia and in New York. The main thoroughfares, before the railroads came to this territory, were the Old Boston Post Road and its side roads. Cattlemen drove their cattle into New York by these same roads and often bought various objects from ship captains; sometimes parrots, monkeys, and later, large animals were purchased. The idea of exhibiting animals, singly or in groups, originated in this locality.

Hackaliah Bailey's brother was a sea captain. He bought an African elephant at auction in London for $20, and, on arrival in America, sold it to his brother, Hackaliah, for $1000. (And this not far from Philadelphia, the city of brotherly love.) If the sea captain bragged of his profit, Hackaliah had the last wink, for he exhibited this elephant, named Old Bet, with surprising financial gain. Encouraged by this venture, he added other animals to his show and, after showing in barns and taverns in several counties, he leased the show to Uncle Nate Howes, who took it on tour through New England. In 1828, Nate was joined by his brother Seth. (However, the greatest name of this era was that of Phineas Taylor Barnum.)

Hackaliah's shrewd Yankee neighbors decided there was money in the show business. Three of them, John J. June, Lewis B. Titus, and Caleb Sutton Angevine, local capitalists, started a combine known as "The Zoological Institute," said to be the first organized menagerie exhibit in America. (Pidcock's menagerie was the first on record in England, established in 1708.) Other capitalists and fortune seekers entered the circus and menagerie business. All of these early shows were advertised as educational, entertaining, Biblical, and scientific, in order not to arouse the displeasure of the ministry and puritanical people. However, two elephants, (one Old Bet), and other animals were poisoned or shot by fanatics who thought a menagerie as sinful as the circus or the theater. The menagerie business prospered and owners endowed colleges, gave to churches, and helped their communities in general. Gradually the animals were trained and thus animal acts started, and owners began to buy round top tents. Band wagons were used in their shows and a large number of horses were required to pull ten or twenty animal cages overland. Several good circuses reached their peak before the days of Barnum and the Ringlings. Short sketches of these in chronological order will set forth how these early shows gained favorable public opinion and blazed the way for the firm and appreciative acceptance of the circus.

CIRCUS ADVERTISING

THE EARLIEST known handbill printed in the United States was in 1797, announcing the arrival of the first elephant. The most historic document of this era is the twenty-four page "P. T. Barnum's Advance Courier," printed in 1872, informing the people of Mr. Barnum's return to the show world after a temporary retirement. Barnum possessed the shrewdest advertising sense of all early showmen.

A great amount of printing was required to operate a circus fifty years ago, and there is a tremendous amount used today, most of it high quality advertising.

For a number of days before the circus arrives in a town, there are newspaper advertisements. These were formerly known as "Heralds" and then there were the "Advance Couriers," publications of many pages done in the style of the magazine of the day and telling the whole story of the show. These gave way to the programs used by the modern circus.

In the early days of the circus, there appeared what were known as "Rat Bills." These were circus papers in the form of handbills in which rival circuses often attacked respective owners by what would now be considered libelous statements, purported to be facts. Honesty, morality, and truthfulness were questioned openly and some of these bills were even vulgar. This form of "vehement" publicity at times left the field of business competition and became intensely personal. Advertising by "billing" is an old art; Charles Dickens describes it as flourishing in 1850. However, circus publicity mushroomed, as it were, from the rat bill and early billing days to the modern method, referred to in circus parlance as "Six High in the Wind."

"SIX HIGH IN THE WIND"

MR. F. BEVERLY KELLEY has written an enlightening article by this title, from which the circus enthusiast may learn much.

From the sides of barns or on boards at dead-end streets, one is apt to see tigers snarling or clowns grinning, because the circus bill-posters have passed that way or tacked the news in glaring picture and letters that all may read: "THE CIRCUS IS COMING."

A bill-poster describes any tough job or assignment from posting banners on a skyscraper to medical or dental operations as "Six High in the Wind." Work on smooth walls was described as "all velvet"; or, if walls were rough, they were said to be "covered with shingles" or they "wore whiskers."

Circus banners, posters, and cards are grouped into one term, "sheets." A one-sheet bill is 28 inches by 42 inches. A 24-sheet stand, the size of the usual circus billboard, contains the equivalent of two dozen single regulation-size sheets, and on the sides of this are posted date sheets, which makes the whole display job 28 sheets. Hence, these large poster displays have led to the circus and theatrical synonym for bragging as "three-sheeting" or "putting up paper" for yourself.

Banners are usually put about eight feet above ground, this height spot being a "good hit" — which stares you in the face.

The Circus Advertising Car of Ringling Bros. and Barnum & Bailey rolls into a town a few weeks ahead of the show and remains exactly the same number of days as the show intends playing the town. A fleet of circus-owned station wagons meet the car each morning, load, depart, and post in haste, covering the territory nearby and "feeder" towns and villages. About one dozen 60-gallon cans of paste are needed daily by the Ringling crew. Much of the show's success depends on their "spotting" to advantage. Good artists are employed to design circus posters and the best printers are secured to bring out the finished product.

PARADES - FLOATS - WAGONS

THE CIRCUS-DAY PARADE

James Whitcomb Riley

Oh, the Circus-Day parade!
    How the bugle played and played!
And how the glossy horses tossed
    their flossy manes and neighed,
As the rattle and the rhyme
    of the tenor-drummer's time
Filled all the hungry hearts
    of us with melody sublime!

How the grand band-wagon shone
    with a splendor all its own,
And glittered with a glory
    that our dreams had never known!
And how the boys behind,
    high and low of every kind,
Marched in unconscious capture,
    with a rapture undefined!

How the horsemen, two and two,
    with their plumes of white and blue,
And crimson, gold and purple,
    nodding by at me and you,
Waved the banners that they bore,
    as the Knights in days of yore,
Till our glad eyes gleamed and glistened
    like the spangles that they wore!

How the graceless-graceful stride
    of the elephant was eyed,
And the capers of the little horse
    that cantered at his side!
How the shambling camels, tame
    to the plaudits of their fame,
With listless eyes came silent,
    masticating as they came.

How the cages jolted past,
    with each wagon battened fast,
And the mystery within it
    only hinted of at last
From the little grated square
    in the rear, and nosing there
The snout of some strange animal
    that sniffed the outer air!

And, last of all, The Clown,
    making mirth for all the town,
With his lips curved ever upward
    and his eyebrows ever down,
And his chief attention paid to
    the little mule that played
A tattoo on the dashboard
    with his heels, in the Parade.

Oh, the Circus-Day Parade!
    How the bugles played and played!
And how the glossy horses tossed
    their flossy manes and neighed,
As the rattle and the rhyme of
    the tenor-drummer's time
Filled all the hungry hearts of us
    with melody sublime!

—From *Rhymes of Childhood*
Reprinted by permission of
The Bobbs-Merrill Company

THE ORIGIN of the parade is ancient, dating back to the triumphal processions of the Romans and to religious festival pageants. Over two thousand years ago, wheeled vehicles were used in parades, and on these ancient flattopwagons-of-parade appeared royalty.

Later floats were decorated in lavish manner depicting tableaux of historical and religious events. Early in the nineteenth century, the idea of these pictorial processions reached America. They had been used throughout Europe, in India, and the Orient with unusual fanfare success. In 1838 in New Orleans, the Mardi Gras festival parade used floats which marked the first organized parade in that city.

From these processions the American circus luckily and advantageously conceived the idea of the street parade as a means of attracting people to the show. The oldest illustration of a circus parade, discovered by the late Colonel Sturtevant, C.F.A. historian for many years, is that of Purdy, Welsh, Macomber & Co.'s parade band, taken from the Albany, New York, *Argus,* of May 1, 1837. This shows twelve wind instrumentalists mounted on horses, riding four abreast, and the drummers follow, riding in a howdah on an elephant's back.

Another early parade attraction of the 'fifties was a team of four elephants – three small ones in front and a large one following, drawing a band wagon. This was used in the Mabie Bros. Circus.

The growth of the circus after the Civil War was phenomenal. Circuses vied with each other as to the elaborateness of their wagons, floats, chariots and other equipage. About this time, the Howes and Cushing Circus made a most impressive entrance into the American circus life. Having gone to Great Britain on a sailing vessel in 1857 and remained there seven years, this great circus returned to the United States with added experience and advanced ideas. This was toward the end of the Civil War, and Howe was very enthusiastic over the future of the circus. Soon after his return to the United States, Mr. Seth P. Howe purchased Cushing's interest in the circus, and expended much money in splendid and unusual equipment, and renamed it the Great European Circus. This name was changed, in the 'seventies, to Howe's Great London Circus.

Being a man of great wealth, Mr. Howe started a movement in the glorification of the circus wagon that stimulated all other circus owners to quick thought and action, and thus kept the circus world highly competitive. He applied the wood carving art, which he had seen in Europe, to the beautification of the circus wagons. He contracted for the carving, gold leaf work, and painting with French and Italian artists, and for the wagon work with experienced mechanics. From 1866, for a period of about six years, Mr. Howe received two or three wagons at a time. These wagons became the talk of the entire circus world. Some of them were built on the novel telescope plan with sections fitting inside one another. By using a windlass, the nested sections were elevated to a great height, showing gold and silver carving, mirrors, and allegorical paintings.

This display of grandeur started an era which could be called The Golden Age of the Circus Parade. Other circuses jumped into the market, and American designers and artists accepted the challenge; thus the great and historical wagons, which hold such an important place in the life and lore of the circus, came into being in this highly competitive era of the circus.

Gradually roads became pikes and bridges were built stronger, and the difficulties of show transportation were lessened greatly; and when the big shows went on the railroad cars in the 'seventies, most of the travel hazards had been eliminated.

However, travel by train had its problems. Sometimes rail delays made parades impossible, but most of the time the parade went on even if the performance was necessarily delayed several hours. The public loved and demanded the parade. The span of the parade's life was 1880 to 1920, in small towns until 1931, or a little later in some places and by some shows.

During the golden years of the circus parade, it grew

until it reached the length of five miles, representing a gigantic expenditure and displaying a splendor unimaginable to those who missed that era.

Captain Anthony Greenhaw gives the following information. "The last circus parade in the United States was at Guthrie, Oklahoma, on October 6, 1939, by the Parker and Watts Circus." However, in recent years some parades have been given by special permission in certain towns. In 1958, Ringling Bros. and Barnum & Bailey gave a benefit parade down Broadway in New York.

To all intent, though, the curtain has been rung down on one of the most spectacular and beloved traditions in American life. The old parade call, "Hold yo' hosses — the elephants are comin'," created a blood-tingling moment of excitement, just as the first strains of the calliope heard in the distance acted as a hypodermic of circus enthusiasm.

Wear and tear on the streets of the cities was a minor cause for the discontinuance of the parade, the main cause being the blocking of the now heavy traffic in all the cities.

Many of the circus performers rode on these parade floats. With the speed of the parade slowed by traffic, hours were consumed, and these performers, exposed to heat, sun, wind, rain, grew tired. They resented such fatigue since, so soon after the parade, they were to risk their lives in difficult acts. At times the streets over which the parades went were rough, and due to bouncing, the musicians on the band wagon suffered bruised lips and even loosened teeth.

Cities charged higher and higher license fees for a circus to parade, so by 1920 parades had become impracticable. It was a sad day for most grownups, and a real tragedy in the lives of children, when the death knell was sounded for the parade. What Courtney Ryley Cooper described as "that ponderous procession of mighty magnitude and multitudinous marvels known as the grand free cavalcade of worldwide wonders," the Circus Parade, is NO MORE!

THE CALLIOPE

JOSHUA C. STODDARD, of Pawlet, a Vermont farmer, an amateur inventor, who did not bother with patents, invented the first calliope in 1855, an unwieldy contraption of two parts coupled together. On one end was a charcoal-burning boiler that had to be stoked continuously to provide steam for the whistles. One hundred and fifty pounds of pressure were required in order to start whistles.

Nixon and Kemp's Circus had the first calliope, in 1858. Sands, Nathan and Company's American and English Circus was probably the first to use a calliope in a parade — in 1859.

The word "calliope" is derived from the Greek language, and means "Beautiful Voice."

FIVE GRACES BAND WAGON

THE WAGON of the Five Graces is truly one of the finest and best-known of all circus wagons. It was built in 1878 by Mr. Forepaugh, at the tremendous cost of $20,000. On its sides are panels of wood carving depicting the Five Graces: Humility, Faith, Hope, Charity, and Purity. All of this panel figure-carving, and also all the trimming, was plated in pure 14-carat gold.

The wagon of Five Graces, the first to be pulled by the Forty-Horse Team, was an immediate sensation, and its fame spread to two continents. It is now housed in the Museum of the American Circus.

THE WAGON OF TWO HEMISPHERES

THE "Master Showman of All Time," P. T. Barnum, not to be outdone by the Wagon of the Five Graces, purchased at a tremendous cost The Wagon of Two Hemispheres. It is the largest and, probably, the most famous of all circus wagons. Eventually it will be housed in the Museum of the American Circus at Sarasota, Florida, since the present owner, Colonel B. J. Palmer, has so stipulated in his will.

This glittering band wagon, in gold relief, pulled by forty horses, dazzled all who beheld its glory as it rolled along majestically in parades. It weighs more than 10 tons, is 27 feet long, (35 feet if the tongue is included), is 8½ feet wide, and 12 feet high. Its most famous driver was Big Jake Posey, who could gather all 72 pounds of reins into his hands and drive for hours. The initial cost of the wagon was $40,000, and Colonel Palmer spent $30,000 on its restoration.

On each side of this enormous wagon is a hemisphere, with bas relief continents as central figures, flanked by lions and bears, which are four times their natural size. The driver's seat is upholstered in red, and is supported by eagles; life-size wooden elephants hold up the rear end of the wagon. Along the sides are huge coats of arms of many nations, elaborately carved in wood. The circles concealed the lower part of the seats on which the musicians sat.

THE WELSH CIRCUS 1818

THE WELSH CIRCUS was not a large show, but it was a good one and was favorably received wherever it played. The three Welsh brothers had been fruit vendors and carousel (merry-go-round) operators before entering the show business. They were known by many for having started the ten-cent circus. Their programs boasted the names of many of the great stars of circusdom.

Of the three Welsh brothers, Rufus remained in show

business for a number of years. He endured miserable mud roads, showed under canvas stretched between trees, but the show grew.

In 1837, Welsh brought several giraffes from Africa, the first to be seen in this country. After several partnerships, he joined with L. B. Lent, and the Welsh & Lent Circus toured far and wide, and most successfully. John H. Glenroy, the first rider who ever turned a somersault on a bareback horse in motion, was with the Welsh Circus in 1846.

The first time the five-high act was done on three horses was on this show in 1845 by J. J. Nathans, Cadwallader, Ed Woods, Ed Kincaid, and John Glenroy.

Welsh never counted the cost of a show, preferring to concentrate on pleasing the public. He left but little money, never married. He is accorded a prominent place in American circus and dramatic history, as a man who set his goals high, and accomplished much. He blazed a trail for those circus greats who followed.

VAN AMBURGH CIRCUS 1821

VAN AMBURGH was one of the earliest in the show business and was the first to carry wild animals along with his show — this in 1821. In the 1830's it was considered quite courageous to step quickly in, and as quickly out, of a cage of lions. To Van Amburgh, who was the first to step into a cage of lions, the quick entrance and the quick exit seemed tame, so he set about teaching his lions a routine of tricks. When he was nineteen years of age, he entered a cage with a lion, panther, tiger, and leopard, each a natural enemy of the other. This difficult task of even mixing the big cats, much less teaching them tricks, was immediately hailed throughout England and France. Young Queen Victoria visited his circus six times in six weeks. She ordered a command performance, January 29, 1839, with full court regalia. By 1834, he had become famous and was advertised as, "The Original Beast Conqueror."

In 1846, Hyatt Frost became identified with Van Amburgh Co. He was a genius when it came to writing high-powered press material. He more or less pioneered with the idea of interspersing, with his circus features, advertisements of all manner of household remedies and recipes, maxims of conduct for the young, almanac matter, stories, proverbs, and jokes. Frost estimated that during his circus career he had traveled over 100,000 miles – and that in a buggy.

COLE CIRCUS 1825

THE COLE NAME clings to the annals of the American circus as much as any other title that came forth. The first Cole Circus of record was that of Ira Cole, a Yankee, who started a wagon show in 1825 and exhibited mostly in Eastern territory until around 1840. It was, at one time, known as Cole, Miller, Gale and Co.

For thirty-three years, the name of Cole was not used until the widow of an English performer, William H. Cole, started her son, William Washington Cole, in a circus of his own in 1871. This W. W. Cole Circus was a great success and ran until the close of the year, 1886. Beginning with the year 1889, the Cole name was used almost continuously down to the present day, but not since 1886 was the W. W. Cole name used.

In 1935 Zack Terrell and Jess Adkins organized a show, taking the title of "Cole Bros. Circus and Clyde Beatty's Wild Animal Show." The prize fight which was staged during the 1940 season of this show between the two clowns, Otto Griebling and Freddie Freeman, was star comedy, a knockout fight. The audience screamed with laughter as Griebling, from the very start, was forced to fight two — Freeman and the referee. Hubert Castle was their foremost performer — a wizard of the tight wire.

The show was purchased by the men who owned the Chicago Stadium, and they discontinued touring, using the Cole title for a special, assembled circus, in exhibits at the Chicago Stadium for a few weeks at a time and at other large city indoor shows.

THE CIRCUS IN NEW ORLEANS

NEW ORLEANS has always been a good circus town. Located, as it is, almost at the mouth of the Mississippi River, it was a favorite city for river shows, as well as for some of the first circuses. The Raymond and the Waring Shows had started in 1829, and in 1839 they combined their menagerie companies and had planned to open in the city of New Orleans. Each company had a big elephant. These shows joined forces just north of Algiers. Only a short distance on the way, the two huge tuskers engaged in a terrific fight. The elephant-keepers finally separated them and Hannibal quieted down, but the other old elephant, Columbus, was still on the warpath. He killed his keeper and the horse the keeper was riding, a Negro man, nearly a dozen horses, mules, and cows, and a man and the two horses he was driving. This fight cost the management $21,800.

In 1840, Ludlow and Smith built a circus amphitheater in New Orleans, and John Robinson, who had been with Raymond and Waring in 1838, came there to open the new building for them. They presented the famous Niblo family of acrobats and the world-renowned Ravels. The Ravels' versatility in talent was the talk of the show world. They were the first to introduce rich and bizarre costuming, scenic transformations, and blackouts. They played New York in

1832 and returned there annually for a quarter of a century.

Some weeks after John Robinson opened the amphitheater for Ludlow and Smith, he organized the first circus bearing his name, Robinson and Elred. Gil Elred was a famous English clown. This firm lasted until 1856. Three generations of Robinsons owned circuses, "Uncle John" being the first.

RICHARD SANDS Before 1840

RICHARD SANDS was fired with a dual ambition: to excel in the stellar role of performer, and to be the manager of a circus. He was most successful in both of these ambitions and, along with Dan Rice, was considered one of the great leading examples in American circus history of performance and management.

Richard Sands was born in 1814 in America. He designed and used, so far as is known, the first colored poster, which greatly excited the entire circus advertising world.

White Tops tells us:

"Until this beautiful piece of old printing was found in perfect condition in 1934, no mention of this kind of color printing was ever noted in any book or periodical that deals with printing or the show business." This Hippoferæan Arena poster is considered one of the finest pieces of early show printing in existence in America. It is now under glass in the Hertzberg Circus Collection in the Public Library in San Antonio, Texas. It cost $200 and is valued at $1000. This poster was found being used as a folded paper lining in the drawer of an old chest in a secondhand furniture store.

Sands took the first American circus to Europe in 1840. The magic touch of all Sands' career, and the one for which he will be best loved and remembered, was the fact that he put the calliope (invented earlier, 1855) on wheels and used it in the circus parade in 1858.

THE JOHN ROBINSON CIRCUS 1840

THE ORIGINAL John Robinson, known variously as "Uncle John" and "Old John Robinson," was born at Little Falls, New York, on July 22, 1802. At the age of fifteen he secured the position as nightwatchman at the winter quarters of Rockwell's Circus. Each night he trained the baggage horses for the ring and astounded his employers when he became a four-horse rider by the time the season opened; he was engaged as a performer in 1818 at the salary of five dollars a week.

Young John, at the age of twenty-two, had acquired a magnificent physique, was an experienced performer, and had saved his money. In 1824 his big chance came. The employees of a show in eastern Tennessee mutinied and drove the owners away. The proprietors met young John, observed his Herculean stature, and immediately offered him an interest in their show at a bargain price, if he would go on the lot and straighten out affairs. He secured a gun and suddenly appeared on the scene. Taking the crowd by surprise, he quickly reorganized the show, with himself as boss.

The Robinson Show secured a strong hold and was a favorite in the South, the trade slogan being, "Southern Men, Southern Horses, Southern Enterprises, Against the World." This made an appeal, and especially after the Civil War when the show returned to the South with the same slogan. This circus was one of the first institutions to reestablish a common bond between the battle-scarred peoples of the North and South.

Mr. Robinson's sons, John F., Gil, and Charlie, were brought up with the show. Active management passed to John F., in 1863, and he was succeeded by his son, John G.; a few years later the title passed to Jerry Mugivan and Bert Bowers. In 1931, the show made its one hundred and seventh annual tour, under the Ringling management, as John Ringling had bought all the Mugivan interests about 1929.

An expression of Uncle John Robinson is still used today by circus folks. When a storm was approaching or there was an imperative reason to cut a show short, Robinson sent to the performers in the back yard the word "Quick Show" – meaning, cut the show to the bare essentials. This term, "Quick Show," was replaced by the term "John Robinson." Even today the management of any show has only to send out an order for a "John Robinson" and all performers know that it means a quick show, cut as much as possible. John Robinson once ran his show in twenty-nine minutes without leaving out a single act. A cloudburst was imminent, and if the show was not finished, ticket money would have to be refunded.

All three generations of Robinsons owned and loved Tillie, an elephant that ranks as one of the greatest animal actors of all time. Tillie was the first elephant to carry a man in her mouth; the first elephant to work in moving pictures; and Tillie was the only elephant that could speak our language. Mr. Robinson taught her to say "Papa." Tillie was the leading elephant member of a squad of elephants that gave a military performance for the benefit of the Red Cross. Tillie sold over $1,000,000 worth of Liberty bonds during the First World War. She died in 1923, at the age of 120 years, and was given a military funeral. The other elephant actors who performed in the military act with her acted as pallbearers, and lowered her into her huge grave with their strong trunks. One of these elephants then fired the cannon which Tillie had fired in this act. These elephants trumpeted all night, grieving for their Tillie. A beautiful marble monument marks the place of her burial.

ROBERT T. STICKNEY
1841

IN MARCH, 1841, the Fogg and Stickney Circus, managed by S. P. Stickney, came down the Mississippi River and pitched their tent in the lower faubourg where their excellent company played to full houses, enjoying a phenomenal success in this exclusively French district of New Orleans.

While the Stickneys were here, the most famous of their children, Robert T., was born in 1846. At the age of two years, young Robert made his debut in the play, "Rollo." Later, he became known as the "Apollo Belvedere of the Circus Arena."

Robert T. Stickney was a dyed-in-the-wool trouper. He was considered by many as America's greatest rider and tumbler. He did a double-somersault over 21 horses, also a forward feet-feet on a running horse. He trouped and rode superbly until he was seventy-five years of age, at which time he retired from riding and trained an animal group to take on the road.

SANDS AND LENT CIRCUS
1842

THE SANDS and Lent Circus, a high-class company, with some financial backing from L. B. Titus, was formed with the main idea of touring the British Isles. After an American summer tour, they opened in Great Britain in 1842. Lent ranked with Seth B. Howes as one of the two best and most important circus promoters of his time. He must have been very diplomatic in his dealings with the creative, artistic, and extremely energetic Sands, whose expensive ideas and youth met just the proper check in the caution and experience of Lent. This show remained in England during 1843, 1844, and 1845. This circus was conducted on such a high scale of showmanship, artistry, and talent that many notices of praise and appreciation of the merits of the American Circus appeared in periodicals in London and throughout the provinces.

The personal charm of Sands, his great versatility in many acts, as well as the excellent company he carried, brought successful showings in the leading Eastern cities and command performances before royalty of Europe.

Sands perfected the ceiling walk, head down, which was splendid and daring. During Sands' trip abroad, learning this upside-down walk, Lent withdrew from partnership with Sands and formed the strong, contending circus, Welsh and Lent.

Upon Sands' return from England, the firm, Sands, Nathans & Co. came into being. By this time, the Spalding & Rogers Circus had become highly successful, so there were three excellent circus companies in strong competition. But the country was growing, transportation improving, wealth and leisure increasing, and there was an eager demand for amusement. Steamships, with regular and frequent crossings of the Atlantic, brought over new talent and ideas to add to American activity, talent, ingenuity, and progress.

Sands, Nathans & Co. Circus was touring the West Indies, playing in Havana, Cuba, when yellow fever, the scourge of the tropics, struck down several members of the circus, including Richard Sands, on Feb. 24, 1861. His untimely death at the age of forty-seven was a great loss to the patrons and lovers of the circus world.

DAN CASTELLO AND OTHERS OF HIS DAY 1846

DAN CASTELLO was well-known to the American circus world and throughout Europe. He entered the ring in 1846 as a tumbler, equestrian, and general performer. He secured and trained "Don Juan, The Educated Bull," as he was billed. He took Don Juan to Europe and there delighted his audiences, especially the English, with the novelty of a bull who performed in the same manner as a trick horse.

Castello performed as a member of several circuses; and while in Sheffield, England, with the Hengler Circus, he exhibited a wild buffalo which he had trained. It was there, at an evening performance, that the animal came near killing him. This buffalo had been a good and willing actor when, suddenly, all the native ferocity returned. He tossed Castello high in the air with a roar that made the audience tremble. Terror seized upon all and a rush was made for the exits. No one dared go to Castello's assistance as the infuriated buffalo dashed across the ring, head down, foaming at the mouth with rage. When Castello reached the ground after the first toss, he had the presence of mind to dodge the mad animal. But the beast was at him again, and amid the shrieks of the spectators who remained, Castello was tossed again in the air, falling this time outside the ring and thus narrowly escaping death. He was severely but not fatally injured. The buffalo could never again be subdued enough for the act, and soon sickened and died.

Coming back to America, Castello organized his own circus, known as Castello's Overland Circus, which was highly successful. It was the first circus to travel over the new Pacific Railroad.

Mr. Coup, P. T. Barnum's manager, was forced to take

shelter during a snowstorm one evening in Castello's house, and it was on this occasion that Coup induced Castello to become Hippodrome Manager for Mr. Barnum. The show became known as Coup, Barnum, and Castello Show.

DAN RICE, CIRCUS OWNER 1847

AMONG THE CIRCUS OWNERS of the Civil War period were some of the most popular pioneers and colorful personalities in the entire history of the entertainment world. Dan Rice was certainly one of these. He was born Daniel McLaren in 1823, but took his mother's maiden name of Rice. He reached popularity and success seldom achieved in the American amusement field. He was endowed with super-personality. His trick horse, Excelsior, though blind, possessed a great amount of equestrian personality. Rice turned in a superb clowning act with his pet pig, Lord Byron. His performing rhinoceros was a hit of the day, and his elephant, Lolla Pookh, was a sensation in her tightrope walking act.

While Rice was convalescing from yellow fever in New Orleans, he met General Zachary Taylor; later he electioneered for the "Rough and Ready" general from the ringside of his circus. Having thus become interested in politics, he had amazing success in mixing a little politics with his circus life. When Taylor was elected President of the United States, he made Dan one of his aides with the title of colonel.

During this era, the showboat business flourished. The Ludlow and Smith Circus was one of these River Shows, and for the season of 1852, Dan Rice signed his show with them. Mr. Ludlow writes, "On January the thirteenth, 1852, there was a heavy fall of snow (that is, heavy for the Southern town of New Orleans) in fact, greater than had been known there in the memory of the oldest inhabitant. In places, where the wind had no force, it was six feet in depth."

Mr. Ludlow continues, "As I was going from my lodging to the Saint Louis Hotel, in the center of the city, passing down St. Charles Street, I beheld Dan Rice, the celebrated equestrian manager, in a sleigh with a fine span of horses with bells, driving north on St. Charles Street. I will venture to say it was a sight that no man living in that city had ever seen there before. The sleigh was composed of a large dry-goods box on a pair of temporary runners made of two-inch plank. This was not a splendid turnout, but it produced as great a sensation as would the Lord Mayor's carriage driven through the streets of New Orleans."

In the early 'sixties, during the war period, Dan Rice's Circus failed and he signed with the Spalding Circus in 1864. In 1865, he joined the Howes Circus which paid him the unheard-of salary of $1000 per week, to clown.

Dan Rice and President Lincoln were close friends. Each of these men loved a good story, and each could tell one in superlatively inimitable style. Rice was always a welcome visitor at the White House.

For war needs, General Fremont seized one of the steamers on which Rice had shown his circus. Dan petitioned the government for compensation and was awarded $32,000. At Dan's request, this money was spent by President Lincoln in caring for wounded soldiers and their wives. Later, Rice, at a cost of $35,000, erected a monument in his home town of Girard, Pennsylvania, in memory of the departed soldiers of the Civil War.

Dan Rice reached immortality in the annals of circusdom as a clown — one of the "Big Three" often mentioned in the three eras of the circus and clowning. Grimaldi and Emmett Kelly were the others. Dan clowned in the day of the one-ring circus, when talking and singing clowns were in their heyday. Dan's voice was clear, strong, and magnetic.

He possessed a ready wit, was extremely clever in repartee, and commanding in appearance, with the intellect to mobilize successfully all of his talents.

Rice's finances were forever changing, and in 1879 he lost all in a disastrous fire. He died at the age of seventy, poor, but famous and beloved.

SPALDING AND ROGERS CIRCUS
Before 1848

AS THE POPULATION of the United States moved westward, the circus went West. The Spalding and Rogers Circus used a new method of transportation which surpassed all others for sheer magnificence and grandeur. During this "Golden Age of the River," their floating palaces and river showboats became the rage of the era.

With all his experience and background as a performer and famed scenic rider, Charles Rogers became a good manager. These qualities of Rogers, coupled with Spalding's astute business ability, made circus history as an example of a perfect team. The stringer-and-jack type of eleven tier seats, with extra seats in front, was an invention of Spalding's. This circus gained recognition as a wagon show and then leased river steamers for a period of time. However, in 1849, they had their huge, enclosed, floating amphitheater built in Cincinnati, Ohio, not on a river steamer, but on a great barge that was towed by two steamers. Thus the hazards of explosion and fire were almost eliminated. The "Floating Palace," as it was called, had a grand total seating capacity of over 2500 spectators. Dazzling crystal chandeliers, using artificial gas, provided brilliant illumination. There were velvet hangings and draperies, and rich appointments and furniture. And there was a spacious orchestra pit. It was an outstanding and a most unusual showplace of that era.

On the decks of the two tow-steamers the horses and animal cages were kept, and were taken aboard the Floating Palace only for performances. The river steamer Banjo (they owned several in their day) preceded the Floating Palace, carrying a staff which handled the advance publicity. The cost of the Floating Palace was $42,000, the towing boats costing an equivalent amount.

Only once did the Floating Palace venture out into the Gulf of Mexico, giving performances along the Alabama coast. On the return trip it was struck by the historic storm of 1853. The heroic and successful attempt of the tow-steamers to save it is depicted in a rare lithograph. Landing safely below New Orleans, it enjoyed a successful show season until river traffic was practically stopped by the Civil War. At this time, the Floating Palace docked at New Albany, while Spalding & Rogers took the circus to South America and the South Indies. Returning home after several years, this show was wrecked at sea off Barnegat, New Jersey. All of the people reached shore safely and only two horses were lost, but the ship was completely wrecked and the circus property a total loss.

With new equipment and courage, they opened in Albany, New York, in June, 1864. They were renovating the Great Floating Palace and steamboats for the year 1865, when the Floating Palace burned to the water's edge. Undaunted, they changed plans and put their show on wagons for an overland tour. However, after a good season. Spalding and Rogers went out of business in October, 1865.

THE SCHUMANN CIRCUS
1848
Copenhagen, Denmark

THE SCHUMANNS train only horses and are known the world over for their expert horsemanship and their skill, ability, and technique in training. Their horses all but speak — it is evident that they understand the language of the Schumanns, who talk to them as though they were guests in their home. Their liberty and high school horses are examples of precision-training and elaborate execution. Their clown horses — well, when they finish an act you wonder if you are the clown and they are the audience, since you have indulged in such clownish antics and fits of laughter.

The Schumann Circus is the oldest circus in the world under the continuous management of one family, having run over one hundred years, their first performance being given in 1848. The family has been most fortunate in having male heirs to carry on the name. The present Albert Schumann has two fine sons, Benny and Jacques. But it is the little daughter of Max Schumann, Katherine, called "Katcha," who is the Wonder Child of the Circus Ring. She is thirteen years of age. For years she has been known to many as "The Little Princess of the Ring." She has a little brother about five years of age.

When Katcha was only three, she started riding with her daddy. She walks in, around, and under all the spirited Schumann horses, and they seem to feel it their special duty to protect her. One large white horse has designated herself as nursemaid for Katcha. She follows her, and whenever the child halts, she places her head and neck protectingly around her. Little Katcha will call out to the white horse, "Kiss me," and the kiss is immediately forthcoming, with a tenderness that is amazing.

Little Katcha is the seventh generation to ride in the Schumann Circus. She rides in correct dress — red coat, tight pants and boots. The buttons used on all of Katcha's clothes are replicas of horses, and also her hair clasps.

Katcha's parents never ask her to go to the circus — she must ask if she is to be taken; otherwise she plays in the garden or around the house. She knows the name of every one of the eighty-odd horses. And not one of the eighty will come to the Schumanns unless called by his name. Max advises that all horses in an act should have names as entirely different in sound as possible, so that it will be easy for the horse to detect his own name when called.

The old clown horse simply "stole the show," to put it in our American way. He clearly showed that he did not want to go to bed when he was reminded that it was his bedtime. He would shake his head — lower it and plead with dreamy eyes — then pout with his lip hanging down. When Albert turned down the cover for him, he flopped into bed. Albert would straighten the cover and he would take his mouth and pull it awry. This took place about six times, and after a severe scolding and a slap on the cheek, he allowed the cover to remain and was soon fast asleep. Presently a clown came in and, try as he would — pulling the horse's legs, tickling his feet — he could not make the horse get up. Then Albert stepped up and told the clown it was easy. Of course, the clown argued and talked, and showed Albert what he had done in order to make the horse get up. Albert went over, spoke to the horse, and he awoke immediately, got up, and looked so sleepy that one expected him to yawn the next minute.

It is unbelievable the number of horses the Schumanns can control in one ring at one time and in one act. This is considered their most famous achievement.

The basketball game is another daring innovation in the training of horses. The Schumanns say the horses get so excited and have so much fun out of this act that they themselves need not be around except to call fouls or settle disputes. The horses are taught to use their noses and also to kick the ball in order to make the basket. This basketball game is one of the most thrilling animal acts, both for the animal and the audience, ever executed or witnessed.

Along with these excellent and unusual performances of their horses, the Schumanns present many other circus acts

– which are rented. All of the acts are presented in one ring in a theater, as are most all of the European circuses. The circus occupies this theater eight months of every year. Then the Schumanns play Norway and Sweden, sometimes France, for two months, then rest by the seaside for two months.

When Max Schumann was only three-and-one-half years of age, he was in an act with six black ponies. On five of the ponies were dolls, and on the sixth sat Max, dressed in exactly the same style. He rode jerkily, exactly as the dolls, without the flicker of the eye to give away the secret. He was always on the last horse and at the moment his horse was making its exit, he waved and smiled. The audience was left speechless – and their applause began after Max had vanished behind the curtain, only to return and receive a thunderous ovation. The Schumanns never sell, or rent out, an act. When their horses appear, one may be certain that one of the Schumann family is showing them.

When the Schumanns celebrated their one hundredth anniversary, congratulations, felicitations, and flowers were sent from all over the world. Copenhagen took a holiday. It was a celebration second only to the coronation of a queen. The theater had been so remodeled as to allow the horses, profusely garlanded in flowers, to parade around the ring, then out under the spectators' seats and on out to the adjoining plaza, making their fancy turns and steps so that the thousands standing outside in the courts could see.

The Danes love the circus passionately. and yet they are its severest critics. If an act meets with the approval of the Schumann audience, it can be sure of bookings anywhere. And the Danish audience shows its approval wholeheartedly. They are generous with applause and laughter, but they are also hard and exacting. The crowd will boo or hiss a seal that drops a ball or strikes a sour note, as quickly as they will an actor who does not meet their standards or expectations.

The Schumanns have played to packed houses eight months out of each year for over a century. Superb performers — charming and hospitable people — these Schumanns of international fame!

THE HAGENBECK ZOO AND TRAINING CENTER AND CIRCUS 1848 – Zoo 1887 – Circus

THE HAGENBECK CIRCUS really started in 1848, as George Bria tells us in *The Sarasota Herald-Tribune* and *White Tops,* when a Hamburg fishmonger, Gottfried Carl Hagenbeck, by name, noticed that the people of Hamburg showed great interest in a public exhibit of seals which some of his fishermen friends had brought to his market. Hagenbeck had a contract with these fishermen to buy everything they caught, so when they came in with some baby seals, he stuck to his word. He put the seals in a tub and soon the market was overrun with people wanting to see the "fish that barked." Gottfried decided to charge admission if people were that eager. Money rolled in and soon he bought a parrot, some goats, a cow, and a polar bear. The collection continued to grow; so it was that Gottfried Hagenbeck set up the first privately-owned commercial zoo in Europe. He and his five sons were caught up with enthusiasm and went on wild animal hunts in Africa, Burma, Ceylon, and many faraway places.

O. K. Armstrong has published in *Reader's Digest* an exceptionally penetrating study of this talented family. All the Hagenbeck boys loved animals, but Carl had a genius for understanding and for training animals. At the age of fourteen, Carl left school to help with the zoo, and at twenty-one he became head of the Hagenbeck Enterprises, which had grown rapidly into big business. Carl trained not only animals but trainers. His methods were kindness, understanding, patience, and the reward system for lessons well learned.

Carl and his hunters and trappers used humane methods in the wild, never killing to capture, and never capturing more than the amount they wanted. Orders for animals poured in from zoos and menageries. People came from all over the world to buy from Carl. P. T. Barnum, on his first visit to the Hagenbeck Zoo, bought $15,000 worth of animals, among them the first giraffe ever to be shown in the United States.

In 1887, the Hagenbecks started a traveling circus, using orange and blue wagons and cages, and performances were given under huge tents. Their performing animals became the talk of Europe, and the news spread to other countries. They also exhibited people from faraway lands, persuading these people to come along with the animals which the Hagenbecks brought from their respective countries.

The Hagenbecks came to America with the same kind of wild animal show which they had been giving in European countries, and were highly successful. After a time, Hagenbeck and the other directors of this U.S. company sold the show to Ben Wallace, John Talbot, and Terry Mugivan, and it was operated in 1907 under the name of "Hagenbeck Wild Animal Show." Ben Wallace bought out the other owners in November, 1907, and the title was changed to "The Hagenbeck-Wallace Show" (or circus), which became one of the "great circuses" of this era.

After Wallace died, this show was sold to the American Corporation, then to Ringling in 1929; 1937-38 was its last year on the road.

In 1902, Carl had bought about 3000 acres of land at Stellingen, Germany, and established the zoo of his dreams. There were no walls or fences, the different animals being separated by deep ditches. The native habitat of each species was copied as nearly as possible. Carl believed in fresh air and exercise, and he built what were known as "acclimatization halls" connected to the great out-of-doors. In such environments, animals mated, and the zoo grew. This idea revolutionized the building of zoos throughout the world.

When Carl Hagenbeck died in 1913, his sons, Heinrich and Lorenz, carried on. They organized a great circus and took it to every continent, with the exception of Australia. Then came World War II.

The Hagenbeck losses, during the air raids, were tremendous; by 1949, only 600 remained of the 5000 animals they possessed just ten years earlier. In one raid, monkeys escaped and embarked upon a raid of their own. They stole, frightened, confiscated, harassed the dogs and cats, and frightened the children.

The Hagenbecks did not despair. They hitched their few remaining elephants to plows and scrapers and filled the bomb craters. They used their old circus tent (which seated 3000), organized, and went on circuit with a light opera company. They made enough money to begin buying animals again. By 1949 they were on the long trail back up, buying ninety-five new wagons and a new tent which seated 4000. They went on more animal hunts. Friends from other countries shipped them animals on credit — a brave and big beginning on the road back to the place of prominence which they had occupied.

Success was theirs again and, in 1952, Dietrich Thomas Hagenbeck, great-great-grandson of the founder, Gottfried Hagenbeck, was mastering every detail of the circus, zoo, and wild animal trade.

THE FAMILY SHOWS 1850

THE SMALL FAMILY shows and early wagon shows, which bogged along on miserable roads during the nineteenth century, deserve a place in circus history. They were the training and testing grounds for acts, actors, advance men, and managers who moved on up to the large shows. Foremost among these early shows was that of Mollie Bailey; others were The Whitney, Orton, Wixom, and Ezra Stephens. These early shows had excellent blackface minstrels, who enjoyed their heyday later in vaudeville.

Many of the smaller shows touring the countryside were called "Medicine Shows," because they advertised and sold different medicines.

EZRA STEPHENS
"The Barnum of Maine"
1850

EZRA STEPHENS, known as the father of the "Side Show," conceived the idea of those colorful banners, known as the "Bannerline," which, in gaudy color and bizarre outline, depict the mysteries which are yours to visualize when you "walk right in, ladies and gents, walk right in. The show is just ready to start, and what you see on the bannerline, you'll witness in living reality on the inside." Such was the "line" thrown out in stentorian tones by the spieler of the side show, as John C. Kunzog tells us in *Bandwagon*. Ezra Stephens was really "the boy who got 'em told, got 'em sold, got 'em in, and got their money." He started the lucrative "fad" of getting two admissions from one person, one for the main show and one for the side show.

Ezra's slogan was "Watch the overhead," so he decided on four tents — one for the main show, one for the horses, one for the other animals; and the fourth tent, called the annex, was for the trained bear and other rare exhibits. Ezra was confident that, by using a touch of Barnum's ballyhoo, he could induce the public to pay an added admission charge to enter the annex. The scheme worked, and the side show was born. Ezra was a master in mob psychology. He agreed with Barnum that "a fool is born every minute." He emulated Barnum in every manner and method possible. He watched Barnum's exhibits. When Barnum exhibited Zeo in her famous slide down a rope from the tent's center pole, hanging by her hair, Ezra found a Circassion beauty who copied Zeo's act to perfection.

When Barnum offered Tom Thumb, Ezra secured Major Robert Harner, eighteen years of age, 40 inches in height, and weighing 48 pounds. How Ezra could so often match Barnum with a similar act was amazing, as though he, magician-like, pulled them from a hat.

Ezra did not use a "bally" stage. Since he was 6 feet 2 inches in height, he could be seen and also see over the heads in the crowd. He always, according to Kunzog, "wore a checkered suit of the latest design, a tall, black beaver hat, and his fingers were adorned with a wealth of diamonds." A mustache of the handlebar type completed the physical appearance. In those days, ballyhoo was known as "Outside Work," and Ezra was a genius in attracting crowds.

The Dancing Turkeys was considered to be Ezra's best act — his outstanding brain child. Old-timers scratched their heads and rubbed their chins. The turkeys in that part of the country, as Kunzog tells us, were worked overtime by aspiring young showmen — all to no avail. What they did not know was that just before the turkeys were put on exhibition for their "Turkey Trot," a coal fire was placed under the steel platform on which the turks were to perform. After a given number of seconds, the turkeys were taken from their coops and put in the large cage with the heated floor. They would stand on one foot and then the other. Soon an organ struck up a tune, timed to the steps of the birds, which became faster as they felt the heat more acutely. This act always "het the audience" to a frenzy of laughter.

His name should have been Ezra "Economy" Stephens. He secured from the Sandwich Glass Works a large piece of transparent glass resembling a chunk of ice, and this stroke of imagination worked psychologically, as thirsty patrons quenched their thirst for many years on Ezra's glass-cooled lemonade.

MOLLIE BAILEY CIRCUS
About 1859

WILLIAM KIRKLAND, 6 feet 2 inches, and weighing 300 pounds, married petite, impetuous, French "Mary." William was a Southern gentleman, owning a plantation in Alabama. Mary and William had a baby girl and they named her Mollie Arline. She grew up on the plantation knowing all the joys and luxuries of such a life. She was a tomboy—climbing trees, sliding down the barn roofs. She had black pigtails and snapping black eyes. She developed rapidly and her father thought it best to send her to a "ladies' academy" in Tuscaloosa. On her return home after the first year in the academy, she brought a letter from her instructor telling of her unusual ability in dramatics and tableau work.

William Kirkland studied his daughter—yesterday a child, today so changed. About this time a circus came to town. His mind turned quickly to that letter from the academy: "Excellent in dramatics and tableau work." Immediately he gave out the word that no one on the place was to attend that circus. Mollie seemed unperturbed. Mollie went to the circus, and no one knew how she managed, or that she had been. Now, there was a rusty, red-haired boy who led the band in that family circus—several children and the parents taking parts.

A few days later, Mollie, only fourteen years of age, packed her little box of quilt scraps, (all Southern girls were taught to embroider and sew, and quilt-piecing was quite an art), and a few belongings, and then, with all the courage she could muster, went to talk with her father. Without hesitating, she announced to him, "I am a grown young lady, Father. I am going to be married."

"Married at fourteen?" And then the storm broke. He forbade it, as did her mother. Again Mollie was unperturbed.

Vivian Richardson, writing in *The Dallas News* of the life of Mollie, tells the story so dramatically and intriguingly: "Moonlight night, whistle at bend of road, two hearts beating fast, swift ride to the minister, and on March 21, 1858, Mollie Arline Kirkland became Mrs. James Augustus Bailey."

The young couple spent their honeymoon on the road with the circus. Mollie was happy with Gus and his family, but she did want to be forgiven for running away. On two different occasions she returned home and asked for this forgiveness, but was turned away. Mollie was ambitious, gifted — a dynamo of energy, and a born manager. She encouraged Gus — she spurred his ambition. She talked of a show of their own, and he was eager and cooperative. They had no money, and she appealed to her father, but was turned down. So at night she showed some very acute business ability. She "borrowed" some horses and wagons from her father's plantation. Gus' brother, Alfred, came with them on the show, and soon Mollie's half sister joined them. They hired one performer. Mollie was leading lady, soloist, organist; Alfred was contortionist and musician; Gus played the fiddle, directed the orchestra, was leading man and comedian.

This courageous little company — a branch family show — went from small town to small town playing in the schoolhouses and borrowing furniture and props in each town. Candles flickered and oil lamps smoked. Candles in tin lard cans sufficed for footlights. But the whole performance was lighted by the heart and soul and indomitable courage of brave little Mollie. Her motto was, "Do it right, or else not at all." There were many dark hours. Sometimes they had to wait until after the show in order to get money to eat. Many times during these dark days, Mollie would call out the one word "Laugh." And then she would add, with a lilt in her voice, "to live without laughing is not to live at all."

Then there came a turn of fate, a mere incident that shaped a great part of the Bailey future. Mollie and Gus were on a main street in a town in Arkansas. A man had stopped his loaded wagon and was talking to some townsmen. "Grass enough for the whole kit and bilin' of you, and some left over. I ain't agoin' to let my shirttail tech me till I get back to Texas, and thar'll be a herd of yearlings astompin'."

" 'Texas,' " Mollie whispered.

"Yep. We'll try it," said Gus.

Before any plans could be made, the Civil War started. Both Mollie and Gus were hot-headed Southerners, and so they immediately disbanded their show. He enlisted in Hood's Brigade, and she volunteered as a nurse. Mollie had an infant daughter, so she took a nurse along and put her baby in a good home in Richmond. Mollie followed Hood's men from hospital to hospital. After several months with Hood's 5th Texas Brigade, she heard that the 3rd Arkansas Brigade was in need of quinine. She smuggled it in paper packages tucked in her hair and sewed in the hem of her skirts, and she secured information, while delivering quinine, that aided blockade runners. Mollie, in later years, never discussed this phase of her war work with her grandchildren, telling them only of her nursing and singing. However, old Confederates spread the news of her courage, and all loved Mollie with undying devotion.

During the war, Gus Bailey wrote the marching song, "The Old Gray Mare," as familiar to Texans as, "The Eyes of Texas." ("The Old Gray Mare" was the official song at the National Democratic Convention in Houston, Texas, in 1928.)

After the war, conditions were so bad that the Baileys could not make a living in the show business for their young daughters and themselves, so they joined a showboat company on the Mississippi. Within a year's time, they had saved enough money to rent a boat and start a company of their own.

However, Mollie still had the burning desire to go to Texas, so after a short time they traded their interest in the showboat for mules. They made the trip in 1869 as far as Arkansas. The hardships — cold and starvation of the war — had left Gus weakened physically; however, he improved. There was little money. But Mollie managed. She fed her family on nourishing hoecake, gravy, and beans. She patched and passed down clothes, she remade her clothes until her fingers ached. Times grew worse, as Gus' health worsened. Mollie had named a son for her father, William Kirkland. And now, in need, but brave, she made her last plea for forgiveness, telling her father of his namesake; but he, as well as her mother, was unrelenting. She never saw either again, from the time she left home a girl of fourteen.

After twelve long hard years following the war, Mollie had better days. They bought a carriage, they stayed in hotels, their six children were healthy. Mollie's supply of energy seemed inexhaustible. She wore dark, rich costumes, had a small corseted waist, was commanding in appearance and manner; she possessed a "swooping stateliness" in her full skirts. She was witty, reserved, charming, and friendly. She could have been a success in almost any walk of life, a great lady in society or business, but she trouped from the age of fourteen to seventy; and not one time did she utter the least desire to leave the show.

She took on the management of the show, since Gus' health was failing, and became known as Aunt Mollie. In 1885, the Baileys left Arkansas and wintered in Dallas, Texas. At long-last, Mollie Bailey was in Texas. In 1887, her circus became a tent show, gradually growing until she had 170 ponies, a number of animals, and thirty-one wagons which resembled prairie schooners. She had tiered seats. In 1890, Gus could no longer travel with the show. She moved to Houston, where the climate was milder, and bought a home there.

Mollie's show became more and more in demand. Country fairs waited for it. Confederate veterans arranged their reunions to coincide with its scheduled appearance. Mollie subscribed to every Confederate monument, bought a lot in every booming town, gave the gate receipts of opening shows to churches, or charitable causes. By 1890, more than half the time she showed on her own lots, thus saving occupation taxes — a new idea in the show business.

In buying groceries for her show, she never waited for the entire order but paid for each item as it was placed on the counter, often making the remark, "I pay as I go."

In 1905, Mollie bought a Pullman and two boxcars. There was always "Open House" on the Pullman. Mollie never failed to have three flags flying at the entrance of her tent — the Texas, the United States, and the Confederate.

There was never a character like Mollie Bailey. The great trouper died in 1918. She suffered tenfold in the troubles and sorrows of her family, but she could throw off her own disappointments; a wonderful mother; a devoted wife; friend to the needy; a true Confederate to her death; unique and aloof in her field having no competition; the only woman in the world to ever operate a circus successfully over a period of time. Mollie Bailey was truly, "The Circus Queen of the Southwest."

ADAM FOREPAUGH
Before 1864

ADAM FOREPAUGH is one of the big names in American Circusdom. Adam Fuehrbach (Vorbach) was born in

Philadelphia, February 28, 1831. From the age of nine he worked hard and saved every penny possible. He prospered and entered the horse-trading business. He was an excellent judge of horses and a good trader. Before he was twenty years of age, he had saved $20,000, and then he returned to Philadelphia where he continued horse-trading.

It was here that he sold forty-four horses to James V. (Pogey) O'Brien for $9000. O'Brien was a well-known circus man but he was not able to pay all in cash, so he prevailed upon the shrewd Adam to take an interest in his circus as partial payment. Adam agreed, and thus he entered the circus business. It was at this time that he changed his name to Adam Forepaugh.

In 1865, Adam bought out O'Brien and concentrated on the Dan Rice Show, which they had previously taken over. In April of 1865, he bought the Mabie Show's menagerie. It had been the custom of all the shows which exhibited animals to tie them just inside the main show tent. Forepaugh found he had a traffic jam on his hands; so he decided to carry another tent, to be known as the menagerie tent. His was the first circus to carry a sizable menagerie tent, in 1869, but soon all the large circuses had added the animal tent.

Forepaugh continued to make money, but continued to travel by the old wagon roads. Finally, in 1875, he took to the rails, although Coup had put the Barnum Show on wheels in 1872. A three-year delay on any progressive move in show business is a long time.

With the Forepaugh Circus and the Bailey Circus growing at such speed, competition was too close for good financial result, so Bailey and Forepaugh reached an agreement whereas both shows, not conflicting as to date, would play in New York and Philadelphia, and after that the towns and territory in the United States were divided and each went on his prearranged way. All went well until the "White Elephant Feud" broke. Bailey had purchased a genuine white elephant (so the story goes), but this elephant was not *too* white. Bailey had paid a very large amount of money for this elephant, because white elephants had always been considered sacred in India and one had never before been sold.

Forepaugh heard of this white elephant. He began planning immediately. He bought an elephant in London, had it painted a glistening white over there (so the story goes) and then shipped it to the United States. Tempers flared — and cooled. However, competition continued between the three shows, Forepaugh's, Barnum's, and Bailey's. In 1888, Forepaugh concluded a most profitable show at the New York Garden, and this was his final brush with the circus.

Two of the most famous posters in circus history came out when competition was at its hottest between Forepaugh and Barnum, and they touched off "The Battle of Adjectives." The famous Forepaugh poster is now in the Hertzberg Circus Collection in the Public Library, San Antonio, Texas. The Barnum poster is in the Bishop Historical Room of the Burroughs Public Library, Bridgeport, Connecticut. Such rivalry became very expensive and unprofitable, and was often quite bitter. "The Battle of the Adjectives" is an excellent example of this intense rivalry.

The two posters which illustrate what is called the "Battle of the Adjectives" between the two men have become two of the most famous posters in all circusdom. The first one, brought out by Forepaugh, shows him a "Giant Among The Pigmys," towering composedly above all of his competitive circus owners.

Barnum had fought long and hard to attain his pinnacle of success. He was not to be outdone. Barnum always rose to the occasion, and usually "went one better." He struck back with clever venom at this Forepaugh poster. He punned with stinging comment on Forepaugh's (four-clawed) name. In the Barnum poster-answer, the head of Forepaugh was on a frog, and Barnum's head on a bull. The sub-caption of this poster was, "The Frog and the Ox." Barnum took his idea for the ox poster from Aesop's Fables. This cartoon really won for Barnum the "Battle of the Adjectives"; and from then on "Barnum's circus proceeded to win the battle for customers."

BEN LUSBIE 1839 - 1884

BEN LUSBIE reached stardom in a role never before or since accomplished. He was a feature drawing card in an act on which he held monopoly. Ben Lusbie was called "THE LIGHTNING TICKET-SELLER CHAMPION OF THE WORLD."

Lusbie was gifted with a mathematical mind, astounding in speed and accuracy. He sold as much as $13,000 worth of tickets in one day's working time. His record was 6,153 tickets in one hour and three minutes.

PHINEAS T. BARNUM Circus 1870

"BALLYHOO BORN OF BARNUM!" Barnum gave birth to the science of ballyhoo, and mastered the art of showmanship in a measure never witnessed before, and with a genius that has made him the pattern of publicity experts ever since. "Barnum" became a household word. He was truly an "IDEA" man.

Phineas T. Barnum was born in Bethel, Connecticut, on July 5, 1810. It was his natural disposition to look on the bright side of life. The story of his life, with contrasts of humble origin and high, honorable success; of great obstacles overcome by courage; of affluence patiently won, suddenly snatched away, and triumphantly regained, is an incentive to anyone who is looking into the future with doubt, fear, or despair.

Barnum started school at the age of six, and was an apt pupil. At the age of twelve, he was called out of bed one night by his schoolteacher, who had made a wager with a neighbor that he could calculate the correct number of feet in a load of wood in five minutes. The dimensions were called out to him and he gave the correct answer in less than two minutes. This incident was most applicable to Barnum, in that he always seemed able to grasp the dimensions of life and give, not only the correct answers, but the answers the people wanted.

Before the age of five, Barnum started saving pennies. At the age of six years, his capital amounted to a sum sufficient to exchange for a silver dollar. He relates that the possession of that huge piece of money made him feel far richer and more independent than he had ever felt since. He always had the Midas touch of changing pennies into silver dollars. The one great word in his life was "ENERGY," which he considered the key word to success. His first salary was ten cents a day, riding the lead horse in ploughing. On holidays he sold homemade molasses candy, gingerbread, and cookies made by his mother, to whom he remained devoted throughout his life. At twelve years, he accepted his first position, helping to drive a herd of cattle to New York. Since he left in a snowstorm, his mother was concerned over his safety. The trip was hard but educational.

When young Phineas left for New York, his mother gave him a dollar. He was sure that amount would take care of every want his heart would wish. The first day in New York he bought four oranges, a toy gun, and a watch, and then a breast pin to take to his mother. These purchases left him with only eleven cents. This went for some very light molasses candy, which was so delicious he bargained for more, giving an extra pair of stockings and two pocket handkerchiefs which his mother had given him on leaving home.

As Barnum grew up, he tried several business ventures, but it was as the owner of a general merchandise country store that he cut his eyeteeth in the business world. It was after being sold bundles of rags, with bricks in the middle, that he declared man's head should be on a swivel so as to watch on all sides. Perhaps it was because he was himself a "sucker" in this business, that he made, later in his life, his world-renowned remark, "A sucker is born every minute." It was this gullibility of man, which he observed on all sides, that helped develop his technique of advertising — the ballyhoo — and the general public has always liked it.

Barnum was a born showman. He learned, early in life, that ever-present, insatiate desire of human nature, the love of amusement. His first venture into this show-world was the exhibition of a Negro woman, Joyce Heath, said to have been the nurse of General George Washington, and reportedly 106 years of age. Barnum had saved $500; he borrowed $500 more and bought Joyce Heath, and thus he began life as a showman. With his innate belief in advertising, he had huge posters and advertisements made of Joyce Heath, sparing no expense. The exhibition of the Negress was a financial success and henceforth Barnum remained in some sort of show business, having found his true vocation.

Barnum next engaged an Italian, "Vivalla," who accomplished remarkable feats of balancing, stilt-walking, and plate-spinning. It was as an assistant to this Vivalla that Barnum made his first appearance on any stage — a stage which widened to a universal one during his lifetime, as Barnum spoke and showed around the world.

While on the stage with the juggler this first night, Barnum heard a man hiss. He immediately detected the one who hissed and in a few minutes he had talked with him, and finding him to be a juggler, Barnum hired him immediately and announced to the audience that there would be a juggling contest between the Italian and the man who had hissed, as he had just hired him. This venture packed the show house.

After a number of successful and some unsuccessful ventures, Barnum bought The American Museum. This firmly established him as a showman. The nucleus of this museum had been started in 1810, the year of Barnum's birth. It contained many rare relics and curiosities. Barnum, with his unbounded energy, launched a real success story. For many years he never ate a warm lunch, always carrying a sandwich in his pocket for a noonday snack.

It was Barnum's monomania to make the museum the town wonder and town talk. He understood the power of printer's ink and advertised extensively. He always seized upon an opportunity as if by instinct. One day a stout, hardy man came into his ticket office and begged some money. Barnum asked him if he wanted to work. He did, volunteering to work for a dollar a day. Barnum employed him at a dollar and a half a day, bought his breakfast, and then gave him five common bricks. These were the instructions which Barnum gave him, and which he records in his autobiography, *Struggles & Triumphs*: "Go and lay a brick on the sidewalk at the corner of Broadway and Ann Streets; another close by the Museum; a third diagonally across the way at the corner of Broadway and Vesey Streets, by the Astor House; put down the fourth by the sidewalk in front of St. Paul's Church, opposite; then with the fifth brick in hand, take up a rapid march from one place to the other, making the circuit, exchanging your brick at every point and say nothing to anyone. Be deaf as a post, wear a serious expression, and answer no questions, pay no attention to anyone and at the end of each hour by St. Paul's clock, show this ticket at the museum door. Enter, walking solemnly through every hall and building; pass out and resume your work."

Half an hour afterwards, at least 500 people were watching this man's mysterious movements. He had assumed a military step and bearing. At the end of one hour, the streets were packed with people excitedly trying to solve the mystery. Many bought tickets and followed the man into the museum. After several days, the policeman, to whom Barnum had confided his scheme, complained that the obstruction of the sidewalks had become so serious that Barnum must call in his "brick" man.

Another example of Barnum's eye for publicity is interesting and amusing. One day, at the age of eighty, he tripped over a rope while walking in Madison Square Garden, where his Greatest Show on Earth was showing. He was slightly scratched. A workman went to help him, but Phineas lay flat and yelled, "Where's the press agent? Tell him I've been injured in an accident." The next day he remained at home, that the show might get the benefit of the publicity.

The transient attractions at the museum were diversified — a miniature Niagara Falls with real water, an attraction for newly-weds of modest means who could not afford a trip to see the real thing; educated dogs; industrious fleas; automatons; jugglers; ventriloquists; living statuary; gypsies; albinos; fat boys; giants; dwarfs; rope dancers; music; the first Punch and Judy show ever exhibited in America; all drew crowds and at the low admission price of 25¢ and half-price for children.

Barnum was the first one to present the temperance play, *The Drunkard,* after it had its premiere in Boston. He also introduced stage plays in his museum but abolished all vulgarity and profanity from such. Many world-renowned actors appeared at his museum. Lecture rooms were added, also a hall which held 3000 people — and still thousands of eager people were turned away. Barnum held baby shows, giving prizes for the finest baby, the fattest, for twins, and for triplets. There were flower shows, dog shows, poultry shows, bird shows. The museum was far more than a "glorified side show." It was cosmopolitan — interesting to the scientist and the educator as well as the layman. The age limit of enjoyment was not restricted. It was clean, safe entertainment for the whole family.

Indeed, Barnum's Museum did become the town talk and the town wonder.

BARNUM AND GENERAL TOM THUMB

IN NOVEMBER, 1842, Barnum was in Albany, New York, where he heard of a remarkably small child. He was not two feet in height, weighed less than 15 pounds, but was perfectly formed, a bright-eyed little fellow, with light hair and ruddy cheeks, who enjoyed the best of health. With the consent of his parents, Barnum engaged him for four weeks at $3.00 a week, with all traveling expenses paid for him and his mother. On Thanksgiving Day, December 8, 1842, he was billed at the museum as General Tom Thumb. His real name was Charles Sherwood Stratton. Barnum named him Thumb from the character in English folklore — "the son of a plowman, as big as his father's thumb, who had many adventures, including being swallowed by a cow and a giant."

General Thumb was an apt pupil in learning the show business and his fame spread throughout the United States. His salary had been increased and, after touring the United States, he was exhibited in Europe. The exhibition of General Tom Thumb proved to be one of twin master strokes in the show life of Barnum. (The other being the presentation of Jenny Lind.) On his European tour (1844) the general was brought in close contact with queens, kings, lords, and illustrious commoners. Such associations were beneficial in introducing Barnum to the great public — and the public's money. Barnum carried Tom Thumb through the streets in his arms dressed as a baby so people would not recognize him, otherwise they would not pay to see him.

Three times the general and Barnum were invited to Buckingham Palace to meet Queen Victoria's friends and visiting royalty. Making the most of such invitations, Barnum would hang a placard on the door of the Egyptian Hall, which he had engaged for presenting the general, reading, "Closed this evening, General Tom Thumb being at Buckingham Palace by command of her Majesty."

It is said that on Tom Thumb's first visit to the queen, after greeting her and her guests in a very polite and courtly manner, he turned to the queen and told her she had a "nice place here," and then asked where her little boy was. Queen Victoria gave Tom Thumb a tiny golden coach (now on display at Cliff House, San Francisco, California). On the third visit, the queen presented the general with a watch which she had made expressly for him. Many gifts of great value were showered upon him.

The general always created quite a bit of laughter as he left Her Majesty's presence. He had been well coached in court behavior. He would bow very low and start backing, showing the proper courtesy to Her Majesty, by backing from her presence. Looking around to find the rest of his party much nearer the exit than he, he would turn, run as fast as he could, catch up, and immediately turn and start backing again, all of which was a very serious procedure with him.

In France, the general was entertained in the same manner as in England, by the King and Queen of France. His fame had gone before him, and the entertaining was more elaborate and frequent. He appeared four times, by command, before the King and Queen of France, at one time wearing his Napoleon Bonaparte costume. The king presented the general with a large emerald brooch set with diamonds. He was literally the pet of all Paris. He also appeared at many charity entertainments. So much money rolled in in London and Paris that a special carriage was engaged to carry it. All of Tom Thumb's appearances were highly remunerative. The same success attended his tour of Belgium. His popularity continued on his return to the United States.

During the early days of General Tom Thumb's touring, Barnum designed, and had made, an elaborate little carriage for him. It was a work of fine craftsmanship and art — painted silver and red, and white and blue, lined with yellow silk. It was pulled by four very small horses. During his European tours, his carriage was always accorded a space along with the royal carriages that it might have safe passage. In touring France, twelve horses and twelve people and several large carriages, and the general's four small horses and carriage, were required to transport in style his petite majesty of 15 pounds, and his baggage. And this style was far beyond that of a field marshal — but what advertising it was! Such an entourage!

Later, another midget, Lavinia Warren, joined Barnum's company. Her real name was Mercy Lavinia Bump. She was born in Middleboro, Massachusetts. She taught school there when she was only 30 inches in height. While with Barnum's company, she met and married General Tom Thumb. He was twenty-five years of age and she was twenty-two. This was a great wedding attended by governors of several states, army generals, and men and women of affluence. Tom Thumb had carried on a classic, diminutive love duel in winning the hand of Lavinia Warren. Although Commodore Nutt was the midget swain who had sought Lavinia's love and failed, Tom Thumb had the gall to ask him to be best man, and with the bigness of a little heart, Commodore accepted defeat gracefully and acted as best man. Winnie Warren, Lavinia's sister, also a midget, was maid of honor. The famed couple were married in Grace Episcopal Church in New York City on February 10, 1863. Fabulous gifts were received from the world's most prominent personages. Their wedding cake weighed eighty pounds. Two thousand boxes of wedding cake were given to guests.

P. T. Barnum capitalized on this wedding. It was a "natural" for a publicity event. The wedding news traveled around the world.

Tom and Lavinia were very happy. One child was born to this union. It lived only two and one-half years. (There are conflicting reports as to the birth of this baby. Some say it was adopted, and others that it was just borrowed.) Tom Thumb died at the age of forty-five and was buried in Mountain Grove Cemetery, near the spot where his devoted friend, the six-foot-two Barnum, was soon to follow.

The great P. T. Barnum and the great General Tom Thumb were the closest of friends during their entire lifetimes. Tom always considered himself Barnum's "little but sympathizing friend." Often Barnum would point to General Thumb and say, "I have sold him hundreds of times and have never delivered him yet." And the little general would reply, "Ah! But in the meantime, I've been kissed by a million ladies."

After Barnum's tours with General Tom Thumb, he built a palatial home at Bridgeport, Connecticut. He named it Iranistan — the name signifies "Eastern Country Place," or, more poetically, "Oriental Villa." Years later this beautiful home burned, and he built two other Bridgeport houses, Lindincroft and Waldemere, but he always looked upon Iranistan as "The Home of His Dreams."

JENNY LIND

BARNUM'S NEXT VENTURE was bold in conception, complete in its development, and astounding in its success. He risked a fortune but made more. He conceived the idea of bringing Jenny Lind, the "Swedish Nightingale," to this country. Although Miss Lind never toured with a circus, her appearance was such a master stroke on the part of Barnum, the great showman, that its effect was profound and deserves space due to the position Barnum held in the circus world.

Johanna Maria Lind was born in Stockholm, Sweden, October 6, 1820. However, she had always been known by her charming name of Jenny Lind. Jenny inherited the musical ability of her father and the strict religious beliefs and business ability of her mother. She was at the height of her popularity in Europe when Mr. Barnum, who had neither seen nor heard her, made his decision to bring her to the United States. A Mr. Wilson was sent to make arrangements and was given the following instructions: "Engage her at any rate not exceeding $1000 a night, for any number of nights up to 150, with all her expenses, including servants, carriages, secretary, and also engage such musical assistants, not exceeding three in number, as she should select; let the terms be what they might."

Mr. Wilson was successful in engaging Jenny Lind for $1000 a night and she brought Mr. Benedict, the composer, pianist and musical director, and Signor Belletti, a fine baritone — also two cousins of hers, two servants, and a valet. According to agreement, Mr. Barnum deposited $187,500 in a London bank, this being a sufficient amount to pay Miss Lind for the stipulated number of appearances and all her expenses.

Miss Lind's arrival had been heralded by Mr. Barnum's own brand of advertising. Never before had there been such a welcome in New York. Banners, arches of flowers on the wharf — thousands of people met the ship; twenty thousand congregated around the entrance to Irving House where Miss Lind was to stay. At midnight she was serenaded by the New York Musical Fund Society, which was escorted to Irving House by three hundred firemen, wearing their red shirts and bearing torches. For weeks the excitement was unabated. Presents were showered upon her. There appeared in the stores Jenny Lind gloves, robes, chairs, pianos—a Jenny Lind phobia held the public. Poems and songs were written about her and to her.

One wit, we learn from *Struggles & Triumphs,* ascribed to Barnum the following lines:

> So Jenny, come along! You're just the card for me,
> And quit those kings and queens for the country of the free;
> They'll welcome you with speeches, and serenades, and rockets,
> And you will touch their hearts, and I will tap their pockets;
> And if between us both the public isn't skinned,
> Why, my name isn't Barnum, nor your name Jenny Lind!

Tickets for Jenny Lind's first performance were sold at auction—the first ticket bringing $225 in New York; in Boston, $625; and the highest bid in any city was $653 in Providence, Rhode Island.

The first Jenny Lind concert brought $17,864.05; the second, $14,203.03. Instead of holding to his contract of $1000 a night to Jenny Lind, Barnum raised it, and after the first two concerts he divided the profit equally. Jenny Lind had never heard, nor dreamed of, such liberality. Her gifts to charity were, in turn, amazing, feeling that such gifts counteracted her mother's fear of the moral corruption of the theater.

Adulation and praise of Miss Lind continued. The morning after her arrival in Washington, President Fillmore called and left his card. The president and his family, along with every member of the cabinet, and many congressmen, attended her first concert in Washington. Jenny Lind, Barnum, and company were entertained at Mount Vernon, where Mrs. Washington presented her with a book from

Washington's own library, in which he had written his name.

Success continued. Jenny Lind not only possessed a wonderful voice but also unusual acting ability. Ninety-five concerts were given. By this time Miss Lind and Mr. Barnum were worn and weary and they mutually agreed to conclude the tour. In 1852, Miss Lind married a German composer in Boston. His name was Otto Goldschmidt. Later they returned to England where she gave her time to church work and teaching. She was in Munich when she died, November 2, 1887.

THE BARNUM & BAILEY CIRCUS

AFTER THE STRENUOUS Lind tours, Barnum retired to his beautiful home, Iranistan, for a much-needed rest. He gave some time to his growing American Museum and Menagerie, which Mr. Seth B. Howes was managing most successfully. This traveling menagerie had been joined by General Tom Thumb, and ten elephants had been added. It became known as "Barnum's Great Asiatic Caravan Museum and Menagerie." The show returned immense profits. Having toured the country for nearly four years, Barnum sold out the entire establishment—with the exception of one elephant, Old Josh, which he retained, as *he* said, for "agricultural purposes."

Old Josh was sent to plow Barnum's farm near Bridgeport. This again was a neat advertising stroke. The steam railway ran by this farm. Old Josh was hitched to a plow and his keeper was dressed in oriental costume. The man was told exactly the times the trains would pass each day. A few minutes before each train time, Josh and the man in costume would start plowing as though they were in the greatest rush to get the crop planted. Barnum estimated that this six-acre plot was plowed at least sixty times. The idea worked like magic, just as Barnum had planned. Heads would pop out all windows of the train. Whoever saw an elephant plowing?! More coaches had to be added to the trains to carry the crowds. The newspapers carried pictures of Josh plowing, with headlines such as, "P. T. Barnum's Elephantine Agriculture"; "Old Mule, the Elephant's Got Your Place"; "Farming to be Revolutionized"; "Elephants Do All the Work"; "Soon the Elephant Will Rock the Cradle and Wash the Dishes." Thousands of people thus became interested in Barnum and went to see his museum in New York, just as he had hoped.

An interesting story is told that showed the great success of the museum, as well as pointing up Barnum's ingenuity. On this particular day, a great many Irishmen were celebrating some special occasion and had carried their lunches, intending to spend the entire day in the museum. (And indeed it would have taken more than a day to see everything.) Great crowds collected outside the museum awaiting admission. Barnum immediately had a large sign painted and hung conveniently near a side entrance. It read, "To the Egress," with a hand pointing toward the door. The Irishmen, eager to see everything, rushed out. The Irish always enjoy a good joke, and once out, they remained to laugh at all others who were so ingeniously lured out.

On July 13, 1865, the American Museum burned, only a few animals being saved. The loss was set at $400,000; it was insured for only $40,000. With that ever-ready courage and determination, dominated by the one word of his life, "energy," Barnum cabled far countries for animals; he bought several museums, and all small collections of any worth, and, in five months, on November 13, 1865, he opened a new American Museum. He had remodeled the old Chinese Museum at Broadway and Pine, and these doors were opened amid much fanfare.

But fire, that haunting demon — especially of the amusement world — struck again. On March 3, 1868, this new museum burned.

1. THE CELEBRATED MIFS WILKINFON, THE FEMALE WIRE DANCER (ABOUT 1784)

2. "PRODIGY 'TWIXT BRUTE AND MAN" (1784)

1784

Extempore, Wrote by a Gentleman on seeing that amazing and singular production of Nature,

The ETHIOPIAN SAVAGE.

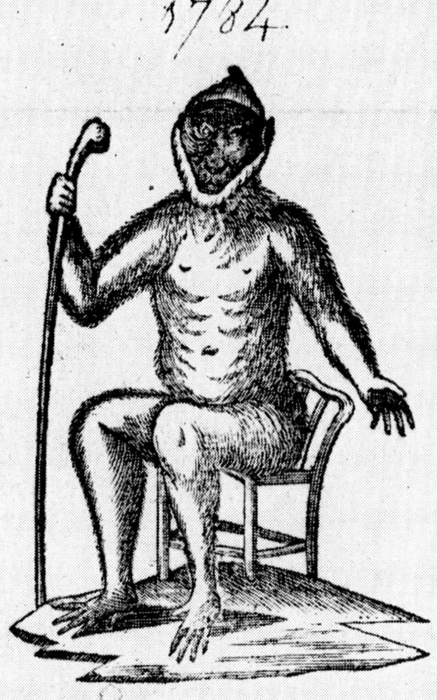

Those who've Arabia's dreary desarts trac'd,
Or roam'd thro' Africa's vast expansive waste;
In search of Nature's deep misterious laws,
Cou'd ne'er with certainty assert the cause;
(In vain their all attempts as yet do scan,)
Whence sprang this Prodigy 'twixt Brute & Man;
No art's here us'd, the Public to deceive,
He all excels.—— Haste, see him, and believe.

To the admirers of the wonderful Production of Nature,
To be Seen alive at No. 99 HOLBORN HILL

A most Astonishing Creature, called the oriental

S A T Y R,

or Real wild-Man of the Woods,

IT may be justly asserted, that this Animal is of a different Species from any Creature ever seen in Europe, and seems to be the Link between the rational and brute Creation. It was brought from the East-Indies to Amsterdam in a Dutch ship, and purchased by the Proprietor for a large Sum.

This astonishing Creature, when he stands erect, is near five feet high, and in many respects is a striking resemblance of the Human species. his Ears are small, but have large apertues, so that he is extremely quick of hearing; his Face is Black with a white Circle round it, which resembles a Mask, his Fore-feet are like the Arms and Hands of a Man, and grow gradually taper till they come to the Wrist, and he uses his Fingers with surprizing Facility, his Body is covered with a fine long hair, perfectly smooth on the surface, he sits in a Chair in a very pleasing and majestic attitude, to receive and eat his Food; he is very affible and obedient to the commands of his Keeper, who can even sleep by his side with safety. This wonderful Creature is a fine display of Nature's amazing Productions, and is allowed to be the greatest Curiosity ever exhibited in Britain.

N. B. Foreign Birds, Beasts, &c. Bought and Sold.

THE ONLY GENUINE LIVING HIPPOPOTAMUS from the WHITE NILE
POSITIVELY LARGEST IN CAPTIVITY.

3. HIPPOPOTAMUS POSTER, BARNUM & BAILEY CIRCUS

4. BARNUM & BAILEY SNAKE WAGON (1888)

5. ASTLEY'S BILL (1786)

Par Permission du ROI, & de Monseigneur le Lieutenant-Général de Police.

EXÉRCICES

SURPRENANS

DES SIEURS

ASTLEY,

RUE ET FAUXBOURG DU TEMPLE,

Aujouord'hui MERCREDI 27 Décembre 1786.

. LION AND SERPENT WAGON

7. THE TWO JESTERS CALLIOPE, HAGENBECK-WALLACE CIRCUS (1934)

8. FIVE GRACES BAND WAGON

9. BARNUM & BAILEY'S HEMISPHERE BAND WAGON

10. JOHN RINGLING NORTH II, AND LOU JACOBS (1950)

11. MERRY-GO-ROUND, BUCHANAN'S YANKEE ROBINSON CIRCUS (1909)

12. FAMOUS RICHARD SANDS POSTER (LONDON, 1843)

13. "KISS ME" — MAX SCHUMANN AND KATCHA

14. HORSES' BASKETBALL GAME

15. DOUBLE DRIBBLE

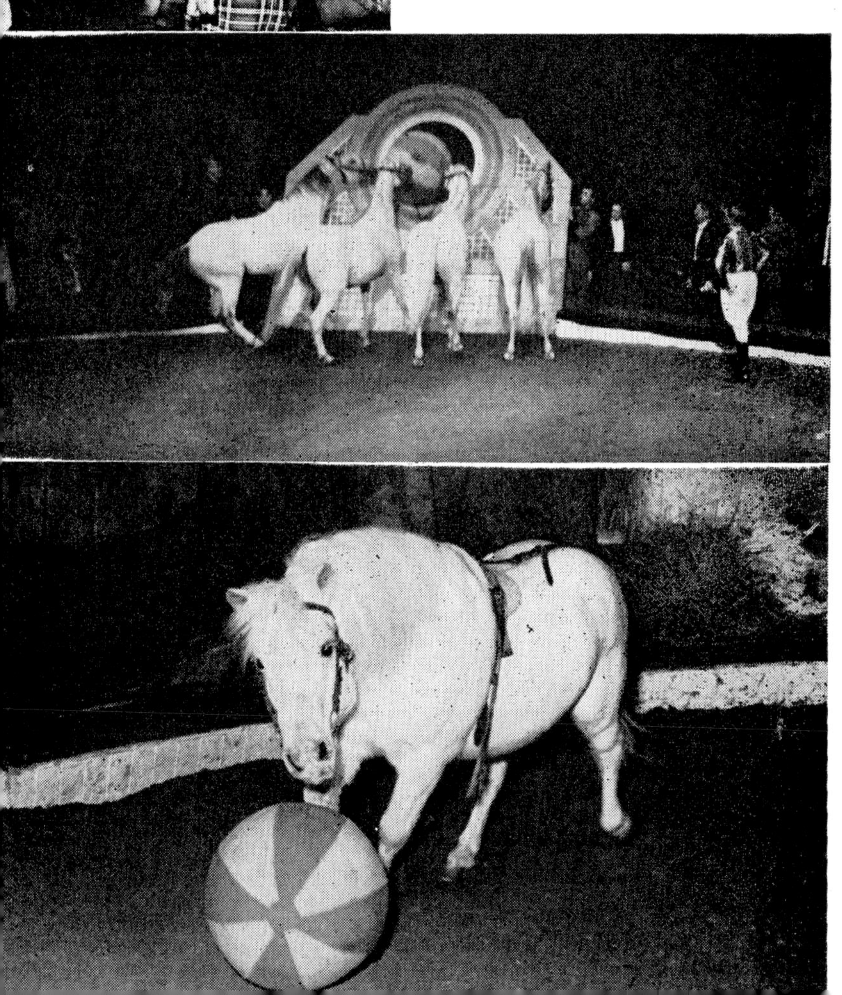

16. A FAMILY OR "MUD" SHOW

17. MOLLIE BAILEY

18. FAMOUS FOREPAUGH POSTER — TOUCHED OFF "THE BATTLE OF ADJECTIVES"

19. BARNUM'S POSTER REPLY

20. THE ONE AND ONLY P. T. BARNUM — FROM AN OLD LITHOGRAPH (1842)

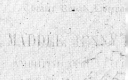

← Jenny Lind.
Photograph taken at
Newcastle on Tyne, by
W & D Downey

21. GENERAL TOM THUMB

22. JENNY LIND (1847)

23. THE DEATH OF JUMBO

24. JAKE POSEY'S HANDS — THE 40-HORSE TEAM

25. FIRST CIRCUS TENTS OF THE RINGLING BROTHERS (1884)

26. JOHN RINGLING

OTTO
ALF T.
CHARLES
John

27. RINGLING BROTHERS FIRST NEW GRANDSTAND TRUCK

28. THE RINGLINGS — SEATED: JOHN, MRS. AUGUST, MR. AUGUST, IDA RINGLING NORTH, HENRY. STANDING: ALBERT, ALFRED T., AUGUST G., CHARLES, OTTO

29. FAMOUS MOUSTACHE CUP POSTER

30. FROM THE TOP: OTTO, CHARLES, ALF RINGLING, BARNUM, BAILEY, JOHN AND AL RINGLING

33. CA'D'ZAN, THE RINGLING HOME

34. A BUDDING EQUESTRIAN

31. JOHN RINGLING

32. MABLE RINGLING

All old-timers remember this fire, for it was so cold the water froze in the hose and what water did get through festooned itself in icicles over the entire building. The people sleeping in the building barely escaped, and animals burned in their cages. The fire was caused by a defective flue in the restaurant in the basement of the building. The loss was close to $1,000,000, with only $160,000 insurance.

Other fires throughout Barnum's long career failed to singe the wings of his enthusiasm or to subdue his energy. One of the worst fires he encountered was the loss of his circus building, animals, and equipment; and then his circus winter quarters at Bridegport burned to the ground. He took the losses with courage, determination, and again called forth his ingenuity. With the great enthusiasm and "ENERGY" – that one word that burned in the very warp and woof of his body and heart – he again toured Europe with General Tom Thumb. He also took Cordelia Howard, who played the role of Little Eva, and her mother, who took the part of Topsy, in the play, *Uncle Tom's Cabin.* Barnum slowly recouped his great losses.

In 1870, influenced by W. C. Coup, an experienced showman, Barnum organzied a traveling show that was the forerunner of the famous Barnum & Bailey Circus. Its success was immediate. Barnum sent agents to all parts of the world to seek out and buy attractions for this show. His name carried weight throughout the United States and in many important countries in Europe. The opening performance was in Brooklyn, April 10, 1871. The tent covered nearly three acres and had a capacity of 10,000, the largest ever used, and daily one to three thousand people were turned away. There were more animals and men and acts than ever before with a show. The success of this show was fantastic – the first year's net was $400,000. Only the larger towns were played, from Maine to Kansas. Excursions were run by the railroads from all surrounding smaller towns for such a circus event. Distant advertising, seventy-five miles away, was a direct cause for such crowds.

This was the first circus or show to travel by rail in its own cars; also the first to exceed the million dollar mark in receipts for a single year. In an old *Herald*, dated July 3, 1879, the story is told of the first electric lights ever to be used in a circus (Barnum's) — operated by 30 horsepower steam engines and boiler and a Brush electric plant, the equal of 35,000 gas jets. This was a big drawing card for the Barnum circus.

Barnum now was able to reach an agreement to combine his show with the circus owned by Cooper, Bailey, and Hutchinson, which show had already purchased Howe's Great London Circus and Sanger's Royal British Menagerie. This combination was a master stroke of business enterprise. After Cooper's death, the show was continued with Barnum, Bailey, and Hutchinson as owners.

Some time later, the great name of the era came from this combination — the name of magic, the name that was to live on to the present day, The Barnum & Bailey Circus. Bailey's background and experience in show business is most interesting to follow. At this time Barnum had already become famous and Bailey was well-known among showmen. Each of these men was fortunate in having the other for a partner.

James Anthony Bailey's original name was James Anthony McGuinness. He was born in Detroit, Michigan, July 4, 1847. He was orphaned at the age of six. He lived with his sister until he was eleven, when he ran away and became a farmer's helper; later he became a bellboy, circus bill-poster, clerk in the Union Army, and finally a genuine and most successful circus man. While he was a bellboy in Howell, Michigan, and only thirteen years of age, he became acquainted with Colonel Fred Bailey who was publicizing the Robinson and Lake Circus. Young McGuinness left town with Bailey and adopted his name. Having served in the Civil War, he returned to the Robinson Show. He was only seventeen, but he was ready, capable, and willing to do a man's work and do it well.

In 1869, James Bailey joined the James E. Cooper Circus as chief agent at $100 dollars per week. In 1872 he bought the privileges, and in 1873 became a full-fledged partner. In Bailey, the circus world was soon to view one of the leading, most astute, and most fair-dealing figures ever to enter circusdom.

In 1876, still under thirty years of age, Bailey had bought out Cooper and had organized his own excellent company. With courage and initiative, Bailey toured 76,000 miles in two years, going to Australia, Tasmania, the Dutch East Indies, and back to Australia. There he bought a boat and transplanted his company to Peru, Chile, Argentina, and Brazil. His ability as a circus manager was becoming well-known. Soon, on his return to New York, he learned that Howe's Great London Co. and Sanger's Royal British Menagerie, were in financial difficulty, and he cabled his agents to buy it. Now he owned Cooper-Bailey and Co. and the London-Sanger combination. It was at this time that P. T. Barnum started laying plans, for he realized that in Bailey he had a worthy foe in the super-circus field.

Forepaugh had enlarged his show, at last putting it on rails, buying thirty-seven cars. Forepaugh negotiated a pact with Bailey for the London Show whereby he would join his for an opening in Philadelphia in 1880, and divide the profits, putting them both in a better position to fight Barnum. However, in August, 1880, Barnum, a leap ahead always, entered a partnership with Bailey whereby their shows and titles were merged for the 1881 season only. Then in retaliation, Forepaugh, in 1882, made an agreement with Bailey whereby they could each play New York and Philadelphia but not conflict in dates, and then they divided the territory east and west. This agreement worked well for two years until, in 1884, it broke with a bang over "The White Elephant War." (See page 41, Adam Forepaugh.)

After several changes in plans, negotiations, and business deals, Bailey finally purchased one-half interest in Barnum's show in 1887, for $150,000, with the stipulation that he was to be in supreme command and Barnum was to cover the world in search of attractions, and "Do the Ballyhoo."

Bailey's greetings, just as he returned to take charge of the Barnum-Bailey interests, was a fire destroying all in the winter quarters at Bridgeport. Undaunted, the courageous Bailey, and the super-energetic Barnum, got the show together for the Garden opening, the title in 1888 becoming "Barnum & Bailey — The Greatest Show on Earth," a title destined to live in fame and glory down through the years.

Bailey was busy with the show, and Barnum, ever alert, was hunting attractions. About this time Barnum made a "BIG" buy — an African elephant named Jumbo. This elephant was purchased from the London Zoo for $10,000. Jumbo was the largest mastodon in captivity. His purchase, and the fact that he was to be taken out of England, raised a storm of protest all over the British Isles, incurring Queen Victoria's disapproval, and also that of the famous author, John Ruskin. This was all just as Barnum would have wished. He turned this "elephant-turmoil" into good publicity purposes. On account of all these objections, Barnum promised to exhibit Jumbo in every important English community, and be it said, this exhibition was most successful.

Barnum had trouble getting Jumbo shipped to the United States on account of his great size. He was 11 feet 9 inches at the shoulder, and weighed over seven tons. He was such an attraction that people calculated he was really worth his weight in gold. "Jumbo" became a household word, and still is, being used to mean anything of unusual size. Jumbo was on tour with the circus for three and one-half years, and Barnum was planning a home-coming trip for him, back to London and through the entire British Isles, when Jumbo was killed by a railroad train at St. Thomas, Canada, September 15, 1885. On the bridge, which is now over the tracks where the old elephant met his death, is a bronze plaque in memory of Jumbo.

Jumbo sacrificed his life for the love of a baby elephant — the little clowning elephant named Tom Thumb. The circus had given its last performance in St. Thomas and the animals were going back to the train to load. Jumbo and the baby elephant, which was chained to him and was his special care, were leading the way. The little elephant had strayed over on the railroad track. Jumbo looked up, saw a huge one-eyed monster dashing toward the little one. Realizing the baby's danger, he rushed over, and with his powerful trunk, threw him to safety.

Evidently angered at this huge demon that was about to attack the little elephant, Jumbo charged full force ahead to meet the locomotive. The impact was terrific and terrifying. He never moved from where he was thrown on the side embankment. The mighty Jumbo had died instantly. Onlookers said he had time to jump off the track, after throwing the little one to safety, but that he charged the locomotive with all the power and ferocity in his huge body, seeming to feel that this monster had tried to attack the baby elephant.

P. T. Barnum gave Jumbo's stuffed (and it really is stuffed) hide to Tufts College. The college made Jumbo its mascot, and Jumbo is the only college mascot that has never attended a football game.

With this show, "Barnum & Bailey, The Greatest Show on Earth," the great Barnum assumed a vital and important place in American history — and a legendary spot in the limelight of the entertainment world. His highly-successful technique of advertising, his business acumen, individual initiative, and firm belief in freedom of enterprise, all had a profound influence on the social history of the country.

Barnum wrote an autobiography, which enjoyed a tremendous sale, going into its seventh edition. Not a dull page in the entire book — neither had there been a dull day in the entire life of Barnum. His latter years were most pleasant. He was happily married to his beloved Charity (his wife's real name) — having married her when he was nineteen. They had three lovely and charming daughters. He had climbed back up the financial ladder and had no worries.

Barnum suffered an acute congestion of the brain and was confined to his bed for several weeks. Every night he looked quietly and yet longingly at his family and whispered, "Thy will be done." Barnum died April 7, 1891. He left an estate valued at over four million dollars. Barnum was immortalized in bronze by his loving friends in Bridgeport, who erected an impressive and magnificent statue in his honor at Seaside Park, Bridgeport, Connecticut. A "Barnum Festival" is held yearly in Bridgeport to honor their distinguished citizen, mayor, state legislator, and super showman. He was offered the governorship of Connecticut at one time but did not accept. The Bridgeport Museum houses relics of this truly "Great International Character."

James Anthony Bailey died at his home in Mt. Vernon, New York, in early April, 1906, when The Greatest Show on Earth was playing in Madison Square Garden. Bailey believed in big attractions, in paying big money for them, and cashing in on big crowds — hitting while the iron was hot, and making it his business to see that the iron was sizzling. He was not a wealthy man when he died, but he left to the world a wealth of business ideas, and he remains the greatest circus manager of all time.

Barnum and Bailey had given to the world the greatest show title of the age, a title which was sold to John Ringling, in 1907. The two circuses were operated as separate shows through the season of 1918. Then, in 1919, when the two circuses merged, the greatest name in all circusdom came into being — "Ringling Bros. and Barnum & Bailey Circus, The Greatest Show on Earth."

JAKE POSEY

JAKE POSEY, the last of the Forty-Horse Drivers, and the most famous, is living at Huntington Park, California. On June 27, 1952, Jake was eighty-nine years of age, hale and hearty. He possesses nobility of character and is a man of trustworthiness. After fifty-six years of gruelling circus duty, he retired.

Jake grew up along with the circus, and the nation. He has fought wind, storms and fires — lived in the very shadow of the tent, and it is he who tells the following story, in the magazine, *Band Wagon*:

"A great deal has been written about the Forty-Horse team. Some very amusing to me. The team was composed of ten units of four horses. They were bright boys, mostly Percherons. Weighing 1600 to 2000 pounds each. They were hitched military style with the exception of one body-pole between the four horses hitched on the end of the wagon pole. The lines on the wheelers were twenty-one feet in length, and eleven feet were added for each additional four, making the lines on the leaders one hundred and twenty feet in length. The cross checks were the same style as used on a four-horse chariot race, a check to each horse bit; twenty lines on the team.

"When turning a corner, I would take up twenty-seven feet slack on the lead lines. When the wagon was around the corner, and the team straightened out, the lines ran through my fingers very fast. If there should be a kink or twist in one of the lines, it would throw all of the lines out of my hand. Consequently, a man sat behind me and kept the lines straightened out. . .

"The seat on the wagon was in the shape of a shell, and when I donned the big livery coat, I filled the seat to capacity. . . If a horse slowed up, I called his name, and he immediately responded. The third man worked the brake. I started driving the team by hitching twelve, the first time, then adding four each time until I had forty hitched. I did nothing but drive and look after the forty.

"I only had one accident of any consequences. In Lynn, England, a 'bobby' (English policeman) became excited, took hold of my lead horses, causing them to back up and put slack in the traces . . . The man at the brake became excited, and tightened up on the brake. I called to him to turn it loose, but it was too late. The right front hub caught in the corner door of a pub and the side of the frame building came out in the street. No one was injured . . . The proprietor of the pub was reimbursed by the circus and he remodeled the house and put up a large sign which read, James Bailey's Forty-Horse Inn. Mr. Bailey told me that I made him a rich man. Said the tourists came to see the house that was torn down by the forty-horse team.

"The last parade was made in Frankfurt a.M., Germany, October 8, 1900. But while showing Paris, France, Mardi Gras was celebrated on March 6, 1902, and Mr. Bailey was asked to be represented in the parade. He sent the forty-horse team, and calliope. I was out eight hours. My arms swelled so much I had to cut sleeves out of the coat to get my arms out. I received a medal from the city of Paris."

Men like Jake Posey are true heroes of the sawdust trail, possessing loyalty and devotion not only to the performers, the animals, and to the owners, but to the circus itself as a great breathing and living institution — "The Show Must Go On."

W. C. COUP
1871

W. C. COUP was an outstanding showman, exemplifying genius, American ingenuity, and initiative. He had the opportunity to talk with many people who stopped at his father's tavern, and a desire to travel became uppermost in his mind. He left home in 1852 with the P. T. Barnum show, and remained with Barnum for sixteen years, and was instrumental in persuading Barnum to lend the prestige of his name to the Castello Show. So, in 1871, this show, under the name, Coup, Barnum, and Castello, became one of the greatest outdoor amusement enterprises of all time. The first year's receipts were $400,000.

Coup also influenced Barnum to put the show on the rails (railroad). This was a masterpiece of business initiatve — a far-reaching, progressive step. Their first loading consumed one entire night, from 8 P.M. until 8 A.M. Coup never undressed from the first loading through the seventh. The railroad equipment in those days was bad. Soon Coup took a most decisive step and one which proved very lucrative — he had all his rolling stock (railroad cars) made. He designed cars and equipment which are still in use today. Thus Coup, in reality, transformed the circus from a trail of gypsy-like wagons to a rolling giant on wheels. Bailey and Forepaugh saw the profit in such progressiveness and did the same.

Another invention of Coup's, the "end loading system," revolutionized the loading of the circus, and is still used by circuses today. About this time a Professor Jukes invented the "jukebox," a mechanical musical instrument or box, which he called, "The Devil's Whistle." Coup was quick to see its merits, and secured the original "jukebox" with which to advertise. He also used stereopticons to project main features of the show. He sent small companies, with brass bands, ahead of the regular show, and these advertised with street entertainment. He also put up posters on dead-end walls. (Thus came into being our modern billboards.) He carried a band and jubilee singers with the show and also a brigade of trumpeters.

Coup was the first to depart from one-sheet lithograph

advertisements to three-sheet; later he used one of 100 sheets, considered an advertising marvel. He was the first to use gasoline lighting, buying this new invention directly from the English inventor, and thus, in 1870, Coup dispensed with kerosene. Later he spent $8000 for a portable electric plant. Coup was not only an inventive genius himself, but he was the first to see potential value in the inventions of others.

In 1876, Coup announced a new partnership with Charles Reiche for the opening of "The New York Aquarium" which he had started. (Animals, even rare specimens, were easily available from the animal farm of Reiche's brother in Germany.) This adventure was successful from the very first exhibition. Scientists thronged the building. Coup was meeting a different type of people: educators, scientists, professors. *Scribner's Magazine* referred to Coup as a "benefactor of science."

Then came one of these peculiar and uncanny moments of life when destiny hangs by a thread. Here it hung by the flip of a coin. Reiche wanted to open the aquarium on Sundays – Coup said an emphatic "No." They flipped a coin to see if the aquarium would open Sundays. Coup lost. And Coup, true to his ideals and convictions, walked out of the building, leaving all for which he had worked for so many years. Then followed twenty long years of trouping for Coup.

Later he established the Chicago Museum. In 1891, he conceived the "Enchanted Rolling Palaces," which created a profound sensation. This show was a popular museum housed in elaborate and expensive, especially designed, coaches. This was Coup's last venture. He died in Jacksonville, Florida, March 4, 1895.

Coup's name is revered throughout circusdom. He was the greatest genius for circus organization, development and management the world has ever known.

The five Ringlings are conceded to be the Circus Kings. But there were *five* Ringlings. The Ringlings profited by all of Coup's successful pioneering.

SELLS CIRCUS
1880 - 1891

THIS CIRCUS, always of excellent quality as to performances, management, and equipment, was known to more or less concentrate on territory west of the Rockies, by no means, however, limiting itself to that area. Sells Circus flourished the last half of the nineteenth century, 1880-1891. It carried an excellent menagerie. It was best known for its unusual and beautiful revolving statuary acts — living statues — on pedestals.

THE FLATFOOTS
Before 1875

THE FLATFOOTS were America's first group of syndicated showmen. It is remarkable how this group approximated modern business methods in circus management. Shrewd, cautious, and mysterious, they routed their shows to the "money spots," disbanded in poor years only to reorganize later. The accepted source of the name is that these managers claimed the state of New York as their show ground and, if disputed by a rival concern, they issued the warning, "We put our foot down flat, and shall play New York State, so watch out." Many famous circus names were connected with the Flatfoots.

THE RINGLINGS
1880

THERE WERE EIGHT children in the circus-famous Ringling family: seven boys, Al, Otto, Charlie, Alfred, John, Gus, and Henry, and the one girl, Ida, who married

Henry North. When the boys were very small, they entered upon their careers of entertaining which continued without change of mind or purpose throughout their lives. The growth from "pin shows" given in their back yard, to fame and a golden jubilee celebration, has been spectacular. They were always clean showmen. They would not countenance any crooks, shady transactions, smutty acts, or off-color jokes. They promised their mother that they would never produce a show of which she would be ashamed. Their circuses were known as the "Sunday School Shows," and they were proud of this title.

The Ringling boys perfected their play shows and soon became juvenile professionals. They hit upon the lucrative idea of charging pennies instead of pins for their performances. They saved pennies and bought enough inexpensive sheeting to make a tent. Larger boys molested them, teasing them and tearing down their tent. Persevering even at that early age, they set up the tent again. Tights were made out of old underwear, dyes being used effectively. Mother Ringling lent a helping hand in assembling these early costumes.

Continuing to save all their pennies, the boys bought an old, worn-out pony, on which they practiced bareback riding acts. They learned to play musical instruments and to do stunts such as somersaulting, juggling, and balancing. The oldest boy, Al, became an expert juggler. Otto gave a good performance with his trained goat. Little Johnnie, then only six years of age, was a clown and sang, "Root Hog or Die," to the accompaniment of a Jews-harp. Charlie was the equestrian, riding the old Mexican pony, and Alfred was the ringmaster. They gave well-conducted parades down the main street of their little town. They were all very serious about their circus work. They lived a normal life, but every leisure moment of thought was of the circus.

Al was the first to become a star. His juggling became

so expert that he played in hall shows with various troupes. In 1880 or 1881, Al had his own show, which played for about a year. He contracted for three outside performers. Al called this show "4-Big-4," an attractive name at any age or time.

In 1882, Al joined a small wagon show, the Parson-Roy Circus, out of Warren, Illinois. During all of his traveling experiences, Al had returned home at intervals to coach his brothers in the show business. So, late in 1882, he thought the time was ripe for them to join him in their professional debut, so they started out in November under the august title, "Ringling Bros. Classic and Comic Concert Company."

In 1883, Al purchased the Parson-Roy Circus with which he had toured early in 1882. This venture is important because it was this show that was the real nucleus or beginning of the Ringling Circus. Some of the old Parson-Roy equipment was used, and the boys also built new, attractive equipment; and so on May 19, 1884, at Baraboo, Wisconsin, they launched forth into the genuine circus business. They had a 45-foot top tent. Their first animals were a lame bear, an eagle, and a hyena. At this time, as well as throughout the successful life of the Ringling Bros. Circus, they adhered strictly to their motto, "to build no bigger than you could operate."

All of the Ringling boys were talented. Al, aside from his ability as a juggler and actor, became proficient on the cornet. Alf was the author of all the skits. Charles liked the violin and played throughout his lifetime. The other brothers played various instruments, but Otto always had his eye on the business end of the show and preferred that the others do the performing. He became treasurer of the circus and proved to be a financial genius. Al, the juggling trouper, became director.

During the early show days, John's speciality was the alto horn; however, he was so versatile that early programs listed many acts in which he was proficient. The Ringling show benefited most from John's services when he took over all the routing duties.

From the very start in the circus business, the Ringling Brothers were successful. They possessed all the ingredients of success. They were natural performers and showmen; had an abundance of energy and determination; the patience to persevere; splendid executive ability; and honesty. But their success was not easy. They underwent hardships, not the least of which was muddy roads. There were practically no good roads and the show grounds were problems even in good weather, but deep mud presented Herculean obstacles.

One of the most outstanding reasons for the Ringling success was the fact that they were always willing to take advice, and, in this willingness, showed great foresight, for on their first real road venture they secured the services of Fayette Ludovic Robinson, who, as "Yankee" Robinson, had been quite successful with his own circus. He was then sixty-six years of age, but he helped the boys until September the fourth, 1884, when he died at Jefferson, Iowa.

Otto was always insisting that they buy an elephant so they could be a "real circus" as he expressed it, and then they could boost the admission price from 25¢ to 50¢. Al heard of two elephants down in Alexander, Missouri, on the Castello Show, which was reported to be hard-pressed financially. They succeeded in buying these – Babylon and Fannie. During the first season all parading had been on foot, but by 1885 they had a band wagon, and twelve other wagons. So it was a most appropriate time for the elephants to make a grand entree in the parade. Some monkeys were added, which, with the bear, eagle and hyena, and now the elephants, made quite a nice road menagerie.

Hardships were not only endured but soon forgotten. Money rolled in so fast that they soon purchased many additions; animals and cage wagons; and in 1889, a cook tent was added. All of the brothers were talking of taking to the rails. Otto and John had long been insisting on rail transportation. So it was that in 1890, Ringling Bros. Circus left Baraboo on its own first railroad train. The Ringling Bros. literally "roared" along the steel rails into the "roaring" gay 'nineties. For the first twenty-five years, the Ringlings went out from Baraboo and back, never drawing any money except their expenses, always putting back into the show what they made in order to build a finer and bigger show each season.

The famous "five heads" poster of the five Ringlings, each with his distinctive mustache, was shown for the first time, July 26, 1900, and soon was seen all over the country. This poster charmed the public and brought in the silver and gold, becoming a great and financially valuable trademark. The use of this poster was discontinued after the death of Otto in 1911.

In 1893, when the Ringlings started their tenth season, it was at the World's Fair in Chicago, Illinois. The brothers looked upon the amusement enterprise of the World's Fair as a great opportunity, and they prepared accordingly. Success crowned their every venture. Their parades were sensational and, for the first time, they staged an "after show," a real minstrel show.

At this time they purchased a fine private railroad car which they named Caledonia. When the Chicago World's Fair celebrated their Golden Jubilee, Ringling Bros. again celebrated with them and gold poured into the circus coffers.

The very first Ringling Route Book was issued in 1892 by a Mr. O. Kurtz, a juggler. In 1893, Alf issued his first elaborate and excellent route book.

In 1907, John Ringling bought the title "Barnum & Bailey Circus" and twelve years later, in 1919, there flashed before the eyes of the world the greatest entertainment title of all time, "Ringling Bros. and Barnum & Bailey Circus." At this time the Ringlings moved their winter quarters from Baraboo to Bridgeport, Connecticut, the old P. T. Barnum quarters. In 1928, the influence and magnitude of the Ringlings' interests in Sarasota, Florida, had grown to such astounding proportions that they moved their circus winter quarters from Bridgeport to Sarasota.

Notwithstanding all of the Sarasota expansion (see next page) and the moving of winter quarters from Bridgeport, John Ringling found time to inspire and assist Tex Rickard in building the new Madison Square Garden in New York City, which has been used for the annual premiere and month's run of the Ringling Bros. and Barnum & Bailey Circus since 1926. The last year in which the Ringlings gave their famous five-mile-long street parade was 1920.

The same year, Mr. Jeremiah Joseph Mugivan (1871-1930) came upon the circus scene in a big way, and had lasting effect on the Ringling interests. By 1929, he owned five fully equipped circuses and had titles to others. His success was spectacular. He organized The American Circus Corporation of Peru, Indiana, with his associates, Bert Bowers and Ed Ballard of West Baden, Indiana. In such a position of strength, he was able to force a showdown with John Ringling in 1929 for the 1930 opening dates for the circus in Madison Square Garden, New York. John Ringling, the Circus King, bravely accepted the challenge and bought the corporation's entire holdings, for, it was rumored, $19,000,000. It was this tremendous outlay of money at the beginning of the financial depression that hung over John Ringling's head for six long years.

In taking over these shows, the Ringlings displayed the same good judgment which they had employed in the past, namely, surrounding themselves with men of similarly good judgment. They retained the men of worth who had been connected with these shows. (Today some of the Ringling department heads have been with them for over forty years.) Combined with their good judgment, the Ringlings have always had super advertising ideas. Alfred and Charles were considered two of the best press agents the country ever knew, and John learned from them. The Ringling Brothers' partnership was begun without a written contract of any kind and continued for forty-three years without a scratch of the pen.

It was in 1911, when John Ringling was only forty-five years of age, that he went to spend a vacation off the beaten path, in the small town of Sarasota, Florida. The 1910 census of this little town was 840. In 1952 it had more than 20,000 permanent residents and thousands of tourists streaming in and out the year 'round. It was the Ringlings who changed the face of Sarasota, especially John. From the first, the town and surroundings attracted him, and in that prophetic strain that was his, he visualized the future and set about transforming all the visions into realities. Sarasota became his home; at this time he was reputed to be worth fifty million dollars, one of the fifteen richest men in the world. Only by looking at a map of Sarasota and the outlying districts can one gain any idea of the magnitude of the Ringling development.

April 8, 1933, when Ringling Bros. and Barnum & Bailey Circus opened in Madison Square Garden, New York City, was the first time in fifty years that no Ringling was there to see it open. John, the sole surviving Ringling brother, was too ill to leave Sarasota. He passed away December 2, 1936.

John and Mable Ringling, two of the world's greatest benefactors, bequeathed two museums to the state of Florida – in 1936, The John and Mable Museum of Art and the John Ringling Palatial Home, Ca'd'Zan, Museum, the state taking possession of these in 1946. In 1948, The Museum of the American Circus was erected on the grounds of Ca'd'Zan by the State of Florida in honor of the Ringlings. Here, more circusana is collected under one roof than anywhere else in the United States. All three museums are outstanding, each in its own field of interest.

At the Museum of the American Circus, the narrator, Dr. H. Chester Hoyt, is warp and woof of his work; and the magic touch of John Sullivan, Curator of the Museum of the American Circus, Sarasota, Florida, unlocks this storehouse of the land of make-believe to all who are fortunate in passing that way.

MERLE EVANS THE BANDMASTER

ONE OF THE STARS of any circus is the bandmaster. The music of Merle Evans' band with R.B.B.&B. Circus is an eight-star performance. (1) With the first tremendous beat, the audience is lifted from a world of expectancy to one of "glamorized emotional receptivity." (2) The music inspires the actors for the performance of their daredevil thrills and breath-taking displays of skill and precision technique. (3) The music itself is a rare musical treat. (4) The musicians must have "flash-mind" musical talent. The trigger-readiness of the musicians has averted many panics. Actors have fallen or animals have become unruly or escaped into the arena. Immediately the tempo of the music is changed to a soothing waltz or a lullaby, having a relaxing influence on circus performers and animals alike, as well as the audience. The second the panic seems averted, a faster brand of music is played, and from there the music goes on picking up the theme of the act as though nothing had happened. (5) Daring and hazardous as the trapeze act is, the lilting, rhythmic waltz-time music seems to make the flying trapeze actors float through the air with the greatest of ease. The tom-tom music of the wild jungle adds mystery and "goose bumps" as the tigers and lions creep or leap. An acrobat does a flip-flop, and the band goes over and over again that sound, "plang," in perfect time with each flip-flop. The rumba gives that certain "South of the Border" atmosphere. Regardless of from what country an act may have come, appropriate music, and also proper cue-music, must be mutually agreed upon by performers and bandmaster, and all hitches ironed out with practice before the act is given for an audience.

As star number (6) for the band, it is, of itself, a dominating array of color and shining brass — a true glamor spot in the Big Top. (7) The band is a dependable fill-in if an act is delayed or in case of animal misbehavior, or illness, or accident. Sometimes the band fills in with "How Dry I Am," and the psychological effect is immediate. The cold drink vendors have a phenomenal rush. (8) The general public never realizes that one of the band's greatest contributions to the circus life is the fact that it is an ear-clock to the circus personnel. Any performer or workman knows which act is on by the selection of music being played, and each may thus judge just how long it is before time for his respective act or duty.

The executive staff of a circus gathers around the bandstand. Protected by the blare of the music, they can talk without disturbing the spectators, and, at the same time, watch the performers.

Circus musicians do not play any louder than those of an orchestra in the theater pit. It is the acoustics of the Big Top. In the tent the notes are picked up and bounced around, creating an illusion of loudness. During rainstorms, musicians, performing under a tent, play more softly than usual because the rain-soaked canvas amplifies the music to an enormous volume of sound.

A successful circus bandmaster must be alert and agreeable, for he must deal with temperaments of all nations, and he must possess great physical endurance. In the case of the great Merle Evans, he plays two shows, each three hours long, every day the show performs. He only waves one hand, his left — with his right, he holds the cornet which he plays during each musical number — his lungs being a perpetual bellows furnishing wind. And at the same time he is playing the cornet, his mind must possess manifold activities of precision, timing, and talent. His band plays 256 cues to each performance of the Great Show.

During his thirty-seven years with Ringling, Evans has led the band 18,500 times or more. He stands with his back to the band as he watches intricate acts in the three rings so that he may be alert for any needed cues. Mr. Robert Ringling called him the "Toscanini of the Big Top"; James Francis Cook, Editor of *Etude,* referred to him as "Will Rogers with a Horn." Evans is also a composer, having written "Lady of Spain" and "March Symphonia" among other scores.

Sousa's "Stars and Stripes Forever" is the "disaster march" of the R.B.B.&B. circus. It is *un*scheduled music and it tells the performers and attendants that something has gone wrong and to get to their posts and help, as the audience is always dismissed immediately under such circumstances. On the afternoon of July 6, 1944, at Hartford, Connecticut, Merle Evans suddenly noticed a spot of fire flashing toward the top of the big tent. He struck up the "disaster march" and the very first notes alerted the trainers, who drove their lions and tigers through the runways in desperate haste.

Merle Evans began his career on a showboat on the Mississippi River. He is a mild-tempered man, and is a self-taught musician. He is very resourceful. One night in Washington, D. C., a windstorm literally blew the band off the stand. The drum was burst wide-open. Evans glimpsed a water bucket, according to *White Tops,* and the *New York Times,* and yelled, "Spill the water out and beat your sticks on it," and "The Band Played On," because "The Show Must Go On."

At one time he had charge of the band for the 101 Wild West Show. He is a mild-tempered man and is a self-taught musician.

BUFFALO BILL'S WILD WEST SHOW 1884-1913

THE WILD WEST THEME seems to be ageless, appealing to all ages of all times, and remains one of "The Tops" today in all types of entertainment. Buffalo Bill's Wild West Show was the first of its kind, appearing from 1884 until 1913. The show-world knew him as Buffalo Bill, but his name was Colonel William F. Cody. Although the wildest of the Wild West had disappeared before Buffalo Bill's Show began, yet he portrayed enough to make one's hair stand on end.

The blood-tingling event and highlight of the show, as Herbert A. Calkins tells us, was the entry of the overland stage drawn by four or six galloping horses. Just at the moment it seemed the stage had lost in the fight against attacking Indians, a bugle sounded, the curtain was pulled aside, and a United States cavalry detachment, colors flying, dashed in and routed the Indians. Children screamed with fright, and spectators shouted themselves hoarse.

William Frederick Cody was internationally famous as a showman and as an American scout. He was born in Iowa. The family moved near Fort Leavenworth. Here, though still a child, he was employed by express companies to carry packages across country on horseback. He was scarcely out of boyhood when he was employed as a government scout. He became known throughout the country as a fearless rider, a keen, skillful hunter and an expert plainsman.

William Cody was given the name of Buffalo Bill in 1867 when he was employed by Goddard Brothers, who had contracted to supply food for the construction crews of the Kansas Pacific Railroad. He is said to have killed over 4000 buffalo (bison) during one season. Later he became a member of the U.S. Fifth Cavalry as a scout, and saw almost continuous activity with the Indians in the West.

Cody organized his Buffalo Bill Wild West Show in 1883. He had long cherished such a dream, and he made it a reality by putting all of his vigor and vitality, born of an outdoor fighting career, into the success of this undertaking. Annie Oakley was an outstanding performer with his show for seventeen years.

The handsome and striking Colonel Cody made a most impressive entrance into the arena. He would dash in on his magnificent white horse; coming to a halt, he would pull his mount to his haunches, and, with sweeping gesture of salute, remove his large Western hat while his shoulder-length white hair waved in the breeze. And all the time the 40-piece band would be playing, "The Stars and Stripes Forever."

Buffalo Bill's show was disbanded in 1913 and he died four years later. Cody was the last of the six great scouts of America. The others were Boone, Carson, Crockett, Bridger, and Wild Bill Hickok.

ANNIE OAKLEY

IN 1880, the team of Oakley and Butler (Annie Oakley and her husband Frank Butler) "joined up" with Forepaugh & Sells Bros. Circus. This was only a short time after Annie had been officially adopted by Chief Sitting Bull. The lure and magic of his name, and the fact that Annie was such an expert marksman, made her a headliner. Shooting under canvas was a little difficult for Annie and Frank at first. It was necessary to use smaller leads in their guns, else they might damage the tent and circus equipment. However, they both soon became accustomed to living under a tent, and made happy troupers.

When a very young girl, Annie had been a star equestrienne, so she was given a spot as a trick rider with the circus. She was a master at horseback-riflemanship.

One of Annie's most exciting and favorite circus tricks was the shooting of small balls as they sailed through the air. She sighted these balls in the mirror blade of a bowie knife. A record of hers, and not yet known to be broken, was shooting at 1000 balls in succession and hitting 943 of them. She was also most adept at shooting small coins from the hands of her husband (an individual way of taking his money) and at flicking cigarettes from his mouth.

Annie was with Forepaugh and Sells Brothers Circus for four years and then joined forces with Buffalo Bill's Wild West Show. Up to this time, there had been only one solo act in Buffalo Bill's Show, and he filled that spot himself. Now Annie Oakley was given a solo spot and she proved a sensation. She was the first and only white woman (other women were Indians) to travel with a show of this kind. She was with the Buffalo Bill Show for seventeen years — was greatly loved and respected — and shared the happiness and sadness of every member of the company.

Mr. Clyde Wixom tells us that the career of Annie Oakley, billed as "The Peerless Wing and Rifle Shot," came to an abrupt ending in Wheeling, West Virginia, only one day before the official closing of the 1901 season of the Buffalo Bill Show. She was in a terrible train wreck. "She was so shocked by the collision that her hair turned snow-white within a few hours after she was taken from the wreck. She never fully recovered from the shock." She is buried near Brock, Ohio.

THE 101 WILD WEST SHOWS and THE 101 WILD WEST CIRCUS

THE 101 RANCH was the colorful background of the 101 Wild West Show. The ranch was the mainspring and the fountain from which came the inspiration and the opportunity, and even most of the acts of the show. In fact, from the very inception of the 101 Wild West Show, its very life and success were so interwoven with that of the fabulous 101 Ranch that the stories of both form an intensely interesting, indigenous, colorful, and historical panorama of the Western life at its very peak of existence – its people, their mode of life and activities – and of the land itself: a cattle empire.

The three Miller Brothers, owners of the 101 Ranch, formed the 101 Wild West Show shortly after the turn of the century. They started the tour of this show from Maryland in thirty cars; later fifty cars were required. The show became world-famous. The brothers gave to the entertainment world something that was new, exciting, tremendous.

The Millers were very close friends and advisors of the Indians. They had been adopted by the Ponca Tribe, speaking their language as though they were full-bloods. On account of this friendship and trust, they easily secured Indians for their show. The Indian representatives in the show included papooses and their mothers, radiant belles of the wigwam, wrinkled warriors, and renowned chiefs and stalwart braves. The Indians were always a great attraction and made good showmen.

From the annual rodeos at the 101 Ranch, the Millers were able to select the best and most daring feats for their show. Steer wrestling, bulldogging, bronc-busting – those pawing, dangerous devils of thin air and dirt. This was hazardous, but cowboys thrive on this life. Once, when Colonel Zack Miller was in a hospital from an auto accident, and he knew the rodeo was going full force, he (with full force) remarked, "Who wants to be cooped up in this antiseptic air when there's rodeo dust to be inhaled!"

The Millers were always ready for a good act. Ezra Meeker, trail blazer of the Oregon Trail in 1850, was returning East in 1920, and stopped for a visit at the 101

Ranch. The Millers immediately offered him a job with the show. He was a good drawing card, and they knew he could give a good account of himself. The ninety-five-year-old pioneer refused to consider the job unless given a ten-year contract, because he wanted a "permanent job — not one that would play out in two or three years." The Millers gave him the contract.

One of the most hilarious acts of the 101 Show, which produced genuine fun among the cowboys, was the foot race — the cowboys in a wild race and tumble trying to get a twenty-dollar gold piece which had been tied to a Brahma bull's tail.

The first human to "bulldog" a steer was the colored man, Bill Pickett, of the famous 101 Ranch and 101 Wild West Show. Down in the mesquite thickets of Texas where Bill's folks lived, huge bulldogs had been trained to drive cattle out of brush and briar so thick that neither man nor horse could enter. When the dog had succeeded in bringing the steer out in the clear, he would bark and the steer would lower his head to charge. Thus, with his head in reach, the dog would sink his teeth into the steer's nose or lip. The weight of the dog, the tenderness of the steer's nose and lip, and the momentum of the steer, carried his body over and threw the steer flat on the ground. From this position, the steer could be handled by the cowboys; hence the term, "bulldogging."

Col. Zack Miller was watching his cowhands attempting to slaughter an unruly steer when the steer broke loose and ran. Bill Pickett jumped on a horse standing by and attempted to drive the steer, but the "onery critter" wouldn't drive. When the horse came up alongside the steer, Bill unloaded right on his horns. In an effort to stop him, Bill twisted his head around and, seeing the tender nose, sank his teeth in it, threw back his hands, straightened his back, and down came the steer. Colonel Zack realized immediately that here was a "natural" for his 101 Show, and so Bill found himself a featured performer "biting the steer," bulldogging, all over the world. This act of Bill Pickett's became one of the best known and most famous in show history.

When the 101 Wild West Show was in Europe, Joe Miller saw a saddle that had belonged to Napoleon. He was told that it cost $5000. He casually made the remark that he would have one made that was far more beautiful. (He did – at the cost of $10,000.) Although the saddle originally cost $10,000, in 1947, with its 247 diamonds, 120 sapphires, four large garnets, 16 rubies, and 15 pounds of gold and silver, it is now worth $20,000. This saddle is still owned by the Zack Miller heirs.

During the First World War, the 101 Wild West Show was playing in England. By requisition No. 1, the English government took Colonel Zack's horses. They allowed the colonel to keep his famous saddle horse. The colonel could not tell of this without a genuine, boyish chuckle. Then he would add, "But those 101 broncs nearly wrecked His Majesty's cavalry."

The Millers always opened their shows free of charge to the children of the orphan homes, crippled children, and inmates of other institutions. They were also most liberal in gifts to charity.

Colonel Joe Miller died in October, 1927. "Mute witness to the service was Miller's beautiful Arabian horse, Pedro, wearing Miller's famous $10,000 jewel-studded, silver-mounted saddle, over the horn of which were draped Miller's well-worn chaps," is the description given by the newspapers of that day.

George L. was next to go, in 1929, leaving Colonel Zack to meet the oncoming panic years alone. The 101 Wild West Show was successful until the fateful depression of the 'thirties. It was stranded in Washington D. C. – later sent back to the ranch where the headquarters of the show had always been maintained. Adverse business conditions and decreased cattle prices led to the loss of the famed 101 Ranch to mortgage companies in 1930.

Colonel Zack never allowed himself to become bitter, and with his fiery spirit and determination, fought back. By 1946 he was able to reorganize the show and open again under the banner, 101 Wild West Circus. Newspapers carried headlines, "Ex-Owner of Famous 101 Ranch Fame Rides Again With His Old Show." Many an old-timer wiped away a reminiscent tear as he watched a man on a white horse ride into the glare of the spotlight and slowly raise his gleaming ten-gallon white Stetson hat; they knew then that "Old Colonel Zack hasn't lost his touch." The new show was complete with howling Indians, chuck wagon gangs, and cowboy thrillers. The 101 was considered the best Wild West Show and Circus of its day, and it has never been equalled.

The new show played to packed grandstands. Despite his seventy-three years, Colonel Zack stood as straight and erect as an arrow and rode superbly. Then came the auto wreck and Colonel Zack was laid up for many months with broken bones. The show completed its successful 1946 Golden Jubilee tour and then took down the famous banner, "101 Wild West Show." Colonel Zack died in a hospital in Waco, Texas, on January 3, 1952. One of his characteristic remarks to his daughter, Mrs. Blevens Miller Gibbs, was "Just give me about three more days like today and I'll be up and out of here."

And thus passed the last of the three famous Miller Brothers, whose names will go down on the annals of show business and in the history of the great Southwest, making of it a greater, better land, because they had pioneered its acres, had loved its acres, and carved from its acres a cattle kingdom and a fabulous empire.

The Millers built this inland empire through scientific farming, ranching, oil, and the 101 Wild West Show. Truly, they stamped their famous 101 brand around the world.

GENTRY BROTHERS
1885

THE GENTRY BROTHERS of Bloomington, Indiana, poor farmer boys, started out in a very modest way in 1885. They had twenty dogs and gave only matinee performances. By 1889, they had added more animals and eight ponies, and gave two shows a day. Their first overland show was composed mostly of dogs, monkeys and ponies. In 1891, they entered the tent show field, opening with a two-car show. The year 1892 saw their second show go on the road; later they added two more — making a total of four complete traveling shows. Seventy-two cars were needed to transport these four shows.

The Gentry shows were known as, "Gentry Bros. Famous Shows." Later, Professor H. B. Gentry's show became known as "Gentry's Dog and Pony Show," and presented some of the best dog and pony acts ever seen in America or abroad.

THE CHARLES T. HUNT CIRCUS
1892

THE CHARLES T. HUNT Circus, founded in 1892, has been under the same management for sixty-two years, and Charles T. Hunt, in his eighties, is a wiry, active little dynamo. This circus is said to have a great many "firsts" to its credit. Besides Ringling Bros., it was the first circus to own its own winter quarters. These quarters are located between Camden, New Jersey, and New York City, in plain view of a four-way highway.

The Hunt Show is a family show. There are three Hunt brothers who assist their father: Charles Jr., Eddie, and Harry, and they "double in brass" as do the elephants, which is to say that they perform diversified acts and assume many responsibilities.

Its annual season is twenty-six weeks. All twenty-six are under auspices which the circus inaugurated in 1932. This show does not go West — it is happy in its own back yard, playing annually to its same old friends. It plays to turn-away houses, although its usual jump between towns is only about two miles. It is a show that is always "better than ever," — and that is the secret of its success.

LORD GEORGE SANGER'S CIRCUS

WHEN RECALLING the large and elegantly equipped Lord George Sanger's Circus of England, one must go back to the days of the earthen ovens and to naphtha lamps. This circus had a great "draw." The parade was always very long; many times the last wagon had not left the circus lot when the first was returning. It had gorgeous procession cars, their famous "Britannia" being one of the telescope variety.

It consolidated with Howe's Great London Circus in 1876, and later Barnum paid Lord George Sanger $100,000 for his circus wagons, title, and wardrobes.

One most commendable and well-remembered fact about the great Sanger Menagerie was that the Declaration of Independence of the United States of America was printed on the back of every copy of their illustrated history of the animals.

SELLS-FLOTO
1904

WILLIAM SELLS (who was an adopted son of William Allen "Ad" Sells of the famous Sells Bros. Circus) was with a dog and pony show in Colorado. The owner of this show had taken ill and Willie Sells induced H.H. Tammen, of the well-known Tammen and Bonfils, proprietors of the *Denver Post,* to lend the ill man some money. However, the owner of the show died, and Tammen, being a circus fan, decided to send the show out on the road. He named it for Otto Floto, who was the sports editor of the *Denver Post.* The show was sent out in 1904 and 1905 under the name of Floto Circus Beautiful.

Sells applied for the position as manager of this show. He was very acceptable on account of his experience and knowledge of the circus business, so Tammen retitled the show, Sells-Floto.

Sells was an excellent manager and created a great interest in this show. However, it was sold, and the Sells-Floto title continued to be used under the new ownership, the managers being Frank Tammen, Fred B. Hutchinson, and H. B. Gentry. This circus attracted great attention because it featured such celebrities as Bob Fitzsimmons, Jess Willard, Frank Gotch, and Jack Dempsey, of the boxing and wrestling world.

When Buffalo Bill was near bankruptcy, Tammen and Bonfils bought his show at auction and for the next few seasons it was combined as Sells-Floto Circus and Buffalo Bill's Wild West Show. Some of the best acts in the entire circus world toured with this show.

In November, 1920, the Western newspapermen tired of the circus business and sold out to the American Circus Corporation which John Ringling bought in 1929.

"THE BARNUM OF THE PACIFIC" EARLY 1900's

E. K. (EDDIE) FERNANDEZ owns the Mid-Pacific Carnival, playing mostly on the islands, out-of-doors. He selects his actors and animals in America, to be carried on his ocean treks. His company travels in style with all the modern seafaring comforts. His animals enjoy the tropical climate on decks covered with canvas.

Eddie has trouped for more than thirty years, over the broad Pacific. It costs $25,000 to move his circus from California to Hawaii, but once there he is well repaid. Eddie's transportation cost for his entire circuit is $100,000, and his payroll approximately the same. To stand such expense and still make a profit, he must be endowed with the gifts of Barnum, hence his acquired title.

The mid-Pacific Carnival has to be slanted, as it were, to several types of audiences — audiences who are very severe and strict in their likes and dislikes; in their religious and civic customs. When showing in India, the religious taboos must be carefully considered. They prohibit the showing of certain animals. The yellow races of people do not laugh at the same things as Americans. In Japan, where animals are plentiful, animal acts are the most popular. The Chinese like the circus thrills and death-defying stunts. All the yellow races like juggling acts.

Yes, Eddie Fernandez's stage is half the world and he knows every clime — and the likes and dislikes of every race.

THE MIGHTY HAAG SHOWS

THE ONE WORD "hardship" might best describe Haag's show and also his life — "hardest to show and hardest to save" — yet he saved "the mostest from the leastest." He sold juices for a nickel a glass and gave a prize.

Before Haag left home, he had been quite a good musician, so he joined the Robinson Two-Car Show owned by "Windy" Smith. Later he played at fairs, picnics, and old soldiers' reunions, selling juices as a side line with his catch-spiel, "Spend a nickel and take home a prize." He saved

$1000. He invested in a minstrel show which was a failure, so he went back to his "nickel with a prize," and he put away every penny he could. He bought a small tent and a few ropes for twenty dollars, and had a little side show.

After floating to the Gulf of Mexico, Haag bought a cart and three mules, and turned the river circus into an overland show. By 1909, his show had grown so much that he decided to put it on the rails, giving it a deserving name, "Mighty Haag Shows." Staying on rails a while, he decided to go on trucks. He made money and saved money, always feeling successful if he did not have to borrow money. He now owned considerable real estate near Shreveport, Louisiana, Florida and Oklahoma.

From "Spend a nickel and get a prize," Haag moved to the directorship of Shreveport's largest bank, Commercial National. He is truly the "Success Story Boy" of the circus owners, saving the "mostest from the leastest" – "Spend a Nickel and Take Home a Prize."

AL G. BARNES CIRCUS Before 1914

AL G. BARNES, of California, was a soft-voiced, handsome man, courteous, kind and sympathetic. He started his circus career as a boy with a trained pony and a talking dog. He loved animals, had a way with them, and would not tolerate cruelty in training or handling.

He gradually added more animals to his show, and a singing mule, named Maude. Barnes was particularly fond of the intelligent mule. It was Al Barnes who used the first phonograph. Continuing to grow, the show went on rails and later combined with the Sig-Sautelle Circus for a short time. Cheerful Gardner, the well-known elephant trainer, was a valuable addition to the personnel. The "Tiger

Woman," Mabel Stark, and Rajah, her great performing tiger, were star attractions.

There are many great loves between man and animal in the annals of history, but in the circus world few have equalled that of Al G. Barnes and his beloved elephant, Tusko, the largest elephant in the United States after Jumbo's death.

In the early days of the circus, people wanted to see killer-elephants – they were drawing cards. Today the public is not interested in such outlaw elephants. Mr. Bailey, of Barnum & Bailey Circus, was the first to recommend killing outlaw elephants.

The story of Black Diamond owned by Mr. Barnes is very sad. He was a worker and was next to the largest elephant in the country at that time. He was a good elephant and devoted to his former keeper, Mr. Donahue. About three years before this tragedy, when the circus was showing in East Texas, Mr. Donahue had married a woman living there and had left the show to remain in that part of the state. At that time, Black Diamond saw his keeper walk out of the tent with his wife, and never return.

In 1928, when the show was in Dallas, Texas, Mr. Donahue went to see the circus. The minute he walked into the tent, Black Diamond saw him and gave the trumpet call of happiness. Black Diamond even whined as if to ask where he had been, why he had left him, and if he would promise never to do it again. All during that day, Black Diamond would become nervous if Mr. Donahue would walk away, so he stayed with the old elephant almost all day. After he left, Black Diamond grieved all night. Mr. Donahue's wife was not with him in Dallas, but Black Diamond remembered that this woman had taken his keeper away with her.

Sometime later, the circus was in Corsicana, Texas, parading on one of the main streets. Black Diamond was in the parade. He had two smaller elephants chained to him, one on each side, with twenty feet of chain between him and each of the small elephants. Mr. and Mrs. Donahue were there to see the parade. Mrs. Donahue was standing between two cars that were parked on the side of the street. It was impossible for Black Diamond to see her until he was exactly opposite her. The instant he spied her he made a terrific lunge, dragging both of the small elephants along with him, seized Mrs. Donahue with his trunk and beat her to death on the pavement. He stamped on her and tried to stick his tusk in her. He did all this suddenly and unexpectedly. Mr. Donahue rushed up, calling to Black Diamond and trying to save Mrs. Donahue; but Black Diamond, now thoroughly maddened, snatched him up and threw him over two automobiles. He was injured only slightly. At this time the animal trainer who had trained Black Diamond came rushing up, whereupon Black Diamond picked him up and set him aside.

While he was carefully putting aside his trainer, men jerked the mangled body of Mrs. Donahue from under Black Diamond. He was led back to his railroad car immediately. He did not feel that he had done anything wrong; he did not try to go on rampage. Mr. Barnes, the owner of the circus, ordered him shot. So in Kenedy, Texas, the circus men led all the elephants out to a mesquite pasture where there were some large oak trees. The moment they started to chain Black Diamond, the old elephant seemed to realize that something terrible was going to happen. He trembled and whined and moaned. He had done only what he thought he had the right to do. He kept whining and begging, kneeling down — trying to please — and there on his knees they shot him. Poor old Black Diamond, he had loved too well and had grown jealous. His mounted head is now in the Hermann Park Clubhouse at Houston, Texas.

Worries continued to beset Mr. Barnes. The war, labor and transportation troubles, came to this great show. In 1929, John Ringling bought the Barnes Circus. There is no disputing the contribution of Barnes to the American circus.

MILLS BROTHERS CIRCUS 1939

MILLS BROS. CIRCUS winters in Greenville, Ohio. It is an excellent circus with novel and thrilling talent, most of it imported. Their elephant, "Miss Burma, who scored nation-wide hits with her 1953 Inaugural Parade escapades, is one of the show-toppers." The experienced Paul Nelson, of long, famous circus lineage, directs the horse displays and is equestrian director.

Mills Bros. Circus advertises as "Your Major Fund Raising Activity," and it is an excellent three-ring circus. It never plays a Sunday date. It books several hundred towns under the auspices of fraternal, civic, and charitable organizations and hospital associations. A circus of this type fills a definite need in the community and country.

CLYDE BEATTY CIRCUS

THE CLYDE BEATTY CIRCUS has high-class entertainment, presented with expert showmanship in three large rings. The show keeps a fast pace and moves with precision. The band is lively, good, and spicy, and plays many current "hits." All equipment is in splendid condition, fresh looking and attractive.

Thirty-four years ago, Clyde Beatty was with Howe's Great London Circus. His name was not headlined, simply listed. He was no more than valet to Captain Louis Roth's wild animals, and his salary was $3.00 a week. In those thirty-four years, that one-time cage boy, Clyde Beatty, has become the owner and star in one of the largest circuses on tour, "one of the two circuses traveling aboard its own train."

The high spot of the show is, of course, Beatty's own big cat act. Clyde is known all over the world for his ability in training and handling big cats. For many years this has been his chosen profession, and he has certainly succeeded.

Beatty is a five-and-a-half-foot bundle of nerve and courage. A misconception which he resents intensely is that cruelty is necessary in the training of an animal. And he always uses the word "train" rather than "tame." He points out that a lion or a tiger is no different from a human in many respects. Kindness, patience, and firmness will accomplish more than force or cruelty. Beatty studies his animals, their traits, dispositions, and characteristics.

Though the screen, radio, and television take much of Beatty's time during off season, yet when the whistle blows for spring opening of the circus, Clyde, the familiar figure in white, will be right there, and it's "On with the Show."

JOHN RINGLING NORTH and HENRY RINGLING NORTH and OTHER OFFICIALS OF THE GREATEST SHOW ON EARTH

SEVERAL YEARS after the death of John Ringling, John Ringling North assumed control as president of Ringling Bros. and Barnum & Bailey Circus. Henry Ringling North became vice-president. The North brothers are sons of Ida Ringling North, the only sister of the seven famous Ringling Brothers.

John set about immediately bringing modernism to the Greatest Show on Earth. Obsolete ideas and operations were discarded. Arthur M. Concello, the erstwhile star of the flying trapeze, was appointed general manager.

One of the first steps of streamlining was the purchase of a fleet of tractors. These tractors retired 300 baggage horses, thus a great bulk of animal transportation and feeding was out. There was always the problem, in smaller towns, of power plants being able to supply only a part of the power needed. So fifteen diesel power plants were added, now generating the current needed for the thousands of miles of wire network necessary for the greatly improved lighting arrangements. Floodlights and spotlights of 5000 watts each are not uncommon. Thirty-eight men are required to operate these plants.

The greatest innovation in the North modernization came in the use of the portable, fireproof, steel grandstands which are really huge, walled trucks, with upholstered chairs that fold down neatly on the sides. Each one of these twenty-nine portable grandstand trucks seats 300 people.

When location is made for the Big Top, the trucks are formed in an oblong circle around the five performing rings, and the seats are unfolded in a few minutes into complete sections. The amount of baggage was greatly reduced by the use of these grandstand trucks, but more important is the fact that this is the greatest time and labor saving innovation the circus has ever known.

While the last of the guests are leaving the arena, this oblong circle of steel folds its wings and disappears in truck formation — "silver ghosts of pantomime," as they have been called. William Curtis had the idea of this portable grandstand as far back as 1898, and his plans were revised, improved and copyrighted.

In the arena, mesh cages have supplanted the clanging steel bar cages. The tent is fireproof. Aluminum poles are being used in some places to replace heavy wooden ones. An elaborate FM 2-way communication system allows the operating brains of the circus to communicate between the train and the lot, as well as between different locations on the lot.

In 1953, for the first time in the history of the circus, motor winches were used to hoist 21 tons of canvas — the Big Top. We shall never again hear the cadenced chant of the guying-out gang as it made its way around the Big Top, "Ah, heebie, hebby, hobby, hole, golong." This is a phonetic rendition of "Heave it, heavy, hard, hold, next." These instructions are the ones called out by the boss canvasman, usually prefaced by the familiar phrase, "Speak your Latin." With the use of the motor winches, power switches are thrown and the mammoth canvas structure, giant monarch of the tent world, which covers a seating capacity for 10,000 people in air-conditioned comfort, is raised to its commanding position in a matter of a few minutes.

The new air-conditioned tent is 20° cooler than ever before and this has added to the phenomenal "draw." The actors have benefitted even more than the audience by this air conditioning, especially the high wire and flying artists. They no longer have to endure the extreme heat at the top of the tent, but perform in 35° cooler temperature. There is studied symmetry in the interior of the enlarged five-pole tent, the largest in the world. The canvas is so treated chemically as to eliminate glare. The green sawdust on the ground under the big top is a colorful innovation and is easy on the eyes.

The costume department received a large boost on the budget sheet, over a quarter of a million dollars being allowed Miles White, who was secured as costume designer, creating the lavish glitter and spangle. White is well-known in his field. The style of the circus costumes has become a major influence in the realm of fashion. As a rule, three months' time is required to make these costumes. Sometimes two sets are needed, one for fair weather and one for rainy. With Miles White doing the designing, Jimmie Strook (Brooks Costume Company of New York) undertakes this gigantic task of making the costumes. According to Patricia Coffin, each year Brooks sends a fitter and twelve finishers to Sarasota, accompanied by 150 trunks filled with dashing "scarlet coats, spangled tights, dress clothes for monkeys, ballet costumes for elephants," and ostrich headdresses. Brooks might have for his circus slogan, "We dress anything in the circus from an educated flea to a jumbo elephant."

Brooks did the costumes for Cecil B. DeMille's movie, "The Greatest Show on Earth," at a cost of $40,000. One woman is kept busy in the Brooks establishment the year around working only on elephant trappings.

The general director at R.B.B.&B., Pat Valdo, "knows the wires," so to speak, as he was, at one time or another, wire walker, juggler, clown, and ringmaster. He juggles the personnel to perfection, and, conscientiously studying every act, past and present, has become the casting director supreme. He crowds three hours' work into every hour he spends awake — and he doesn't sleep much.

Roland Butler, as Publicity Director, is a dynamo of energy. He has an uncanny knack of finding or giving birth to adjectives, stupendous in import. He is known as the man with the ornate vocabulary. It is said that he has rediscovered or put into the dictionary more new words than any living person.

Allen Lester is another important man with the Big Show. He is a press agent of precision. You may be sure his statistics are correct. He spots his publicity with assurance. It is Lester who tells the world that it costs $20,000 a day to operate The Greatest Show on Earth, that the Big Show has jumped 239 miles in a single night and was on time for the matinee the next afternoon — that the shortest jump in a tour is the ten-mile stretch between the twin cities, Minneapolis and St. Paul, but the trains are loaded with the same precision as though going 100 miles or more. "Safety

First" is practised. The circus is irrevocably committed to system and does not digress. And Allen Lester follows this working motto of the great show, "System and Order, and Order and System — the Watchword" — no excuses, no errors, no tragic results.

Robert E. Reynolds, Superintendent of Properties, has spent thirty-nine years with Ringling Bros. and Barnum & Bailey Circus. His staff of forty men call him "Round-the-Clock Reynolds." It is his duty to protect life, limb, and property. He inspects miles of rope, riggings, many strings of steel cable and swivels (40 swivels support the aerialist act). He has a musician's sense of pitch — as one might sound a tuning fork, he taps each swivel with a sharp instrument. If the swivel has a dull ring, he promptly replaces it with a new one. Frank Braden once said of Bob Reynolds, "Bob could hang a flying trapeze between Mt. Ranier and Mt. Shasta in time for the afternoon show."

Now Frank Braden is one of the big names in the picture of success of this great circus. Braden is known as the dean of American press agents. He lives, breathes, and has his being in excitement, and so good is he that one can never tell whether the excitement is of his own making or actual. Braden is the advance man for The Greatest Show on Earth. He is a Houdini when it comes to publicity gags — he pulls them from an imaginary bag, with imaginary ease, and you don't even imagine such a thing of him. And Fred de Wolfe's interesting articles always afforded a colorful insight into the life of the big show.

John North spends February and March of each year in Sarasota, in close consultation with his experienced manager. Together they "tune" the new show. John North lives with the show while it is in New York, and he travels with it for a time and then hands it over to his manager and goes to Europe for the rest of the year, scouting new acts and new talent, staying a month or six weeks in Spain. He continually "rides herd" on talent in countries abroad.

35. ANNIE OAKLEY (1892)

37. MERLE EVANS

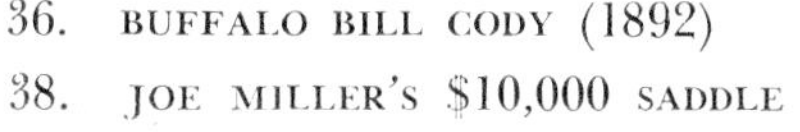

36. BUFFALO BILL CODY (1892)

38. JOE MILLER'S $10,000 SADDLE

39. CLYDE BEATTY AND HIS CATS

40. JOHN RINGLING NORTH

41. HENRY RINGLING NORTH

42. LITTLE MADISON SQUARE GARDEN, SARASOTA, FLORIDA

43. THE HARTFORD FIRE (JULY 6, 1944)

44. GEORGE ESCALANA, BOSS PAINTER OF R.B.B.&B. CIRCUS

THIS IS THE FAMOUS SINGING WHEEL

45. 1000 POUNDS OF CHICKEN — FOR ONE MEAL

46. TRAVELING "HOTEL RINGLING" — THE DINING TENT

47. LITTLE LILLIAN LEITZEL

48. CHARLES F. CLARKE AND FAMILY

49. ALFREDO CODONA

50. LILLIAN LEITZEL (CHICAGO, 1926)

51. THE GREAT LILLIAN LEITZEL ON THE ROMAN RINGS

52. LEITZEL FELL TO HER DEATH WHEN ROMAN RING BROKE

53. LEITZEL AND CODONA — JUST MARRIED, CHICAGO, 1928

54. MONUMENT TO LILLIAN LEITZEL, INGLEWOOD, CALIFORNIA

55. THE FLYING CONCELLOS

56. RENE AND MADELEINE GERALDO

57. THE GREAT WALLENDAS

58. DIETER TASSO, JUGGLING GENIUS

59. LA NORMA, THE FLYING TEMPTRESS

60. MARY JANE MILLER, DARING AND DECORATIVE YOUNG AERIALIST

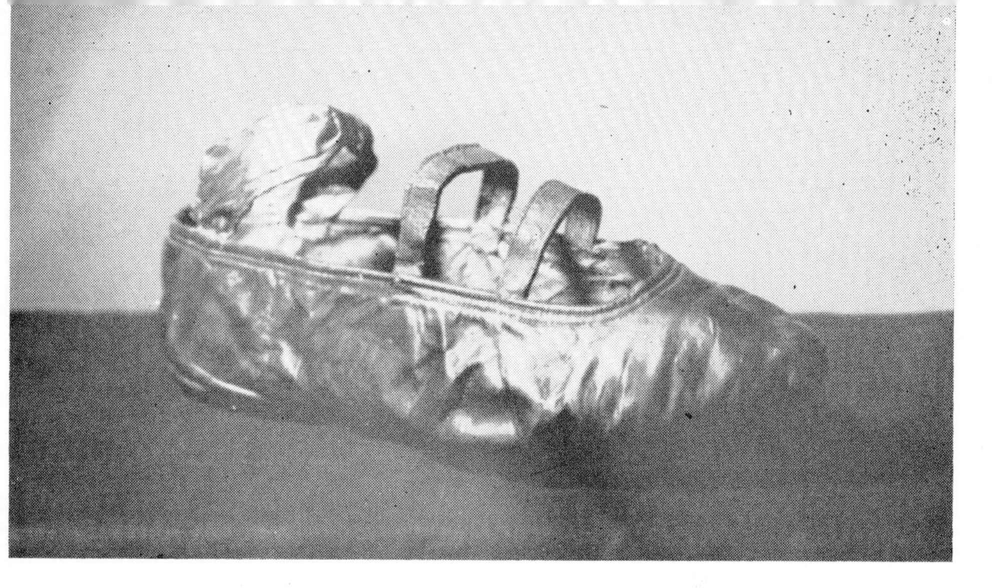

61. "THE SHOE THAT DANCED AROUND THE WORLD"—
BIRD MILLMAN

62. ELLA AND FRED BRADNA

63. KAREFF MANUS

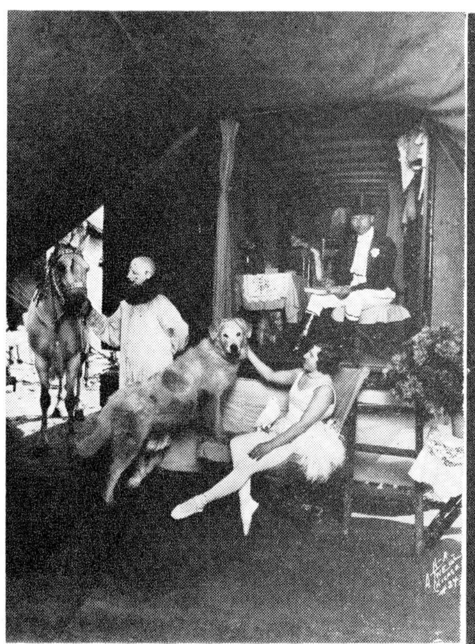

64. VITTORIO ZACCHINI, "THE HUMAN CANNONBALL"

65. THE CHADULIS, "DAREDEVIL CYCLISTS"

66. NIO NAILTO — FOREWARD SOMERSAULT ON TIGHT WIRE

67. PINITO DEL ORO

68. BRUNN, "THE JUGGLING KING"

69. UNUS

70. MR. MISTIN, JR., THE WORLD'S YOUNGEST XYLOPHONE VIRTUOSO

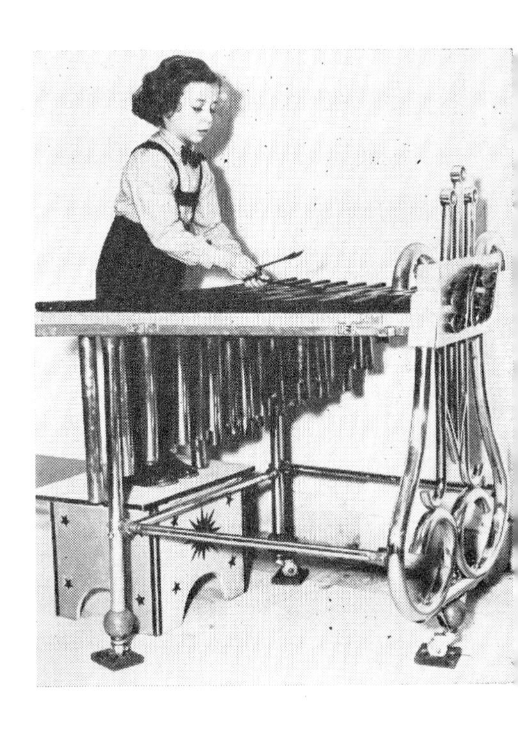

71. POODLES HANNEFORD

72. MAY WIRTH

73. LUCIO CRISTIANI

74. THE LOYAL REPINSKY FAMILY

75. THE GREAT BLONDIN

While John is doing his scouting, Henry North remains in residence in Italy. Having established headquarters there, he covers the Mediterranean area where great acts are born and bred. Italy is the crossroads for international talent, and Spain is not far away.

Henry North gives a great deal of attention to the business side of the show. He is not the glamor man that John is. He is more down-to-earth, fraternizes more with the personnel of the circus. He has one son, who, when on vacation from school, joins the Big Top folks to learn the circus business from the ground up. He is the pet of the entire show.

While the Norths hunt talent, rare animal trainers scour the world on safari or in jungles for additions to the great show's menagerie, which is world-famous.

So when Ringling Bros. and Barnum & Bailey Circus comes to your town and you are seated – eager, excited, waiting – the band will give that electrifying opening fanfare. A void of silence follows – and then the ever-old, the ever-new announcement that brings excitement to finger and toe tips – "Children of All Ages, John Ringling North proudly presents (the 197th edition of) The Greatest Show on Earth!"

CONCESSIONS

LITTLE NEED BE SAID about the concessions on the circus lot. You can hear the clatter, clang and call. "Health by the gallon! Pink Lemonade right here! Come on! Come on!" "Sweet Cotton Candy – come on, Kiddies!" "A mile of hot dogs. Hot dogs and hot mustard! All hot! Get 'em while they last!" "Popcorn for you – peanuts for the elephants! Don't disappoint the elephants! They're waiting for you!" "Soda water! Soda water! All flavors! Tall bottles!" "Eve! Ah, Eve! Here, here! Give Adam an apple – a big red apple! Candy-coated!"

And for entertainment: — "You dunk your bread — now dunk a man! Hit the trigger with a ball! See him drop into the water!" "Lady! Lady! Are you an Annie Oakley? Hit the bull's-eye and take home an eye full!" "Easy! Easy, does the trick! Ring yourself a prize! Right this way!" "Bingo! Bingo! Bingo! You win! We lose!" "Mister! Mister! Your ladylove wants your picture — step in — step out! Your head on an elephant; a giraffe, or if your mouth's big enough — on a hippo! Take home a photo!" "Souvenirs! Souvenirs! Circus Souvenirs! Lookie! Lookie! Lookie! A circus souvenir!"

WINTER QUARTERS of RINGLING BROS. AND BARNUM & BAILEY CIRCUS

The Premiere in New York

IN LATE NOVEMBER, after eight months of trouping from 15,000 to 20,000 miles — having given performances in about 140 cities from coast to coast in the United States — the Ringling Bros. and Barnum & Bailey Circus returns each year to its winter quarters in Sarasota, Florida, bringing home its 1400 troupers and the travel-weary animals from twenty-eight lands.

At the end of each touring season, when the whistle blows at the end of the last act of the last performance, the band plays "Auld Lang Syne" and a thunderous chorus of voices swells the very canvas top. Then, as Frank L. Morrisey tells us, there is a moment's silence before the cheery call rings from every throat, "See you in the Garden in the spring!" And that spoken ritual is more than words — it's a deep, spiritual expression of hope for the family's reunion. So circus people never say good-by. There is a sequel to this "See you in the Garden in the spring," as we learn from "The Circus Catches Its Breath," a Ringling release. Performers will tell you that each year just before the fanfare blares for the customary annual opening in Madison Square Garden in New York City of "The Greatest Show on Earth," there is a "timeless moment in which the whole show seems to draw a breath deep enough to last until the next November" – then it's fanfare, says Frank L. Morrisey, and it's John Ringling North calling, and it's "The Garden in the spring."

The Ringling winter quarters comprise 200 acres of mill and shop activities; sheltered wild animal arenas; ring barns; and many other departments. All in all there are 70,000 tons of equipment which must be rehabilitated each year while in winter quarters. The Big Top alone, with its cordage and 74,000 yards of canvas (canvas enough to cover twelve acres) weighs 21 tons and three times that when wet, or 63 tons. There are 73 miles of rope used in the big show's tent.

Rehearsals start at Sarasota early in February, and a number of days before this, performers of flying and wire acts practice and hurtle outside in the warm Florida sunshine. There is activity in every tent and in every corner – a veritable "big-time hive." Artists come from all over the world to get colorful paintings. Many authors, magazine editors, and feature story writers visit the winter quarters yearly.

In February, the rehearsals move to "Little Madison Square Garden," an outdoor replica, to the inch, of Madison Square Garden in New York. Here the production numbers, large and small, are worked out and spaced as to seconds and fractions of inches. Thus the production, so spaced in Sarasota, fits with precision when presented in New York.

At last the show is ready to start rolling on the long, silver enameled trains toward Madison Square Garden, New York City, where it has its premiere each year. And be it said to the glory of the Ringlings and the Norths that each year all the proceeds from this premiere go to a worthy cause — Red Cross, War Relief, Cancer Research, and many others. Every seat in Madison Square Garden is always taken for this opening show. Stars from Hollywood are flown in to appear and take part in the opening, and many actors from Broadway lend their prestige and assistance. Actors and actresses, writers and artists, and visiting celebrities are introduced to the huge audience. It is a gala night in a gala city, with young and old in high spirits.

This giving of the proceeds from the premiere showing is but one facet of the interest in health and happiness — the civic-mindedness — of the Ringlings and the Norths. Both the women and the men of all these families have worked hard for the Salvation Army, for war bond drives, for all worthwhile projects. Their work in the U.S.O. during World War II was manifested in many ways. Thousands upon thousands of men and women in the service of our country and our allies were admitted to their great show without charge, through the U.S.O.

The Ringlings and the Norths are beloved in Sarasota. The friendly people of that lovely city feel a kind of pride-of-ownership in this big show. Each year almost everyone in the entire city goes to watch the trains leave town, to wave good-by, and to wish them good trouping. The business houses close, the city takes a holiday to express its love and appreciation of this, The Greatest Show on Earth. Father John Elslander, of St. Martha's Church, traditionally blesses the bright railroad caravans. And then the engineers get the "high ball" and the engines roar, and the coaches, silver streamlined beauties of the rails, click, as on and on to big New York the silver streak flashes its way. "The big cocoon has split wide-open and the beautiful, rainbowed butterfly, man-made and destined for an eight-month flight-on-wheels to the music of a circus band, is winging its way."

Every performer feels the strain of gypsy blood take hold, and the long, long road ahead beckons.

THE CLEVELAND FIRE
August 4, 1942

ONE OF THE WORST circus fires in history occurred on August 4, 1942, when more than forty of the Ringling Bros. and Barnum & Bailey Circus animals — some trained — burned to death. Loss was estimated at $200,000.

The fire occurred in Cleveland, Ohio, just after lunch. A Negro boy, sixteen years of age, who had run away from home to join the circus, and who had been fired from the circus for laziness, set fire to a stack of straw near the animal tent. Fire spread as each gust of wind carried a tiny flame to an explosive spot. Flames roared through the animal cages. The holocaust seemed to envelop everything. Animals cried, shrieked, screamed with bloodcurdling jungle terror.

A group of camels, chained together, were burned. Two dozen elephants, which remained obedient to the orders of their trainers, were led from the fire with strips of burnt skin hanging from them. Some of the caged animals were saved by the firemen who managed to pour a constant stream of water on them. Many of these were pathetically burned in spite of the heroic efforts of the firemen, officials, actors, side show freaks, roustabouts, and volunteer helpers.

After it was over, women gave way to hysterics, men fell to the ground exhausted, and hardened roustabouts and trainers wept as little children.

"HARTFORD HORROR"
July 6, 1944

THE WORST FIRE in all of circus history occurred July 6, 1944, while Ringling Bros. and Barnum & Bailey Circus was giving the matinee performance in Hartford, Connecticut. The fire started in the men's rest room, took to the side wall, and in a flash, the entire tent was in flames. In less than five minutes, the Big Top had burned.

Robert Ringling stated that the tragedy would never have occurred had the firm been allowed to use priority fireproofing for the canvas. (The day after the fire, this priority fireproofing was released for circus use.) On account of not having priority, the firm had coated the tent with a waterproof solution of gasoline and paraffin before leaving winter quarters in Sarasota, Florida. This coating was the cause of the flash fire, and on account of this coating several officials of the circus were arrested on charges of manslaughter and placed under heavy bail.

All available help was quickly mobilized and Hartford did everything possible to aid. Most of the circus spectators, who were burned, were trampled in the rush to escape. Ushers, ticket-sellers, actors, officials – all helped as long as humanly possible. The Merle Evans Band played as long as they could remain on the bandstand, then went outside and played. This music was a great help in keeping down hysteria. The people burned or tramped to death numbered 168, and 497 were injured.

Considering the large number, 6500 people in attendance at the matinee, and the fact that it was a flash fire, the evacuation was remarkable. Another factor that increased the rate of death and number injured was the fact that so great a percentage of the audience was made of up children and women.

A husky circus roustabout, twenty years of age, (and by his own words a killer, having committed four slayings, and an arsonist since he was six years of age, having a record of more than a score of fires) confessed setting off the blaze that brought untold suffering and tragedy and sorrow to the entire circus world.

After this fire, the circus went into winter quarters at Sarasota, but remained there only a few days, going out right away to show in the open air. The wind hampered the aerialists, and spectators and actors endured 95° temperature, but the "show went on." Karl Wallenda, ready to go aloft when the great blaze started, said, "The awful fire has called up in all of us the spirit of the circus trouper. Our act is presented now at 42 feet — 12 feet higher than under canvas. I hope it thrills the people as it does us." The famous clown, Emmett Kelly, said, "We must forget the fire. We must entertain. In wartime, it's more important than ever. It's going to be great in the open air."

The circus was considered so important for the "sustainment of morale on the home front" during the war, that the Office of Defense Transportation issued a general permit for operation of circus trains.

The new tent which Ringling Bros. and Barnum & Bailey Circus uses today is completely fireproof, and so are the seats.

The present managers, John Ringling North and Henry Ringling North, have paid off all claims arising from this holocaust, $3,946,355. It took a number of years, and colossal courage to undertake such a staggering debt, but all, to the last penny, has been paid. On December 10, 1950, checks covering the final $690,612.43 payment on claims were mailed out.

PULLING IN – UNLOADING – AND PUTTING UP A CIRCUS: The Trains Pull in For Ringling Bros. and Barnum & Bailey Circus

BEFORE THE SHADOWS form in early dawn, the first of four long trains of Ringling Bros. and Barnum &

Bailey Circus pulls into a town to a smooth, gliding stop, as M. G. Gorrow tells us in *White Tops*. The circus commissary is aboard. However, one of the advance agents of the circus has gone ahead of this train and has contracted with railroad officials for designated unloading spots. He has arranged for planks to be placed between the rails at these spots and for gravel (in early days, cinders) to be put in all mud holes or ruts, and sawdust or sand (formerly cinders) on all slick or icy ways. All the cans, wires, bottles, and rubbish which might hang in the wagon wheels or hurt the feet of the soft-footed camels and elephants, will have been cleared away. Ramps are placed ready to be put on the end of a long string of the 70-foot-long flatcars as soon as they arrive. The cars are spotted (stopped) as near the circus grounds as possible. Train travel of the circus has kept pace with the modernization of other Ringling Bros. equipment. One hundred cars are used.

Since the circus owns all the cars it uses, they are built for specific loads — the stock cars, like the flats, are especially built for all lead stock — horses, elephants, camels, zebra, the hippopotamus, and the like.

Following this first train section, which always carries cooking and dining room equipment and personnel tents, comes the second section which carries the menagerie, with attendants, and the animal tent and necessary parts and units. The third section has the heavy load of the Big Top with all its parts and other equipment and personnel needed for its erection. Sometime later the fourth section arrives, with the performers and officials, who get most of their sleep on these rides between towns.

It is big business, when it comes to bringing a big show to town. Three weeks before the date for the show's arrival, advertising men have pasted the signboards with exciting posters, and other forerunner publicity has been contracted. Then a week or more before the show arrives, newspapers feature star performers and animal acts. Circus enthusiasm starts mounting by the day and then by the hour.

The 24-hour men, those who precede the arrival of the circus by a full day, "make" (rent and prepare) the show lot, its approaches, and block the tent layout of forty-two units, including the Big Top, menagerie tent, and the horse tent. In some cities, these 24-hour men find it necessary to grade, fill, and level the show lot.

At the dawn of circus day, agents are on the ground to direct deliveries of all supplies — fuel oil, stock feed, fruits, bread, vegetables, eggs, water, meats, etc. These must be ready for the dining department because the cookhouse is the first unit to arrive on the ground and "get going." On the day before, such items as hay, straw, smithy coal, and coke are on the circus lot, but most of the supplies of a circus are delivered the day a show arrives. Of course, contracts for these supplies are let weeks ahead by agents who buy everything a circus uses in the town in which it is showing.

Everybody with the large Ringling Bros. and Barnum & Bailey family has a berth, or better, in the Pullmans — even the lowest-paid rookie on the roughest job. The comfort of the personnel is given paramount consideration. A double-length bed makes sleep come easier for the giant, while the fat lady's berth is double in width, and the midgets snuggle down in their baby beds. Laundry and dry cleaning facilities operate on a two-day schedule. Big buses shuttle a "gilly service," carrying all personnel of the circus, desiring to ride, to the circus location.

Soon the circus lot is a beehive of activity. After the cookhouse is in readiness, all the other departments get attention by their respective crews; the menagerie; the horse tents, etc. And so it is that an entire city sets up housekeeping in a few hours and is ready, with best "bib and tucker," and company manners, to receive thousands of callers.

That these callers depart, happy in heart and spirit, is ample testimony to the friendliness of the circus city.

LIFE IN THE BACKYARD
or
ON THE FAMILY LOT OF THE CIRCUS

THE BACKYARD, or family lot, is the private parking lot for the cars, trailers (formerly wagons) and for the tents in which circus performers live. It is just what the name implies — the family lot — home for the huge circus family for a day or two, or for the length of time a circus remains at a stop or town.

It is almost impossible for one who has not been privileged to visit on the family lot to realize how much home life, how much genuine happiness, how many comforts, and how much of the identical home atmosphere which the townspeople enjoy, is present on this family lot. Here are the women and girl aerialists in simple, little gingham dresses, some with their children on their laps, others hanging out a little family wash on clotheslines stretched between wagons or trailers. The "old-timers" are always engaged in "gab-fests" and invariably draw a good audience. Here and there you see a mother and father teaching a child to become a tumbler, a tight wire walker, a bareback rider, or some other act which he will inherit. And these parents beam with pride over each little successful accomplishment of the child.

Schoolteachers travel along with the larger shows and the education of the children progresses normally. Parents with smaller shows (and these shows usually stay for some time in each town or stop) send their children to school in whichever town they are playing. After all, most of the circuses stay for several months in winter quarters, and the educational advantages for the children are given first attention then.

These circus performers lead normal and extremely moral lives, no drinking, dissipation, or late hours. Their bodies are of paramount importance to their profession. A tired muscle that does not respond in split-second precision timing may mean instant death to the aerialist, the bareback rider, or the acrobat. The one thing which actors fear and dread most is old age, and moderate living wards off that silent creeper for a time, perhaps many years.

The interest of the entire personnel of the circus is so compact — one for all and all for one — that it is said that if any member of the family sneezes in front of the main entrance, the vibrations in the back yard start all to worrying over one of their family having a cold.

The family life in the back yard of a large circus is a wonderful and inspiring example. The members have learned to take the storms of the elements and the storms of man's own making. They realize that a storm is a part of the normal horizon of life — they summon courage. With that priceless commodity, they have been able to ride out the storms of life.

FEEDING THE RINGLING BROS. AND BARNUM & BAILEY CIRCUS

THE FEEDING of a large circus has been called "Cookhouse Magic." George Blood is the efficient boss of the little canvas city known as Hotel Ringling, the world's largest land-traveling restaurant. He has been "with it" for more than twenty-five years.

A telescoped system of cooking caldrons was invented for the circus. The U.S. Army benefited by the example of the circus methods and now uses this same type of rolling kitchen and equipment. This modern fold-up and fit-in, quick-change-artist system has taken the place of the Barnum field ranges. The "wash-rag-juggling" workers now glance over their shoulders at an assembly line full of gleaming unbreakable plasticware, as the dish washing machines click with precision. The dishes are washed, sterilized and dried automatically.

Frank Braden tells us of the visitor who asked George, "How do you do it?" George replied, "Just like the restaurants, only I serve the same folks in different cities daily, while your people serve different customers in the same spot." But the man shook his head and said, "Just think of setting up housekeeping in a different town each day and expecting to serve 4200 meals."

George Blood "has about 142 men working for him — " says Braden, "chefs, plain cooks, pastry cooks, waiters, bus boys, machine operators, canvasmen, storekeepers, commissary clerks, and truck drivers." "Hotel Ringling" must function, come hail or high water, because circus folks have good appetites and George Blood gives them good food. Everything that is in season is served — melons, corn on the cob, and all kinds of fresh vegetables. There are no printed menus. The efficient waiters "reel it off" in a "lingo" all their own. Twenty-eight nations are represented in the huge Ringling Bros. and Barnum & Bailey Circus family, yet the waiter, in some mysterious way, understands all orders in "this canopied bower of babel." People from different nations volunteer their favorite recipes, according to Don McNeill, and one such, now used as a standard dessert of the Ringling Cookhouse, is Joyva Halvah, an exotic delicacy of the Near East.

When a meal is ready, a flag is run up on a tall pole and all over the circus lot the words, "The Flag's Up," are called from one to another. There are two tables reserved for staff members. Staff and performers eat at one end of the dining tent. Of course, families are seated together and so are acts, small or large. This all makes for friendly or professional talk during meals. There is much laughter, good-natured teasing, and shop talk, all of which is an important contributing factor to the "Happy, Big-Family Feeling" with the Greatest Show on Earth. There is no smoking in the dining tent and no rowdy or loud talking. The official and the working man have exactly the same menu. Congeniality is the appetizer served in Hotel Ringling. The side show people have tables to themselves and always eat first. Their show must start well in advance of the main performance.

Feeding the animals of the circus is also in Mr. Blood's department. There are many very expensive animals with the circus — the jungle cats, bears, and rare animals including Toto, Gargantua's widow, and her two adopted gorilla babies, Gargantua II and Mlle. Toto.

CIRCUS PERFORMERS

CIRCUS PERFORMERS respect their bodies as bankers do their gold — their bodies are their lives, which they bravely gamble on every performance. They are brave, courageous, self-sacrificing. They bring to the sawdust world the best — perfection, gained through gruelling hours of practice; technique, studied and inherited from generations; precision, such as comes only from that spark called genius.

Space, time, not even energy, would permit writing about all the great stars of the circus, and the thrilling acts of the sawdust ring. The author has taken one, maybe two, representing each field of performance. For omissions, none of which are intentional, forgiveness is implored.

ORIGIN OF THE ACTS

"LEAPING" had its origin among Spanish vagabond players and court jesters. In the beginning, there were cart wheels (turns-feet-to-hands and back) and flip-flaps — next came the backward somersault. Several pioneers broke or fractured their necks, but undaunted, others kept trying. Next, the double-somersault and finally the triple. In 1856, a Mr. George Miller twice accomplished the triple-somersault while practicing, and the very first time he attempted it in public, he was killed. Later John Worland gave three successful exhibitions of the triple-somersault in three cities.

Leapers do these somersaults nowadays, but they use a springboard by means of which they gain enough altitude that the act may be completed in comparative safety. Billie Pape did a forward somersault from a springboard over five elephants, his body catapulting through the air for a distance of forty feet.

"Tumbling" developed from "leaping." Well-known tumblers were the Rubio Sisters and the Yacopi Troupe. There is one tumbling act known as the Risley Act — taking its name from its originator — the basic principle of which is one man lying flat on his back and, with upraised feet, balancing or throwing or rolling another person about. Alfred Fullgrapp juggles two people at once, stacks them, and tosses the two, one on the other's shoulder, to the shoulders of another man waiting nearby.

"Flying" is considered the most sensational of all standard acts. The original flying act consisted of two men on trapezes, hanging head down, and throwing a third man back and forth through a few feet of space. As the space of the throw increased, a swinging trapeze was added so that the flying man might bridge a greater distance. The timing of this swinging was so perfected that the catcher could throw the flying man to this arc and he could, by his own force, return to his original pedestal. Thus the "flying return" came into practice. This was a great step in the art of "flying." Three trapezes were added and six men sailed through the air. The Ward-Belle Flyers increased this number to nine flyers sailing through space at one time.

THE TECHNIQUE OF THE FLYING ACT

AERIAL BEAUTY, which catches the breath and tugs at the heartstrings, is nowhere more patently apparent than in the gyrations of the flyer — the twisting, somersaulting, pirouetting flyer, high above the ground on a swinging trapeze. In his actions, one finds beauty of form, grace, muscle control, precision, and technique, perfected to split-second timing. All of this demands courage and daring — yet, it is all such a technique performance, that not only artistic ability, courage, and bodily perfection are required, but more, a generous supply of good common sense, such as it takes to persevere in any difficult operation from the ground up. And the time of persevering is a period of at least four years to the aerialist.

An aerial act to some is "sheer magic," to some a "thriller," but to others it becomes an "athletic classic." The principles employed in aerial acts have been studied and analysed over a period of eighty-seven years, dating back to 1870, when Leotard conceived the idea of the trapeze.

It is interesting to note how the idea of the flying trapeze first originated. Ted and Taff Volta (twins) had been performing in 1876, at the Casino in the Rue Lafayette at Toulouse, where Leotard had been born and educated. Young Leotard's father owned a gymnasium and swimming bath, "Gymnase Leotard." The manager of the gymnasium told the Volta twins exactly how this act originated. He said young Leotard was ready to plunge in for a swim. Looking up, he noticed parallel cords hanging from each of two roof ventilators, serving to open and shut the ventilators. It occurred to young Leotard that if a wooden bar were fixed between each, he could swing from one to the other without risking more than a sudden plunge into the pool below. He put into effect this idea, and from this developed what we know now as aerial acrobatism.

When Leotard first appeared in his trapeze act in London, a padded mattress was spread the whole length of the stage. Later, a net was substituted, which form of protection is still used today.

When a trapeze actor is performing on the bars, his movements are greatly affected by the slope of the ground. The movement of an acrobat's body will be greatly accelerated over a downward slope, while he must put forth added energy and strength to swing his body over an upward slope. And this phenomenon is true even though the bars and supports are perfectly level.

This point has been argued for years, with many dissenting opinions being submitted, but it is said that the noted Alfredo Codona subscribed to this theory, asserting it to be a fact.

The apparatus or rigging of the aerial act has gone through many modifications, and even today varies according to the particular act, each one of which is technical in detail. One of the highest acts of this kind was that of the Six Hanlon Volters, performed 100 feet from the ground. Intense training for an aerial act is necessary. Work on the Roman rings develops the back, arm, and shoulder muscles, also the neck muscles. Flip-flaps and round-offs on the ground make the body strong and supple so the performer can instantly adjust himself, for the tuck, in turning somersaults in the air. He must learn to fall correctly on the net below — always on the back and shoulders. Then comes the long course of learning the proper timing by the catcher and the flyer. The flyer is the more spectacular of the two, but he could not perform without a competent catcher. On the catcher rests the burden of the proper timing of leaving the pedestal and the bar by the flyer. Eddie Ward, Bloomington, Illinois, who trained around one hundred aerial performers, estimated that the speed of the flyer when caught by the catcher was at the rate of a body moving at forty miles per hour.

The flyer's next schooling step is the polishing of his routine of tricks, and the fitting of the music to his act. And, finally, one of the most important lessons affecting his "draw," or popularity with the audiences, is that of showmanship—poise. Then the final result to be gained is—perfection. The names of many famous star performers appear on the aerialist list.

Some of the pioneer and best-known aerialists were: The Rollande Brorthers, The Rizareli Brothers, The Buislays, Cornelius Silbon's Troupe, Lazelle and Wilson, Carlo and Ross, The Eugenes, The Dacomas, Dunbar and Vernon of the early Ringling Show, The Peerless Potters, Flying La-Vans, Six Flying Jordons, The Becketts, The Herberts, Banvards, Ernestonians, Flying Dillons, The George Troupe, Weitzel, English, Tryan & H. Zorrella, Todd, Beckman & Todd, Moore and Gilmore, Flying Lloyds, The Stokes Troupe, and others.

Later well-known aerial acts are Eddie and Eugene Silbon, Charlie and Edyth Seigrist, Enrico Diaz, Bert Doss, Harold Voise and Roy Deichler, who composed the Flying Thrillers.

The aerialists, Miltemore and Charlie Noble, had heard of the famous Hanlons in Europe and that they used a net. No one here in America seemed to know how a net would work or how to use it. But Miltemore and Noble called in a fisherman and secured his services in making a net, which they used. This net was hemp rope tied with knots. Some onlooker remarked that the boys looked more like fishermen than actors, so the boys immediately decided, as we learn from the writings of Clyde V. Noble, to call it The Fisher Bros. Act.

Charlie's wife, Minnie Noble, added a sensational bit to their act, as she was the first woman in the United States to do an Iron Jaw Act, or tooth act, hanging suspended by a rope, with only a leather strap in her mouth, holding by her teeth while the swivel and other acts were performed.

This act is seen in many circuses now, each girl having her own leather strap, so padded and shaped as to fit each individual's mouth. Emily Becchi Noble, wife of Clyde Noble, was considered one of the greatest women trick cyclists in the world.

When the Ringling Bros. decided to put their show on the railroad, the first act engaged by them was The Fisher Brothers Act. Charlie Noble, in his day, was the greatest leaper in show business, and was the first man to ever successfully do a double-somersault and catch. Another brother joined the act and it became known as The Five Famous Flying Fishers, and, from that date on, all large aerial acts have been called Flying Acts.

The Ward Act was the next aerial act to become famous. Mayme Kimball Ward was the first women to ever do the double-somersault and catch. Eddie Ward, her husband, was an excellent and artistic performer. It was Eddie Ward who popularized the act of "flying" to such a degree that he inspired the well-known song, "The Daring Young Man on the Flying Trapeze." He probably trained more men and women for aerial acts than any other performer.

In trapeze performance, teamwork is all-important. "Knowing when to drop the swinging bar for an aerialist to return to the platform demands split-second timing," and is the very essence of skill. Performers on the flying trapeze grasp wrists, not hands — the famous catcher's grip, wrist-around-wrist, — and up they go, rocketing, swirling, and gliding through thin air.

Trapeze artists are among the highest-paid performers in the world. They do not play to the grandstand, every thought, nerve, and muscle being coordinated in the perfection of their exacting act. Their life is rigid, their profession demanding the best possible care of their bodies, food and sleep being of prime importance. They must have confidence, but not overconfidence, for eternal vigilance is the watchword.

THE CLARKE FAMILY
or
THE CLARKONIANS
About 1630

THE CLARKES go back six generations in the entertainment world, and the last two generations have been in America. John Clarke, a contemporary of Astley in London, was succeeded by his son, born in 1786, and known as Old John Clarke.

The principal dates for the early English shows were at the old English Fairs. For hundreds of years, these fairs were very importart as a historical background. They were the "cradle of the outdoor show business." These shows were later transplanted to America, and the Clarkes were key figures in bringing these to America.

Old John Clarke was a real character and always had a good circus. The son, John Clarke, was a successful showman after the old London Fairs had passed out of existence. He was a contemporary of the Sanger, Powel, Pablo, and other circuses.

John Clarke's sons were Alfred and Charles. Each of these had his own show and there was much friendly rivalry. One of Alfred's sons had become the greatest bareback rider in continental Europe. Family and professional pride became a challenge to Charles and his family. With their iron will, determination, and excellent physiques, Charles knew his sons could excel. He decided on the high aerial flying act as their field. He had watched its development since the time of Leotard.

Day after day, Charles' sons, Ernest and Charles F., practiced in secret for seven years on their flying trapeze act. Ernest was the flyer or leaper, and Charles F. the catcher.

Then the act, a double-somersault, was presented in the Coliseum in London. All Britain proclaimed the act a wonderful success. At this time, the act took the name Clarkonians, for the aerial act only; they still rode under the family name of Clarke. In 1903, Barnum and Bailey brought the Clarkes to America — the Clarkonians. They were a great success here.

After four and one-half years of practice and experimentation, Ernest was able to add a pirouette to the double-somersault. This tenacity lent itself also to his eventual mastery of the triple-somersault. He accomplished and performed on occasions, though not for the public or regularly, the quadruple-somersault. For versatility, Ernie Clarke was the greatest flyer who ever mounted the pedestal. It is said that Ernie would be the first to concede that Alfred Codona did a surer and more artistic triple, and that Eddie Silbon's double cutaway and four-to-the-net were unapproachable, but Ernie and Charlie were the best two-man flying return act ever witnessed.

Many thought the great Alfredo Codona was the first to triple-somersault, but he magnanimously corrected this impression. After pulling a muscle, Codona had retired from the ring. He was equestrian director in a show in California. Ernie Clarke and his son, Ernie, Jr., were with the show. Codona blew the whistle and led Ernie Clarke to the center of the ring, and, as Spence and Fred Bradna tell us in *The Big Top,* Codona announced, "I have often been given credit for originating the triple, but here is the man. He did the triple before I learned to fly," and Codona concluded by saying that Ernie Clarke was the greatest flyer of all time. But Bradna, with his thirty years as equestrian director and, in all, forty-two years with the circus, differs. He says, unquestionably Ernie Clarke was one of the greatest flyers, but that Codona topped him. Bradna and most other competent judges consider Alfredo Codona the greatest aerialist of all time.

The Clarkes appeared with several circuses but they were with Ringling Bros. and Barnum & Bailey Circus from 1906 to 1926 — twenty years as headliners. They are a distinct credit to the circus profession.

THE NELSONS

THEY WERE ELEVEN, these acrobatic Nelsons, all one family. They justly won for themselves the title under which they were billed, "The Most Marvelous Family of Acrobats in the World." Their act required the highest degree of nerve and skill. Perfect confidence, each in the other, was clearly discernible as their acts clicked with split-second perfection and precision. The rapidity with which their whirling bodies gracefully swished through space had the appearance of seemingly reckless execution. The Nelsons appeared with the Great Wallace Show, also with Barnum and then, for many years, they were with R.B.B.&B. Circus.

Mrs. Nelson was greatly perturbed that the famous Nelson canvas bag had disappeared. And one can understand her "mother-love" for this bag. About every two years, as the Nelsons came upon the circus stage for their act, the father carried a canvas bag over his shoulder. He would stop in the middle of the stage, open the bag, and invariably a little baby girl, about a year of age, would roll out, jump up, then turn a somersault and throw kisses to the audience. For six consecutive times little girls rolled from this bag, — and then one year Paul jumped out. When the spectators realized that at last a boy had appeared, the thunderous applause could scarcely be quieted. After Paul, another little golden-haired sister, June, made her arrival by way of the same bag. Then, for several years, no bag on the father's shoulder and no baby. Members of the audience would call out, "Where's the bag?" "What, no baby?" "We want a baby." After skipping about four years, Mr. Nelson again appeared carrying the same bag on his shoulder, and, as a little curly-headed girl rolled out and turned the accustomed somersault and threw kisses, he announced, "My granddaughter." Mr. Nelson could have challenged almost any Indian squaw in the number of papooses he had carried on his back.

CHARLES SIEGRIST

IF EVER AN ACTOR was the combination of all the acts and arts, it was — and is — Charles Siegrist. Many call him the "Iron Man of the Circus." His physical endurance has never been equaled.

To say that Siegrist is an aerial star is correct, his work being outstanding, but one would have to add, quickly, a list of all his other feats of stardom, which would run the gamut of circus acts. He is one of the greatest comedy riders of all time, and is a leaper of renown. He was a vaudeville headliner in the winter when he teamed with Polidor in a clown act. He is a superb tumbler, being considered by many as the greatest tumbler of all time. His physical coordination is perfect in his wire-walking act, and his stamina, poise and grace appear inexhaustible. His every movement is polished and fluid, and he has served as a model for more aspiring young circus talent than could be estimated.

It seems that nothing can stop Siegrist. He broke his neck in New York City along about 1933 in an aerial act, and in 1936 was back flying again. He is five feet, five inches in height and made of brawn, nerve, energy, and stamina. Yes, he is made of steel mixed with rubber, molded with courage, and propelled with jet energy, and is on the lookout for an atomic plug-in connection — for at the age of seventy-two he is still on the high wire performing the double-somersault.

ALFREDO CODONA AND LILLIAN LEITZEL

TO STUDY THE CIRCUS as a circus, is intensely interesting and absorbing, but to study the lives of the two greatest circus stars of all time, transcends all circusdom. These two were the true royalty of the circus. They were the most admired and sought by owners and managers of circuses. Other performers were not jealous of their fame. These two, Lillian Leitzel and Alfredo Codona, stand alone in perfected technique of performance — a performance made the more brilliant by one of the greatest love stories of the sawdust world. Each of these stars should have individual billing for the sake of art, but their love story is so beautiful that, for the sake of the heart, their names are eternally linked.

Alfredo was born at Hermosillo, Sonora, Mexico, October 7, 1893. He became an American citizen in 1933. His family had been in the circus business for about 100 years, but the name passed from the circus programs with his generation. Alfredo had no children and his brother, Lalo, had only one child, a girl, and she did not choose the circus as her career. Yet the name, Codona, will live forever in the annals of circus immortals.

Alfredo's immediate family owned a number of circuses in Mexico. He had made his entrance into the circus ring before he could walk. He was carried into the ring and balanced on his father's hand as the opening number in the act. At the age of five, as we learn from Spence and Bradna in *The Big Top,* Alfredo was in his father's aerial act, doing somersaults and single trapeze turns. His father's great aerial speciality was a gag. Bradna and Spence go on to tell us that, while acting as catcher, "he would swing head down, and as the flyer left his perch, would pull a watch from his pocket, look at it, yawn, pocket it again, and then casually receive the hurtling flyer."

At the age of ten, Alfredo was an all-around acrobat, performing balloon stunts. He also became an excellent performer on the slack wire, a difficult act. But he was destined to reach his fame in the air, as an aerialist. He was considered the handsomest man on the circus lot. He was perfectly proportioned, with dark hair, sparkling black eyes, and a ringing laugh. To the layman, as well as to the aerialist, there were several reasons for Codona's greatness. First, he was a genius in performance; second, he was a born showman, and third, he possessed that great advantage of a wonderfully attractive appearance, a lithe and perfect figure. He executed his pirouettes (to which his natural build lent itself) with the same ease and distinction as he did his famous somersaults.

When Codona first let it be known that he was going to perform the triple-somersault, he was in Berlin, and the manager admonished him of the danger, naming over a list of predecessors who attempted this; it had ended in death or serious injury to all. But Codona's determination was as well developed as the muscles in his body, and with his daring and patience in unceasing practice, he persisted and did the triple in almost every performance until the end of his brilliant career. Codona had figured this act to the tiniest fraction of an inch and to almost infinitesimal timing. He calculated that, at the time he was doing the triple-somersault, he was flying through the air at the speed of 62 miles an hour.

Codona's modesty in discussing the technicalities of his work was proverbial. However, his superiority, in part, is attributed to that wonderful and quite exceptional "lift" which he possessed due to the remarkable muscular development of his arms and back. That "lift" enabled him to rise much higher than the average performer when he released his hold on the swinging trapeze, thus allowing a greater space of time after execution of the somersault, in which to finish the remainder of his act. This gave that distinct air of consummate ease and assurance to his performance.

Having worked with his father in the Wirth Show, Codona, with his sister Victoria, who was a great equestrian, joined the Barnum & Bailey Circus. In 1917, he founded his own number with his brother, Lalo Codona. From 1927 to 1933, he was a star, holding the center ring with the R.B. B.&B. Circus. He was released for a short period to double for Weissmuller in the Tarzan film in Hollywood.

Such competent authorities as Ted Volta, Courtney Ryley Cooper, and others regarded Codona as the finest trapeze artist that has ever lived, possessing the most highly perfected technique. (Many venture to suggest that there will never be his equal.)

LILLIAN LEITZEL

THE LIFE STORY of the great little Lillian Leitzel contains all the joy, accomplishment, pain, glamor, success, and sadness that can be crowded into one lifetime. Lillian's mother, who was Elinor Pelikin, was one of the outstanding acrobats and aerialists of all Europe. As a child of eleven, she was apprenticed to a mountebank. Her father was ill and the family badly in need of finances. As an apprentice, Elinor led a most miserable life. She and another child were taken to the country for training, far out where their cries could not be heard, as they were whipped unmercifully—whips of rawhide cutting the blood.

Elinor reached fame, married, and had one child, born in Breslau, Germany, January 2, 1892. The child was called Lillian, although her real name was Leopoldina Alice Pelikin. Lillian was left in Breslau to be reared by her father's mother, who had been a famous aerialist in her youth. Elinor sent plenty of money for Lillian to have all the advantages of education, music, and private tutoring. Elinor remembered her hard life and wanted Lillian's made easy.

When Lillian was twelve years of age, her mother sent for her to come to New York to appear in a most popular act with her — with the Leamys, a name that had already become a household word in Europe. Soon after Lillian arrived, her mother was called home, but Lillian remained in New York. Sudden changes in the Leamy act left Lillian stranded. She knew very few people and her cash had dwindled. Discipline came to her rescue. She had heard the name of a Broadway booking agent, and after a long search, she found him. Luckily, the agent had heard of her. The late Courtney Ryley Cooper, in his very fine book, *Circus Day,* gives us the following account of Lillian's struggle. The agent asked Lillian, " 'Tell me what you want to do — you give me your address and I'll scare you up a tryout. In the meantime, get your rigging ready!'

" 'But I haven't any rigging,' said Lillian naively.

" 'No rigging? Then go buy some.'

" 'But please, I haven't any money.'

" 'I knew there'd be a catch to this,' and he dug deep into his pocket. 'Get me straight, though — this is just a loan.' (After her death, among Lillian's possessions was found a scribbled receipt from that agent for every cent of the money which he lent her, the money with which she bought her Roman rings.)"

The arranged tryout, as Cooper tells us, was to be for three nights in a suburban theater. On the third night, some New York managers were scheduled to drop in and look over the acts. The first night passed without mishap, but on the second night, Lillian fell squarely on her knees. She was nervous, of course, and had never worked alone before. She crawled gracefully from the stage, smiling at the audience, and then collapsed in the wings, from the intense pain. But the determined little Lillian, the lonely little girl, was at the theater the next night on crutches. She was to enter on an empty stage. She instructed a stage hand in a hasty rehearsal. The spotlight came on, and just as though it were a part of her act, the young man carried her lightly onto the stage, while she held her aching legs stretched gracefully in front of her. She realized that her future depended on this one performance, that the managers were out in front. The attendant lifted her gently to the rings as though she were a Dresden doll and would break. (She looked the part.) Catching the rings, she could now work without strain on her legs.

Her determination and courage brought results. Just one hour later, while she was still in her dressing room, she signed a contract for a ten-week Broadway appearance at $300 a week! Her vaudeville star had risen and she was booked in other towns. The Ringlings saw her and immediately engaged her as a center-ring attraction for the Greatest Show on Earth, and here she remained a center-ring star until her death. Each winter she would tour Europe in vaudeville or with circuses, while the R.B.B.&B. Circus was in winter quarters.

During Leitzel's early circus career, she was married to the side show manager, Clyde Ingalls. After about three years, they separated. He seemed jealous of the love and admiration showered upon her. Leitzel, as she was affectionately called by the entire personnel of the circus, worked continuously at improving her act. She never became conceited. She was deft, possessed a beautifully formed body, and stepped with such rapidity that her feet literally twinkled. She was a star of stars. All activity in the big top ceased when it became time for her entrance. Groups watched her from the outside in deference to the greatness of her performance.

After every ring in the Big Top was emptied, an absolute silence of expectancy followed. Suddenly, a spotlight played about the arena and then focused on the tiny figure, only four feet and ten inches in height and weighing ninety-four pounds. There she was, standing at the performers' entrance. Her footman, Willie Mosher, was six feet and four inches — in uniform of brilliant color. On muddy days, he picked up this little beauty and carried her into the ring. Leitzel's maid, Mabel Clemens, always present, always attentive and faithful, followed close behind the two. Music filled the big top, keeping time with Leitzel's twinkling, dancing feet. Then, with all the grace, charm, and airiness of a butterfly, Lillian Leitzel stood, flooded in light. She gave the appearance of a rare and scintillating gem set in platinum. A very small, but strong hand grasped a canvas-covered rope. She always gave the rope two or three quick twirls in front of her, and then, with a leap, she began her ascent to the very top of the tent. She had an original motion in effecting this ascent, seeming literally to roll herself up — up to forty-five or fifty feet with only the strength of her wrist holding her safe as she transferred her weight from the rope to the rings. There she swung, rolled and cavorted with childish delight and spontaneity. Then, standing head down on her hands, she would sway wildly and drop so suddenly, as to break the grip of any hands except those tiny hands of Leitzel's. She laughed, threw kisses to the audience and did it again and again, always with such grace and, seemingly, without effort or fear. She would descend, and almost immediately be jerked, by the full strength of a dozen property men, to the very top of the tent. There she would plunge into the act for which she was most famous — a series of turning motions in which her body swung over one arm in a continuity that seemed never to end. Her tiny legs flying, her free hand swinging gracefully, yet with a purpose, for it aided the momentum needed to keep her body twirling. There in the top of the tent, this whirling mass of humanity went over and over — fifty — 100 — 150 times, while the shoulders of the spectators ached. Once she made a record test of her endurance and completed 249 one-arm flange turns.

These rhythmic gyrations were the most sensational exhibition of endurance ever seen in a circus. Her Titian hair flying in clouds to her waist, she became a beautifully colored ball. A loud drumbeat sounded at each turn. People could not resist counting turns. And then she descended to the thunderous applause of thousands who could scarcely believe their eyes — so physically poised after such a strenuous act — to bow gracefully, smile, again throw kisses, and with twinkling feet, depart as rapidly as she had entered. The entire audience felt the magnetic pull of her dynamic personality. Everyone who knew her admired and loved her. She was "The Darling of the White Tops." Fred Bradna, who was equestrian director twelve years of the time Leitzel held the center ring of R.B.B.&B., said in his and Spence's book, *The Big Top,* that Leitzel "commanded a pre-eminence never attained by another star in any circus on earth. She was the fiercest, hottest-tempered, most furious — and at times the most lovable individual I ever met . . . As a hostess to her admirers she was at her astounding best." She was a most enthusiastic trouper and possessed a positively encyclopedic knowledge of everything bearing on the sawdust ring, with which she had been connected since childhood.

Leitzel held a spotlight as a conversationalist possessing a mixture of wisdom and charm. She discussed with authority almost any subject in which she thought her guests and admirers were interested. The consummate skill with which she juggled information and coquetry, and signed off with wisdom, left her listeners speechless with admiration. She summarized contemporary news with linguistic ease, speaking seven languages fluently. No one envied little Leitzel her position — all were proud of her.

There were always throngs of people waiting at her tent after each performance — literally heroine-worship. Her private chauffeur was delayed an hour or more before he could drive her to her private Pullman car.

Leitzel occupied an entire, commodious railroad car which was elegantly furnished, containing a very small piano, especially built for her. Some evenings she played very late, mostly classical music, for she was an accomplished musician, having received her master's degree in music before she was twelve years of age. She was a most precocious child, becoming proficient in languages, history, and literature before she was twelve, at which time her mother sent for her to come to New York.

Lillian Leitzel's rise to stardom did not come easy. Many hours of tortuous practice – practice which she kept up daily – went before her rise to supremacy in her field. Great as the strain was on the muscles of her arm, still a greater strain tortured her brain. The rushing of the blood to the brain was so terrific that uncontrollable tears always gushed down her cheeks upon descent. It was this strain which caused those little flashing fits of temper, over which she seemed to have no power, and for which she was always sorry. But Mabel Clemens, her faithful maid to the end, understood perfectly and was a great comfort to her.

Lillian Leitzel was truly an aristocrat of the air, an immortal in the ranks of stars of circusdom.

THE LEITZEL-CODONA ROMANCE

LILLIAN LEITZEL and Alfredo Codona were both center-ring stars with R.B.B & B. Circus when Codona's marriage with the Cincinnati girl, Clara Curtin, broke, and she left him. Possibly this sympathy for Codona re-focused Lillian's eyes on Alfredo, for they had been childhood sweethearts many years before. They were both with the same circus in Europe – were both very young – and the rules of the circus discipline prevented them from doing little more than stare at each other. Alfredo, in describing these days of first young love, said, "We just used to sit and look at each other. She was so beautiful to me. I was afraid to even talk with her."

Theirs had always been a mutual attraction. Alfredo was the one man in the world whose skill, prestige, and temper were the equal of Lillian's. They were supreme in their fields. They each received enormous salaries. Lillian's private tent was always spotted most advantageously for her comfort on the lot. Her tent was elegantly furnished—Oriental rugs, rare hangings, screens, furniture, and always a bower of flowers from admiring friends. She had a man and a maid servant. Codona had not been reared in a cultural environment, yet a finished education was the one thing Alfredo most earnestly desired besides the love of Lillian. He longed for literary and musical knowledge and understanding. So he became Lillian's willing and enamored pupil and lover.

Lillian Leitzel was beloved by the entire circus personnel, from Mr. and Mrs. Charles Ringling to the workmen and the roustabouts. She was most generous. She gave boots to workers when she noticed theirs were worn, she heard with interest and understanding all the troubles, illnesses, and vagaries of other actresses and actors, and also of the lowliest roustabouts. She loved and cared for the children of mothers who were performing in the ring. She conducted classes for the children of the circus that they might learn not only the three R's, but proper deportment, poise, the ways and exigencies of life. She was not only the "First Lady of the Air," but the "First Love of the Circus."

Lillian was a bundle of beauty, grace, and affection. She charmed men from coast to coast. Millionaires vied in entertaining for her. All of this attention and admiration worried Codona. It seemed to him that he was forced to love from afar. His love for her was overwhelming and consuming and he was jealous. Would she ever be his? He fought for her love morning, noon, and night. Press agents were inspired by this beautiful, yet tempestuous love affair of the two great stars.

At last Codona won her, and on July 20, 1928, they were married at the Embassy Hotel in Chicago, between the afternoon and the evening performance. Although Leitzel was the orchid of the social and idolizing world, yet fate seemed always unkind. For publicity reasons, the circus expected her to accept invitations and attentions. Notwithstanding all this, the marriage survived, though with difficulty. Codona was jealous – he wanted her for his own – his love was furious and devastating. Lillian could not give up the adulation to which she had become so accustomed. She did try to be a kind, good, and loving wife, and yet at the same time do all that was expected of her by the circus publicity department. Leitzel and Codona had each reached the pinnacle of professional success.

In 1939, as was her custom, but very much against her wishes, Leitzel went abroad for winter bookings. So did Codona – for an engagement in Germany. Lillian was in Copenhagen. This was the first time they had been separated since their marriage. On Friday 13, February, 1931, Lillian was aloft executing her famous over-arm twist when something in her apparatus broke – some say the Roman ring crystallized, the same Roman ring which she had bought in New York for her first act, with borrowed money. Lillian plunged downward. She arose immediately. She protested against being taken to the hospital. Her courage was great. Again fate had been unkind, since she had almost finished her act. She fell at the only second during her entire act that the property man was not watching her. He had reached back to get the rope on which she was to descend. Had the fall not come at that one split second, he could have caught her, or at least have broken the fall. Her injury was serious.

Codona came rushing from Germany by plane to be at her bedside. It was either his great love or her great courage to brace up in his presence, for they were truly and forever devoted, that caused a rally in her condition. Codona went back to his act, feeling that she would soon recover. Almost at once, upon his departure, she relapsed. Upon reaching Berlin, Codona received word that she had died. He cancelled all further European bookings at once. All the circus and entertainment world mourned the greatest woman star of all time.

Leitzel fell to her death on February 13, and on February 17, in New York City, the opening of the hockey match in Madison Square was held up while all lights were dimmed, as they were when Leitzel appeared there. The spotlight fell on a man on the ice in the center of the arena. He said, "To the memory of Lillian Leitzel. God rest her soul." The band played, "Auld Lang Syne," the last selection always used for the last night of the circus season, and the drums rolled one hundred times as they did when Leitzel did her one-arm, giant half-flange act — then the lights went on — and the hockey game began.

Two months after Leitzel's death, an airplane roared over the "Mauretania," dropping wreaths on the large ship — wreaths of flowers from her circus friends and numerous admirers in every walk of life, for Alfredo Codona was returning, bringing home the ashes of his beloved Leitzel.

In a few days, The Greatest Show on Earth was preparing to open at Madison Square Garden in New York. Courtney Ryley Cooper, the great circus writer, tells us the following conversation with Codona:

" 'You'll have to buck up. Lillian would have wanted you to go on.'

"Codona replied, 'Yes, she always watched my act — and waved her hand to me. She gave me ideals. She said she wanted me to be the greatest aerialist in all the world.' An unseen power seemed to lift him, and his chin stiffened."

That evening at the circus a halt came, a dramatic silence, just as there had always been when Lillian Leitzel entered, and then the floodlight and flashlights enveloped Codona as he stood on his high aerial perch. Next came the clear words from the equestrian director, "Your attention, everybody — Alfredo Codona, the only man in the world to so perfectly perform the triple-somersault from the flying trapeze, three complete revolutions to the hands of his brother." The drum rolled. The silken form of Codona flashed from his pedestal higher and higher. He released, going into the dizzy revolutions and pirouettes. Then he sped downward and the smacking of flesh against flesh was heard as he clasped the wrists of his brother.

The Garden literally went into hysterics; thunderous applause continued. Alfredo Codona swung back to his pedestal and bowed — not toward the audience but toward the place where Lillian Leitzel had always stood to watch him. He had triumphed and the Queen of the Sawdust Ring acclaimed, in spirit, her King of the Flying Trapeze.

TRAGEDY STALKED AGAIN

FOR WEEKS AFTER the Copenhagen tragedy — the death of Lillian Leitzel — Codona walked as though he were half asleep. The shock had left tragic lines on his face. His great love of a lifetime was gone. His timing was not so perfect in his act. However, time passed, and time does help to heal all sorrows, in a way. A little less than two years after Leitzel's death, Codona and Vera Bruce were married, in San Antonio, Texas. Vera was a beautiful bareback rider from Australia — blue-eyed and slim of form. Wanting to become an aerialist, she had joined Codona's act.

Spence and Bradna have written a poignant account of this period in the great aerialist's life. Codona was now the most publicized star of the G.S.O.E. In spite of the ovations, the applause — almost adulation — there was still a void in his life which nothing could fill — that love since childhood. He was melancholy and quiet. He was not the same Codona.

He paid little attention to his guests, was always preoccupied, and, whenever opportunity permitted, he would look at the accustomed spot where Lillian's tent had stood — the tent where his great romance had grown to culmination.

Although Codona was a performer supreme, yet in 1932, acocrding to Spence and Bradna, during the Madison Square Garden opening, less than a year after his marriage to Vera Bruce, he fell and tore a ligament in his shoulder while doing the famous triple. Again, in Madison Square Garden in 1933, he seriously and permanently injured the remaining muscles of both his arm and shoulder. He and Vera went back on the road, she as an equestrienne and he as her hostler. Then one night Codona just left — disappeared — later to show up as manager of an act including his brother Lalo, and Clayton Behee, whom Codona had trained. Those who knew Codona said he seemed lost, was bitter, could not find himself — he did not seem to fit anywhere. In 1935, he became equestrian director with the Hagenbeck-Wallace Circus, and in 1936 of the Tom Mix Show. Ever restless, he moved on to the same position with indoor circuses.

Codona seemed completely miserable. His unhappiness bore heavily on his heart — his very existence seemed an effort.

Then on the 30th day of July, 1937, Vera Bruce sued Codona for divorce — the charge, cruelty. The lawyer had called Vera and Codona to his office to discuss and arrange a settlement of their property. During the discussion, Codona suddenly asked the lawyer if he would leave him alone with Vera. The instant the lawyer closed the door behind him, Codona shot Vera five times, "mortally wounding her, and then put a bullet through his own head." Thus does *The Big Top* bring to a close the tragedy of Alfredo Codona.

The book tells us also that, after Lillian's death, Codona had erected a magnificent and most impressive monument, seventeen feet in height, in Inglewood Park Cemetery, Long

Beach, California. On a tall pedestal are life-size statues of Lillian and Alfredo. The monument symbolizes "Reunion." Alfredo, with outstretched wings, holds Lillian in his arms, "The Eternal Embrace."

In the crypt of this monument Codona had placed the ashes of his Leitzel. So it was, at his own request, that he was buried "beside the ashes of his wife, Lillian Leitzel, his great love."

ARTHUR AND ANTOINETTE CONCELLO

ARTHUR AND HIS WIFE, Antoinette Concello, will go down in history as two of the world's great trapeze performers. Antoinette is one of the most famous women performers in showdom. As a schoolgirl, she visited, annually, the world-renowned Lillian Leitzel. Holding Leitzel as her ideal, Antoinette has risen to feature rank; her "two and one-half" is especially graceful. In this, the catcher catches the flyer's feet after she has completed two complete somersaults. She is the only woman in the world successfully to complete a triple-somersault to a hand-to-hand catch – her husband's – making three complete revolutions to the jackpot catch. Antoinette is known as the "Big Top Goddess of Flight."

RENE AND MADELEINE GERALDO

THE GERALDOS, known as "the barefoot boy and girl," are guaranteed to bring fright-perspiration in freezing weather. They work with bare feet from two trapezes forty feet in the air in what is known to circusdom as the "double trap" act and also as a "lump-in-the-throat" act.

They literally risk their necks by trusting their all to

their educated feet. This beautifully proportioned husband-and-wife team specializes in "catches" — hand-to-hand, hand-to-foot, and finally a foot-to-foot hold. At the climax, Rene hangs by one heel clasped in Madeleine's locked ankles.

"THE SHOE THAT DANCED AROUND THE WORLD" BIRD MILLMAN

IN 1941, we learn from Janet Sterling, who coined the above phrase in her *White Tops* article, the museum in Canyon City, Colorado, received an interesting gift, a little metalized shoe. Mrs. Millman gave this shoe to the museum shortly before she died. It had been worn on that famous, tiny foot of her daughter, Bird Millman O'Day. Bird's name had circled the globe as one of the world's great wire dancers. Her grace, her personality, and coquettish charm and beauty, together with her skill and originality in performing, placed her name among the immortals in the show world.

Literally this little shoe had danced around the world, for Bird had danced before the crowned heads of Europe when she was only fourteen years of age. She had appeared at Madison Square Garden; in the Greenwich Follies; in the Ziegfeld Follies on Broadway, New York City; and with Ringling Bros. and Barnum & Bailey Circus. This same little shoe was one of two which saw her to safety as she walked and danced across a wire stretched twenty-five stories high above Broadway, New York, that pulsating boulevard. Bird, as many show people are, was just a wee bit superstitious, and always wore this same pair of shoes when doing a special dance or unusual feat.

These shoes were made from the softest elkhide, from which all the oil had been removed to prevent slipping. Even after this little shoe had been metalized, the patches and stitches on the side showed — it had been mended countless times.

Janet Sterling reminds us of the occasion when Bird needed a new pair of shoes, so she called at a leather goods house in Boston and carried the little shoes with her to show them what she wanted. Mr. Joe O'Day, a member of the firm, came to take the unusual order. As the making of these shoes progressed, so did a beautiful romance. The impish little shoes danced their way into Mr. O'Day's heart, and he and Bird were married soon. Bird retired and they lived happily in Boston until his death, when she returned to her home in Canon City, Colorado, where she passed away in August, 1940.

CON COLLEANO (CORNELIUS SULLIVAN)

CON COLLEANO has been called the "Toreador of the Tight Wire," and "The Wizard of the Silver Thread." Millions of spectators have applauded his intricate Spanish dancing and his somersaulting on the tight and the slack wire. Con comes from a circus family. His brother, Maurice, was successful in doing the double-somersault in a ground acrobatic act, and his sister, Winifred, was a star, having mastered the heel catch on the trapeze.

Colleano decided he was going to become a star and he wanted to think of some original accomplishment. So he did a feat no one had ever done before — the forward somersault on the tight wire. The backward somersault had been done, but in doing the forward somersault it was impossible to see the wire as one came out of the somersault, the performer's feet hiding the wire from his view. Suicide was the word for such an attempt, because the head may be slashed from the body by the taut wire. Con was determined, and hours and hours were spent in practice. On his first night to try this forward somersault before an audience, he attempted it three times without success. Then a fourth try and he stuck the wire with his chest. Blood spurted and the Hippodrome curtain was dropped. Con begged the stage manager to ring up the curtain. The applause of the audience did not abate. At last the curtain lifted and Con, determined, made his fifth attempt—his feet found the wire but he fought hard for balance. Finally he stood erect and still, and the audience screamed their frenzied applause. A few other wire walkers and performers have since accomplished the forward somersault but Con Colleano originated it. Con Colleano is listed with the Wallendas, Bird Millman, and Hubert Castle, as one of the great wire artists of the modern era.

When Con was a young boy, his grandfather had him sit at a table upon which was placed a bowl of sugar. Con's job was to catch all the flies that attempted to light on the sugar, and he was told he must use both his right and his left hand. This was excellent training for the boy's eyes and also made him ambidextrous. To train and improve his footwork, the grandfather gave him a skipping rope and had him jump in and out of a row of eggs.

"The flies helped the most," says Con. "They really gave me the 'eye' for the forward somersault."

HUBERT CASTLE

THE NAME OF HUBERT CASTLE is listed among the truly great of all tight wire performers. He "threw his act away," meaning that his technique was so perfected that, to the onlooker, his performance looked easy—almost without effort. This requires precision, perfection and genius. It is superb showmanship. He is a quiet family man, and is a Texan.

One of Castle's outstanding single features is his appearance as a drunk in top hat and dress clothes. He staggers to the wire, gives a hilarious imitation of a drunk walking a tight wire. This has been described as "sheer magic." Then he takes off his dress suit, and gives a speedy, whirlwind exhibition. The distance which he can leap in the air from the wire is most unusual.

THE WALLENDAS

THE GREAT WALLENDAS – the name Wallenda is rarely mentioned without the adjective "great" preceding it. It is a name that became well-known in 1874. Later, Karl's father organized and performed in a flying act at the age of sixty-five. When he became too old to catch humans in a flying act, he went to Africa and caught big game and "brought 'em back alive."

The present Karl began his aerial career in 1921 at the age of sixteen. After performing only a short time, he decided that he and his brother, Herman, should develop something original, which indeed they did – the cupped rims on a bicycle, these rims overlapping the tight wire, which is about three-fourths of an inch in diameter. Experienced and practiced performers begged them to abandon such an insane idea. But with determination, courage, and nerves of steel, they persevered. At seventeen, Karl rode this bicycle on a wire stretched sixty feet above the ground, carrying his brother on his shoulders. At eighteen, this fearless lad bicycled across the Oder River at Breslau, where his wire had been stretched eighty-five feet above the water.

In Vienna in 1927, Karl saw Helen Kreis perform. Karl was impressed with her ability, finished technique, and poise. As his brother, now weighing 185 pounds, had become too heavy for him to carry on his shoulders, he engaged Helen as a "topper." After carrying her on his shoulders for seven years in this act, he assumed the carrying charge for life, and they were married.

In 1932 while the Wallendas were performing in Glasgow, and were in the final part of their act with all members out on the wire, one of the landing platforms collapsed, the sudden jerk unbalancing all performers. As they fell, all except the girl at the top managed to catch the wire. She hurtled too far away from the wire, but as she passed by one of the men, he managed to catch her body between his legs and hold her. This was hailed as a superhuman feat — not only for split-second thinking and muscle reaction, but for sheer strength, for she was dead weight, having fainted. She regained consciousness quickly — even before they reached the ground; and along with the others, who were cut and bruised, came to the front of the ring and took her accustomed bow.

Only one year later, in 1933, tragedy, terror, and sorrow struck. The back wheel of Willy's bicycle came off and the family watched, helpless in that awful instant, when he plunged downward to his death.

The Wallenda act is performed seventy feet above the ground without the protection of a net. Joseph and Herman each ride a bicycle, with a pole balanced between them on their shoulders, and on this pole stands Karl. Above the exact center of the arena, Helen mounts to Karl's shoulders, and thus balanced they cycle on across. On their very first appearance in Madison Square Garden, they were a sensational success, the crowds screaming and stomping their feet. This noisy acclaim of an act means failure and disapproval in Europe.

Spence and Bradna in their book, *The Big Top,* tell us how the Wallendas took their bow in grief and hastily retired to their dressing room and took off their costumes, while the audience clapped and stomped. Bradna, the ringmaster, hastened to their dressing rooms, explained the situation — the American custom. The great crowd clapped and waited for fifteen minutes while the Wallendas dressed and returned to take a bow for a thunderously acknowledged success.

ARTURO TROSTL

"THE GREAT ARTURO" was the Ringling billing under which Arturo Trostl became famous in this country, but this noted circus family had held the spotlight for over 150 years in Austria. When "The Great Arturo" appears on the wire completely encased in a sack, the audience sits spellbound. No cry, not even any breathing, is heard, yet many sighs of relief are audible when he has safely crossed over. He is a most versatile performer on the high wire.

DIETER TASSO

DIETER TASSO has justified his billing, "The Incomparable Slack Wire Juggling Wonder of the Century." On a low slack wire, Tasso balances on his left foot, and with the other foot he tosses a saucer to his head, which takes its place as though his head were a magnet. Again with his right foot he tosses a cup into this saucer. This maneuver is kept up until the stack of cups and saucers, balancing precariously on his head, reaches eight in number. Then into the last cup, with this same right foot, he tosses a lump of sugar and finally a teaspoon. During all this tossing, he is swinging back and forth on this low slack wire, a balancing feat in itself.

LA NORMA - TRAPEZE ARTIST

ONE OF DENMARK'S most delightful products is La Norma, a beautiful young woman who streaks through the air as though she were a Fourth-of-July firecracker. Her blond beauty and grace reminds one of the bird of paradise.

La Norma works on a single trapeze and she has added "another hazard to an already death-defying profession." She does all of her routine with bare feet. The "bare-heel-catch" is the climax of her act. This quick catch depends on hair-trigger balance, and the slightest change in wind current or temperature must be matched with a corresponding muscular adjustment by this "Flying Temptress."

ELLA AND FRED BRADNA

ELLA AND FRED BRADNA are two magic names in the circus world. Ella Bradna appeared in the center ring of R.B.B.&B. Circus for twenty-nine consecutive years, a record for center-ring stardom. Her last circus appearance was in 1942 when she was sixty-eight years of age, still lovely and exciting, her grace, charm, and beauty matching the fire and rhythm of her horse, Proud Eagle. (Fred Bradna's name was Frederick Ferber, Jr. Ella Bradna was well-known in the circus world, so when they married he took her name, Bradna.)

Fred Bradna has to his credit forty-two years in show business, the last thirty years of which he was Equestrian Director for "The Greatest Show on Earth," Ringling Bros. and Barnum & Bailey Circus. Bradna's book, *The Big Top,* as told by him to the eminent author, Hartzell Spence, is one of the best circus books ever written, authoritative, informative and thrilling. It contains the following anecdote:

One day in the spring of 1901, Fred Bradna and two lieutenants took "French Leave" from the German cavalry and went to Paris to see the Nouveau Cirque. They were seated in a red velvet box. A Viennese waltz heralded the debut of "Ella Bradna, the youthful mistress of the earth's most daring feats of equitation." This dainty, phenomenal girl appeared. With no ringmaster to monitor the horse, with no reins with which to control the sixteen-hand stallion, depending entirely on a few voice signals and her personality to cue this intelligent animal, she went through a series of dazzling gymnastics — toe dancing on a running horse, pirouetting holding the horse's tail. Then she was handed a gun, and firing at a target, a flock of white pigeons was released. They alighted on her outstretched arms. At a given word the horse knelt, a white Saint Bernard dog came in drawing a small horse-cart, labeled, "Hotel des Pigeons." The birds flew into the cage and the dog, with an understanding of showmanship, made a majestic exit with his feathered stars. Ella's next act was to jump from the ground to the back of a galloping horse while wearing a full-length evening dress, making this a daring and difficult feat never accomplished before.

It so happened that on this occasion of Bradna's visit, the audience became excited and someone tossed a flower into the ring. The horse shied and, to quote Bradna, "The beautiful Ella toppled over the ring bank into my box. I do not believe in miracles, but suddenly there I was, my arms around the little equestrienne.

" 'Are you hurt?' 'I'm all right,' she replied in German. Pushing her curls back from her face, she returned to the ring, completed her trick, blew me a kiss, bowed and ran from the ring. And I, stunned by the perfection of her performance, her grace and beauty, and her parting gesture, made two spontaneous decisions. I would marry this beauty, and I would join the circus." So three years later after his enlistment was finished, Fred married Ella. Theirs was a life of love, hardship, and success.

Ella Bradna had been in show business since she was three years of age, and she continued to give of her unusual talents for over fifty years Although she was an excellent performer — an artist in many fields — it was as an equestrienne that she gained her greatest fame.

Ella and Fred Bradna had spent many years acting and trouping. Finally, on May 31, 1915, Bradna took over the full responsibility as equestrian director of R.B.B.&B. Circus, a position which he held for thirty years, until he retired to make his home in Sarasota, Florida. During that time he signaled the G.S.O.E. into the arena for 27,500 times, played to audiences totaling 705,000,000 and traveled a little less than one million miles.

The duties of an equestrian director are many, varied, exciting and trying. He must see that the show consumes just two hours and twenty minutes — no more, no less. He encourages performers, giving "pep talks," and gives helpful praise and constructive criticism. He must be prepared to cope with all kinds of weather; tragic accidents; illness; and temperaments both of undependable man and unpredictable animal. Substitute acts must be ready. The old elephants' act can always be pushed up or delayed. Each act, no matter the importance or earned prestige, must be only twelve minutes in length. It makes the actors in the following performance very unhappy to have their time cut. It is easy to understand how an equestrian's brain must be "clock-wise." He must be resourceful at all times and he must also be most diplomatic. Many celebrities, politicians, actors and just plain folks, ask to be allowed to clown, to ride the elephants or camels. All these situations must be handled with finesse by the alert director. In *The Big Top* there is the story about Woodrow Wilson, who was a most enthusiastic circus fan. Mr. Charlie Ringling invited President Wilson to ride on an elephant. "President Wilson was game but his advisors would not permit a Democrat to ride on the symbol of Republicanism."

When a president visits a circus, there are certain provisions which must be made and met. Secret Service men appear early in the day to inspect the grounds and ask questions. The show must not start until the president and his party have arrived. They use the performers' entrance and are usually escorted by the equestrian director to Section E–first row. The Secret Service men occupy the second row.

Ella Bradna will long be remembered as one of R.B.B.& B.'s center-ring star attractions, and Fred Bradna as one of circusdom's most magnetic officials. His complete command of nine languages was a tremendous asset. The tremendous force of his personality lives on in the gallant and dignified, the penetrating and exhilarating spirit of the circus.

THE CANNON ACT

THE RINGLING BROTHERS were leaders in offering sensational acts, but several years before they entered the circus business, Zazel was shot out of a cannon for the first time in 1877 at the Royal Aquarium, Westminster, London. Zazel was one of the first to do the human projectile stunt.

Vittorio Zacchini, as real live ammunition, was one of the most spectacular to perform the cannon act. The Zacchinis are an Italian-American family and there are about thirty-five members of this family – cousins, sisters, brothers, aunts, uncles – a most unusual family. When each attains majority, he or she is shot from a cannon, the traditional method of bringing the family up in their circus act. They originated the modern version of this cannon act and are the foremost performers. There have been fifty outside the family who have tried to imitate this act, and thirty-two who were killed. No Zacchini has ever been killed, but several have been injured.

The Zacchinis use a cannon aluminum tube, twenty-three feet in length, mounted on a light gun carriage. They invented the mechanism by which they and others are propelled. It shoots the human cannonball the length of the Ringling big tent. A Zacchini who has been injured usually acts as trigger man. The human bullet wears a white horse-hide suit, white crash helmet, and an asbestos mask. He covers himself with talcum powder so he will have an easier "slide" or "shoot" out the chute. He lowers himself feet first into the cannon barrel.

On occasions when something jams, this human bullet has almost become asphyxiated by fumes of black powder, which is ignited for effect. The "bullet" often suffers a blackout, but he can't afford to stay out long, for he has only three seconds in which to turn a half somersault in order to land on his back in the net, which is 200 feet away. The maximum height shot in the air is 100 feet.

PINITO DEL ORO

PINITO DEL ORO, (literally translated, Little Pine Tree of Gold), is a Spanish beauty with nerves of steel, and a phenomenal sense of equilibrium. She literally stakes her life two times each day on her sense of balance. She works on a narrow trapeze bar, without assurance of a net, balancing for ten minutes, first on her toes, next on her knees, then on one knee, and finally on her head. At no time does she reach for support.

Most swinging trapeze actors concentrate on swinging forwards and backwards, but Pinito also swings sideways and in a dizzy arc, as well.

NEO-YU-NAITTO

WHEN NEO-YU-NAITTO turned a forward somersault on a tight wire, she had mastered the most difficult of all acrobatic stunts. It is said that she and Con Colleano are the only two people to ever successfully accomplish this suicidal feat, the forward somersault, where one misstep would sever the head — (the feet hiding the wire as one comes out of the somersault facing forward). Years of practice, precision, and sheer instinct must guide the feet to land safely on the wire.

THE CHALUDIS
Daredevil Circus Cyclists

"WHERE THERE'S A WHEEL, there's a way," is the motto of the Chaludis, daredevil bicycle riding quartet with R.B.B.&B. Circus.

Circus folks call this three-high, head-to-head act the "Eyeful Tower," because the two girls, Lucia and Gerda, are such lovely blondes. They whirl around the ring at a steady seven-mile-an-hour speed. They are wonders of the wheel.

UNUS

UNUS IS ONE of the most talked of stars who has ever appeared with the R.B.B.&B. Circus. He has been described as the equilibristic mystery man, possessing uncanny balancing skill. He has been hailed as one of the foremost feature stars of all time. He has also been very successful on television.

Unus can balance the entire weight of his body on the end of his forefinger, and this forefinger-balancing is done on a ball. John Ringling North watched him do this handstand, this one-finger balance, on his cane atop the Bon Marche store cornice in Brussels. Mr. North engaged him immediately for The Greatest Show on Earth.

Unus possesses an abnormal sense of balance and timing, and he has perfected this gift until his feats seem superhuman and incredible. While doing this single-finger balance on a can on a ball, high up on a stand, he juggles five circles, one on each leg, one on his free arm, one on a stick held in his mouth, and one around this single finger which is supporting his entire weight with the juggling movement added. It has been truly said that while watching this sensational "single," you freeze as a bird dog watching prey — you become spellbound.

BRUNN – THE JUGGLING KING

TO FRANCES BRUNN, every single movement has a meaning all its own. The flick of a muscle in the calf of his leg starts a ring into spins, the muscles on his forehead turn a ball balanced on a holder, his lips turn another ball, to say nothing of his ten nimble fingers and ten twisty toes. His is a new art in dexterity — an art which he has practiced for over twenty-two years to bring it to the peak of perfection.

Brunn started his career when about seven or eight years of age. He is an acrobat, a dancer, and an equilibrist. With all these accomplishments as a basic background of advantage, he has become one of the greatest jugglers in the world, is, in fact, considered by many as the greatest throughout the amusement history. He was a center-ring attraction with R.B.B.&B.

He has proved a sensation on television.

MR. MISTIN, JR.

TRULY GARGANTUA the Great heads the list as the top-ranking attraction to lure the crowds of circusdom, advertised as "The World's Most Terrifying Living Creature." Then in 1953, The Greatest Show on Earth sprinted from such a Gargantuan heavyweight to the tiny musical prodigy, Mr. Mistin, Jr., the Child Wonder of the Musical

World, who has astounded circus and show crowds throughout Europe, Asia, and Africa, with his musical prowess.

This little, five-year-old, golden curly-haired boy made his official debut with a Belgian Circus in Brussels, his home town, at the age of two years. This "pint-sized wonder is the world's youngest and greatest xylophone virtuoso."

Under the direction of his father, Mistin practises one to two hours each day. He speaks five languages fluently, but, like all little boys, he hates to go to bed, and loves ice cream, toys, and soda-pop.

He is a master of the classics and yet swings with equal ease into the rhythm of the modern songs. Every muscle and fiber of his fine little body seem attuned and in tune. When he asks the audience to sing a modern song with him, an aurora of animated melody envelops him, and his tiny body sways in rhythm with the thousands of voices.

HORSES

THE HORSE is still king of the circus performing animals and there are many types of horses, each fitted by nature for the task and work he does. The good old faithful baggage, or work horses, have been replaced almost entirely by tractors.

The most famous hitch in all circusdom and horsedom, the world over, was the Forty-Horse-Hitch. But the proud stamp of 160 feet, in perfect rhythm, is heard no more — drowned out by progress, when the parade died. Progress is man's future, but thanks be, man has the privilege of nostalgic backward glances, and thus, for many, the Forty-Horse-Hitch lives. But the youth of today is cheated in that his memory holds no such oasis of circus memory as the street parade.

Other horses that occupy important niches in the life of the circus are the lovely dressage horses, the tiny Shetlands, the rosinbacks, and many other breeds of equines. The bluebloods, however, hold a deserved spotlight. Many of them are from the most aristocratic families in the land of the bluebloods of ol' Kentucky's blue grass.

Not all of the horses used in the rings of the circus are thoroughbreds, and there's a reason. Thoroughbreds are often too highstrung, too nervous for the circus ring. They are used only in the hippodrome track and rings during high school and dressage display. Even then, standard breeds perform along with them. These horses show their steps while hitched to swanky, little pneumatic-tired sulkies.

Closely akin to the liberty horse is the high school horse who seems to have a human brain. He adds and subtracts; picks out blues and reds from varicolored scarfs; identifies flags; answers "Yes" and "No" to questions; gallops backward; cake walks; capers and poses, all to undetected signals from the rider — maybe a shifting in the saddle, maybe a touch by the hand or the heel, maybe a pat on the neck, a slight pressure of the knee, foot (toe or spur), and perhaps an unnoticed finger pull on the reins, or numerous different words or low-voiced commands may do the trick. High school horses are taught in academies, and the rules established by the Spaniards in olden days are strictly adhered to today. Modern trainers and riders have added to the Spanish routine and rules the very latest in all the dance steps.

To do a manege act is the same as to do an act with a "high school" horse.

Horses that live with the circus and perform under the Big Top learn not to pay attention to unusual sounds, horns, or commotions. Due to that horse sense and that highly developed natural sense of duty, it is unusual that a horse's attention is diverted from his act.

A horse lives as long in the circus as anywhere else, with the possible exception of the rosinback. Yet one rosinback, owned by the great Poodles Hanneford, was still performing strenuously and perfectly at the age of twenty-four. A horse's life span usually depends on treatment and food, and in the circus he gets the best of both.

The famous P. T. Barnum imported thoroughbred stallions and mares — and Arabian horses — in the 1870's. Many of these became progenitors of the Kentucky bluebloods of this generation.

Beautiful horses are always vital to a circus scene — with tossing heads and manes and sky-pawing hoofs.

THE ROSINBACK

THE "ROSINBACK" horses are considered by many as the aristocrats of the ring. On their common sense and sure-footedness depend the lives of bareback performers. They are a little larger than the average white or dappled horse, and in breed, are most likely Percherons or Belgian geldings. A rosinback has perfect conformation, and the canter is his gait. He does the standard sixteen paces to the regulation forty-two foot circus ring (and eleven for a fast finish) until he is signaled to stop by the ringmaster. So great is the rosinback's sense of duty and knowledge of the act, that the tent could be taken down all around him and he would never stop until told. This intelligent horse does not vary his pace or gait — he even seems to hesitate a split second in expectancy of the soft footfall of the bareback ballerina or acrobat on his accommodating back — for they do have nice, broad, roomy backs. His name comes from the fact that a little rosin is sprinkled on his back so that the rider may have surer footing.

The leaping, somersaulting, dancing, bareback performer risks his very life on the step, distance, and timing of his cantering rosinback. So great is the need of teamwork between the animal and performer that most rosinbacks are owned and trained by the performers themselves. The requirements of a good rosinback are many. He must be intelligent, have a good disposition, and be willing and most patient, for the training hours are long and exhausting, as well as exacting. The rosinback has a great arched neck and deep, soft eyes, such a picturesque opposite in power to the dainty, ballet-costumed equestrienne whose efforts must be so closely coordinated with his. These horses have an unusual distinction; some of them have the initials of their rider (who is also owner) carved on the foresides of their front hooves.

Some of the deepest man-animal devotion is found between performers and their trusted rosinbacks. The measured gait and timing are hard on the horse's joints, and leads to lameness and necessary retirement. With rest, this lameness usually disappears, but when final retirement comes there is sadness and gloom around the circus.

The roster of horses who number among the great performers in circus history is endless, and the antics of these animals have given rise to stories which are told and retold among those who love the circus.

Mr. Kenneth H. Dunshee, editor of *News From Home,* published by Home Insurance Company, tells the story of an old horse named Bill, upon whose broad back one of America's greatest bareback riders learned to perform. He had grown old and had to be pensioned. His mistress found a good home for Bill, where a kind farmer agreed to take the best of care of him. Although the star visited him as often as the scheduled season permitted, Bill grew restless. One morning Bill jumped the rail fence like a three-year-old and was off into the hills. He wandered over the country, never allowing anyone to approach him, nor was he even seen often. His former mistress heard of his escape, and she became almost frantic with worry. Later a report came of a mysterious, pure white horse which was found standing contentedly in a little gospel tent in a timothy meadow many miles away. Yes, they took old Bill back to the farm, but he had shown them that he "knew what he had been missing," — and that what he wanted most was his old life under a tent.

MAY WIRTH

MAY WIRTH was Australian by birth, her circus lineage dating back six generations. Her maternal grandfather was one of the very first bareback riders. She started her riding career at the age of five, performing in the ring with her mother, who was one of the world's great equestriennes. In the act with her mother, May appeared in rompers, wearing a big pink bow in her hair. This bow in her hair almost became her trademark.

At thirteen years of age, May was a star in her own right, having reached stardom so young on account of her very early training by her mother. The great rider, Orin Davenport, was also one of her instructors, teaching her to somersault from one horse to another, being the only woman who ever accomplished this. Her backward somersault was a feat of unusual beauty. Her contemporaries willingly granted that she was the greatest equestrienne.

May Wirth rode so fast that her horses had to be changed to keep them from getting dizzy. She carried a whole stable — fourteen horses — Arabian and Australian steeds. Her acting was so fast that it was almost impossible for the camera lens to catch any image. One of her most unusual feats was leaping from the ground to the bare back of her flying horse with her feet encased in baskets, and then turning a backward somersault, baskets still on her feet. Four years were required to perfect this daring trick. May Wirth rose to fame as the supreme equestrienne of the day, another immortal in circusdom.

May was performing, lying flat on her horse's back, head down on one side, her foot secured in a strap. The strap broke, and in the Spence-Bradna book, Bradna tells us, "In my long circus career this was the most heart-rending accident I ever witnessed, coming when May Wirth was at the height of her career. The horse had circled the ring five times before he could be halted, May's head banging against the ring and her body dragging." Her death was a great loss to the entertainment and circus world.

POODLES HANNEFORD and THE HANNEFORDS

TRUE PEERS of the equestrian world! Hanneford is a famous family circus name, dating back nearly two hundred years in Ireland, when the first Hanneford decided to become a bareback rider, and later a circus owner. The Hannefords have always been rated "tops" in bareback riding. However, to old circus fans, it is doubtful if any future generation will ever equal "Poodles," the greatest equestrian clown of modern times.

The Hannefords brought their fine stock from Ireland. They carried seven horses, three grooms, and a transportable ring with a heavy felt floor mat. Only four horses were used; the others were reserves, or understudies.

Mrs. Elizabeth Hanneford, the mother, is said to be the first female ringmaster in history, and the first to ever appear in Parisian frocks. She became famous for her clothes, her jewels, her ostrich plumes and egrets. They became her stock in trade — she was even more celebrated for these than for her graceful popping of the whip in the ring. She performed more than seventy-six consecutive years.

There were six principals in the famous Hanneford act: mother, father, two daughters, and two sons. Their performances as a family were breath-taking in beauty as well as skill, and the clowning of Poodles punctuated the whole with fun and frolic. He is the comic supreme. His leaps, his somersaults, his antics, all seem to run in reverse — if he is supposed to land on his feet on the shoulders of his horse, he is sure to complete a somersault and a half, and land on his head on the tail of the horse. If he is supposed to mount catching the mane of the horse, he winds up barely holding on to the horse by the tail. His clowning "brings the house down."

Poodles' clown costume is only a camouflage. Shedding this coon coat, he executes some of the most amazing acrobatic bareback stunts — somersaults from ring to back of galloping horse and back again in continuous wheel to the ring floor a dozen times. He is an original, turning in a precision-polished performance.

KONYOTS

AS THE LARGE AUDIENCES in Madison Square Garden applauded the Konyots and their horses, little did they realize that these very same horses carried their masters to safety as they fled their native Czechoslovakia which the Nazis were about to occupy. The Konyots' decision was quick — giving up fortune and home. Carrying no baggage and under cover of darkness, each riding a horse and guiding another by reins, they made their way across a treacherous stream of swift water about seventy-five yards wide.

The reputation of their horse act was known all over Europe; and in effecting their escape, friends took care of them along the way. They played engagements in Scandinavia, and finally, after much difficulty, arrived in the United States.

Arturo Konyot presented something new in equine training in his "painstaking schooling" of a group of draft horses in the intricate routines of the sleek liberty horses.

When Teddy Roosevelt said, "Give a boy a horse he can ride," Konyot took him seriously, and when his boy turned out to be a pretty little girl, he gave her a horse just the same, but he left it up to "Dorita" to show how she could ride. Many a skilled horseman sits up and takes notice when Dortia, in Spanish costume, dashes into the arena on

"Bouncing Bomber" to the strains of "Lady of Spain." She is one of the brightest stars to bespangle the hippodrome.

LUCIO CRISTIANI and THE CRISTIANI TROUPE

THE CRISTIANI TROUPE is an Italian family whose great-great-grandparents were famous equestrians. There are ten — these versatile Cristiani stars under canvas. But it is Lucio, however, who has made the name, Cristiani, immortal in the annals of circusdom. His acts were varied, and he was a superb artist, reaching the peak of perfection in all phases of his work.

Somersaulting on a horse is a difficult feat. A horse, while trotting, moves slightly up and down as well as forward. In somersaulting on a horse, the rider must time his return to the horse when the animal is in downward motion. This requires split-second timing. In Lucio Cristiani's incredible somersaulting act, he used three horses, and he returned, not to the back of his own mount, or the second, but, passing completely over the second horse, to the back of the third horse, as the movement of the third horse was downward. He must not only go high enough in the air to allow time for the passing of the second horse, but he must twist his body in a curving motion, since the diameter of these circus rings is only forty-two feet. Thus it is, as Spence and Bradna tell us in *The Big Top,* that he "allows for this arc by somersaulting not merely backwards but sideways as well and then alighting" on the horse that is moving forward, upward, and downward — and yet Lucio always knew where he was going.

The death of Lucio was a great loss to the Cristiani family, as well as to the circus world.

"THE RIDING RUDYNOFFS"

ERNA RUDYNOFF RIDES into the ring on one of her magnificent horses. She is lovely, gracious, graceful and is a dashing rider. Her costume is of the most fashionable; and the rhinestones glitter, all this belying the circus tragedy — Erna's artificial limb. Fred H. Phillips has provided us with much useful information regarding this fabulous family.

This tragic trick of fate happened while Erna was with the Old John Robinson Circus back in 1928. A horse stumbled, causing a compound leg fracture for Erna, resulting in amputation. But she was brave, and there is always the beginning where one may start all over. Erna had married the featured young rider, Rudy Rudynoff. Due to the leg injury and amputation, she was forced to remain away from circus life for five years. The spring following the accident, Rudy went out with the circus. Erna had to be left behind. She and one old retired rosinback horse were about the only living creatures in the deserted winter quarters. The old horse and Erna became more than a team; they became fast friends. He seemed to realize that Erna's determined little heart needed cooperation, and this he gave with almost human understanding. Success crowned their efforts. When Rudy returned, he was delighted and immediately bought for her a five-gaited Arabian stallion named Color Flash, and broke him to a dancing routine. For two years, Color Flash and Erna appeared with R.B.B.&B. Circus. Then came 1937 and the final rehearsal before leaving for the opening of the circus in Madison Square Garden. Again a horse stumbled and Erna fell against the ring curb, breaking five vertebrae. Her neck was put in a cast, which, the doctors said, must remain for a year. Erna challengingly replied, "I'll be riding again in eight weeks."

Erna went to New York with Rudy and the circus. It was cold there, such a change from the warm Florida weather that she took a cold. She had been forced to wear a cape, not being able to get a coat on over the cast. The cold developed into influenza. The doctor could not treat her sore throat on account of the cast. She begged him to remove it, which he finally did. She suffered no ill effects, and Erna rode again. She was so proud of Rudy that fateful year. His accomplishment helped to boost her. He introduced sixty-two horses, an elephant, and four camels into the ring in one act. Such success was to be expected of Rudy, as he was born to the circus, in Stuttgart, Germany. His father was a bareback rider and his mother a wardrobe mistress with the great Schumann Circus, the largest on the continent and the most famous.

JUSTINO (GIUSTINO) LOYAL (REPINSKY)

JUSTINO LOYAL is the worthy head of a great riding clan, dating back several generations. He mixes comedy with difficult roles. He does all sorts of somersaults on single galloping horses, and in all directions. Then he goes into high hurtling somersaults from horse to horse in column — twisters straight and twisters through hoops. The height he attains from the back of a horse seems impossible. He is one of a very few riders to ever complete successfully the horse-to-horse somersault.

The Justino Loyals are noted for the superior quality of their "rosinback" stock. They have ten of the finest horses ever seen in a ring performance, superb animals, magnificently trained.

ROPE WALKERS

THE YOUNGER GENERATION of today is not so familiar with rope walking, an art which has developed into the tight and loose wire walking. Blondin's rope-walk over Niagara Falls (see p. 158) made this act popular, and rope walkers began appearing in many large towns. The performers would stretch a rope between two tall buildings, and, after passing the hat for collection, would remove street clothes under which they were wearing tights and spangles. With the aid of a balancing pole, they would climb up and walk the rope, literally causing the onlookers to hold their breath.

One performer who stood out above all others in their early and novel profession of thrillers was a one-legged veteran of the Civil War, a Mr. Van Hoone. He would walk the rope with seeming ease, and as a part of his act, when about midway between the two tall buildings, while in mid-air, would produce the wherewithal as if by magic, would break a number of eggs into a skillet and fry them over an alcohol lamp.

A modern counterpart of this act is that of Mr. Camillo Mayer, past sixty years of age and weighing around 200 pounds. His age and weight give the spectator watching him, as he swings ponderously from side to side, with seeming great effort as he climbs a rope ladder, the impression of a joke in the making. The circus crowd always laughs heartily at his clowning, then becomes very quiet, afraid to believe its eyes, when, picking up a chair, a table, and a stove, he ambles out on the wire. He is completely at ease on the wire, but the audience, by this time, is "anything but." He stops midway on this wire, stretched forty feet above the ground in the top of the tent in center ring, and there, with no protecting net underneath, sets up housekeeping.

He balances the chair, then sits down; next balancing the table and stove on the wire, he lights his stove, takes a frying pan out of the table drawer and cooks some phony flapjacks, flipping them in the air for a quick turn.

In 1911, a pioneer flyer in a Wright Bros. plane made a daredevil flight over the crest of the Canadian side of Niagara Falls, down into the gorge, under Honeymoon Bridge, and up and out. Here was a competing thrill to rope-walking skill.

About this time, balloon ascensions came into popularity, and dimmed the exploitations of rope walkers for a while. There was also a law passed which prohibited rope and wire crossings of the Niagara Falls. This had been the one glamor spot of solo perfomers.

BLONDIN

BLONDIN (EMIL GRARELET) was born in France. When he was only five years of age, he went to see a traveling company of actors, rope walkers, robots, and equestrians. As soon as he reached home after the show, he stretched a string between the upper rungs of two chairs and tried to walk it. Of course he fell, and there were tears. The tears were soon gone, but the ambition and desire remained steadfast.

In time, Blondin became the greatest rope walker of his day. He came to America, and, during the winter of 1859, made plans for the crossing of Niagara Falls — 1100 feet across the raging, boiling waters, 160 to 170 feet below. At last he had his hempen cord twisted and ready, and it spanned the distance. The eventful date set for his crossing was June 30, 1859. He was the first to attempt to cross this boiling cataract. One misstep was certain death. The turbulence of air over Niagara Falls created quite a problem, but Blondin reckoned with this successfully.

Blondin selected as a location for his feat, a point halfway between the falls and the suspension bridge. His rope was three and one-quarter inches in diameter and 1300 feet in length. This rope was skillfully manipulated and pulled across the river by a cord carried across by a boat. Many guy ropes were used, but with such great length that there was a sag of sixty feet in the center of the rope; yet Blondin successfully calculated this. (At first he used a balancing rod, but later used only his arms as means of balancing.)

The date was publicized and a crowd befitting such a daring feat gathered on both sides of the river. Canadian steamers came with excursionists from Toronto, and many other cities and railroads ran specials from Buffalo and surrounding territory. 2500 persons swarmed the vantage points — statesmen, judges, editors, members of Congress, capitalists, artists, professors, and socialites; all classes and all ages came eager-eyed and remained to gasp at his artistry. Many scaffoldings were erected for the event. These did not accommodate the crowds, and all housetops and windows were overflowing. Blondin was attired in pink tights, a yellow-spangled tunic, and buckskin moccasins. As he approached the rope, the thunderous shouts and cheers rose to such magnitude as to rival the crescendo of the falling waters. Blondin picked up his balancing pole and started across. Halfway across, he stopped, sat down on the rope and calmly viewed the surroundings.

During the months to come, Blondin made many, many crossings, each time introducing some new feat. Once he carried a picture-taking apparatus — a camera on a tripod. Lashing his balancing rod to the rope, he took pictures of the crowds on each side. On another occasion, he brought a heavy chair, and, halfway across, balanced the chair on the rope, sat down and calmly took in the situation. Then, adjusting only two legs of the chair on the rope, he again sat down, then stood in the chair. People screamed and turned rigid; some fainted. Eighteen minutes were consumed in the first crossing over to the Canadian side, and he calmly walked back in less than half the time, although he lay down for two minutes on the rope in returning — as though to take a rest.

On July 4th, Blondin crossed the falls blindfolded and in a heavy sack made of blankets. On July 16 (and many other times) he crossed rolling a wheelbarrow with which he performed unprecedented tricks, at times carrying human or animal freight in his wheelbarrow. He also turned somersaults midway on the rope. On another occasion he carried a man on his shoulders the entire way across. Blondin made headline news around the world with his memorable caution to the nervous man whom he was carrying on his back. "I must request you to sit quiet," said Mr. Blondin, "or I shall have to put you down." He reached such perfection that he would pretend to be slipping, as if his position had become insecure, which always brought chills of horror, and ice to the veins of the spectators.

On September 14, 1860, Blondin performed his last crossing before the Prince of Wales and many nobles and notables and thousands of spectators. He crossed, performing varied stunts, and then announced that, in honor of the prince, he would do what he had never done before, cross on stilts. His Royal Highness insisted that he not endanger his life in such a manner. Blondin reassured the prince and then offered to carry the prince over; and it is reported that, had it not been for the Duke of Newcastle, there is no telling what might have happened. Blondin mounted the stilts and made a successful crossing, although with great difficulty. After this performance of unmatched skill and great, great courage, the prince and party talked at length with Blondin. Later the prince sent him a check for a very handsome sum; the letter was dated September 15, 1860.

The citizens of Niagara had previously sent Blondin a gold medal, bearing this inscription: "Presented to Mons. I. F. Blondin by the citizens of Niagara Falls, in appreciation of a feat never before attempted by man, but by him successfully performed on the 19th of August, 1859, that of carrying a man upon his back over the Falls of Niagara on a tightrope." Blondin received other handsome gifts. He was hailed as "King of the Rope" and was driven through the streets that all might acclaim his great bravery and skill.

Since Niagara Falls could not be carried along as a stage

for Blondin, he continued his breath-taking feats at different places.

Blondin's fame preceded him to England. Boots, hats, cigars, neckties, perfumes, articles of confectionary, stationery, millinery, and many other articles bore the name of Blondin. As Jenny Lind was received in this country, so was Blondin accepted across the way, over all Europe. He continued to add new stunts, more astounding and breath-taking. Dressed as a chef — with cap, table, chair, frying pan, and plates; glasses, flour, eggs, milk, and carrying a stove, he would stop halfway across, set up housekeeping, and cook an omelet. He also perfected his stiltwalking to such perfection that he was able to turn somersaults on the rope in stilts. Considered by many as his greatest feat was his musical accomplishment, playing the march, "Guillaume Tell," on the fiddle, while dancing on the rope, and continuing to play while turning somersaults, without once stopping the music, keeping his bow arm in steady motion, and his left-hand fingers working with the velocity of steam.

Blondin's last performance was given in Belfast, Ireland, when he was seventy-two years of age. He was a perfect gentleman, and highly respected. His unmatched skill, his hardihood, and courage, gave him the title of "Hero of Niagara."

II Welcome to Clown Alley

and many, many others ☞

Isn't it strange that princes and kings
And clowns who caper in sawdust rings
And common folk like you and me —
Are builders of eternity.

To each is given a bag of tools
A shapeless mass and a book of rules,
And each may make, ere life has blown,
A stumbling block or a stepping stone.

— R. L. Sharpe

CLOWNS
"Merchants of Mirth"

The Clowns! "Zealous Zanies, Jumping Joeys, our leaping, tumbling grimacers are on the loose! Merchants of Mirth, they'll trade you a bruise for a chuckle or a laceration for a belly-laugh any day, a riotous, reveling, rollicking roundup of roisterers who know that a good sense of humor keeps us young." Thus does Ken Dunshee sum it up in his R.B.B.&B. program article.

Rex de Roselli, in his "Clowning — A Serious Business," published in *White Tops* and *Studebaker Wheel,* says:

"It is a sign of sanity in a troubled world that we can still find time to laugh at the time-honored insanities of circus clowns. Inheritors of an old tradition — privileged to lampoon and satirize the dignified, the pompous, and affected — a world without them would be a world that had forgotten how to laugh."

The two tributes above, though expressed in entirely different manner and mien, are both true of that ageless, international, and universally-beloved character—THE CIRCUS CLOWN.

The earliest history of clowning goes back to the Sanskrit days of the Indians. Some records argue that the comic actor, the ancestor of the clown, appeared as early as 800 B. C. It is recorded that some of these actors covered their faces with soot. (Probably this gave rise to the blackface minstrel.)

We find clowns mentioned in the Latin classics, and on down to the court jester — Panteleone of France being the first to use the slapstick method. So we see that through all the ages, man has felt the need for laughter. The clown enjoys making the other person laugh at him, his predicaments, his lack of comprehension. He is willing to cajole himself that he might excite laughter, and the ones who laugh find it funny even to the point of hilarity, to see a fellow human being in such comical situations.

The question is asked often, "Why and how do so many men become clowns?" or "How did the art of clowning start?" There are many stories as to its source, but since the circus is primarily for children, and since parents desire to please their children and make them happy, let us tell the story of the little daughter of a mountebank in France. This little girl dreamed that she saw her father with a white face, white pantaloons and peaked hat, performing before a crowd — and everyone was laughing. Wild-eyed and eager, she repeated her happy dream to her father. He was so impressed that he dressed as she had dreamed, and became the first circus clown.

Clowning is one of the oldest and yet one of the most unspoiled professions in the world. It is exacting and difficult, and a highly respected profession. Being funny, to clowns, is a serious business. Timing is as important to a clown as to an actor. Today, the clown depends on pantomime, and must produce by concentrating all his efforts on visual gags. Hours of study and practice go into a seemingly guileless act that captivates an audience.

Clown faces — their make-ups — and their individual costumes, are what Bing Crosby calls "their treasured trademarks." Each clown feels, not without justification, that he is ethically entitled to his own peculiar style of make-up. Among the clowns themselves, this feeling is very strong. Universally clowns respect this property-right of make-up and clown act. So important is this to the clowning profession that they literally will, or bequeath, their "faces" to their offspring or succeeding generations. And, once a clown's own particular type of make-up is established, it is very seldom changed.

If one doubts the seriousness of a clown as to his profession, he has only to listen to conversation along Clown Alley, a certain section on the circus lot where the dressing wagons of the clowns are parked.

As long as 300 or 400 years ago, clowns were known to go from town to town on the European continent doing original stunts, impersonations, tricks, and antics. They were truly the forerunners of the circus clowns of today.

The oldest clown make-up is the whiteface. The other two types of clown make-up are: august, and character. There are two types of whiteface — the neat, which is a large expanse of white, with reasonably normal-sized nose, mouth, and eyebrows, using the traditional red and black. The grotesque type uses the same color scheme with features made larger, more absurd and outlandish — the mouth may go from ear to ear, with a gigantic nose, or eyebrows reaching to the hairline.

The august (auw-goost) style originated in the middle part of Europe, having the same exaggerated features as the grotesque white, but on a pink or reddish face instead of pure white. (Traditionally, as the R.B.B.&B. program tells us, the august is the "butt' of a clown gag, the white face the "straight man.") The type known as "tramp" in America, is called a "Charlie" in Europe (English nightwatchmen — seedy, tattered individuals, for the most part, are called "Charlies").

Make-up is a real problem for the clown, with the weatherman the cause of most of his worries. On hot summer days, the clown-white gets sticky and putty noses are inclined to lose their shape — and charm. Chilly weather stiffens clown-white and makes it hard to manage, and putty noses congeal and deal the funsters misery when they must be removed. On rainy days, water trickles down a clown's chalk-white, but a good clown "knows his face" in any kind of weather, and can do an artistic make-up even in the dark.

The last clown of the old school, before buffooning was curtailed, was Polidor, a Barnum & Bailey august of classic stature. He featured his pet sparrow, his pig, and his dog.

We are told that Uncle Sam looks like he does in caricature because the idea of his costume was copied from the make-up and dress of Dan Rice, a famous clown. (See Dan Rice, p. 25.) Others who had become famous as clowns in this old school were: Harry Wentworth, Tony Denier, Joe Pentland, Dick Sands, Dan Stone and George L. Fox. Tony Pastor and Pat Rooney were among our first clowns; Billie Burke became a favorite jester in the 'eighties, especially known for his act with a mule. (Billie Burke, his daughter, a famous stage and screen star, wife of Florenz Ziegfeld, producer of Ziegfeld Follies, was named Ethel Burke, but so proud was she of her father's fame and rank as a clown that she took his name.)

With the advent of the modern circus, which has outgrown the old, intimate one-ring circus, the technique of clowning has changed. The talking and singing clown has passed on. He could no longer be heard in the large circus tents, and the audience wanted more action and speed. Now several circus acts are given in the same period of time formerly consumed by a singing clown. So the clown was put "on his own" with his props, having to depend almost entirely on pantomime, a difficult art. The fun of today's circus has to be "condensed into capsules of concentrated convulsions." These are the days of "digest reading, headline scanning, aerial touring, and chemical concentrations." This is the atomic, satellite and outer space era.

The clowns "bust out" in the walk-around, seeming to be propelled into the circus arena, so real is their zest and zeal. Besides being an integral part of the circus, clowns perform what might be termed a fundamental part. They relieve tension caused by daring trapeze and high wire acts. They fill in where perhaps some emergency has prevented an act from appearing. They entertain between acts when time is required for changing props. They are an ever-ready reserve of the circus. And clowns are ever watchful of any hindrance to an act, or person, or animal — such as a broken bottle, a loose rope, a stray dog.

Making good in Clown Alley, as Rex de Roselli points out, is far different from making good on the stage, or in pictures, or on television. In these three entertainment fields, "gag" men write the funny situations, and authors and directors put the comedy on the stage. Every clown is wholly dependent upon himself, his ability and ingenuity — he "cooks up" his own pantomime jokes, plans his own costumes, and supplies his own props.

An excellent example of this planned, modern, individualism — this trademark of distinction — is Felix Adler's "birthstone nose." For many years Adler, a star clown with R.B.B.&B. Circus, has worn the birthstone of each current month in the end of his putty nose — in November, he wears a topaz; in April, a diamond, etc. Adler is one of the few top clown stars who has several costumes. As has been said, once a clown's costume is established, he seldom changes. Adler advises, "A modern clown must make up his act with the precision of a scientist. I perform in what I call 'international terms,' and I never use any objects in my act that all people in all lands couldn't understand."

The best example of the established costume is that of the great modern circus and motion picture star clown, Emmett Kelly, dressed in rags, eating a cabbage leaf. (See p. 178.)

One of the younger clowns, Ernie Burch, also with R.B.B.&B. Circus, has become known for his eyelashes. They're made of bright green metallic paper, and pasted just above his real eyelashes.

The universal name of the clown is, "Joey." It originated with Joseph Grimaldi (see p. 172), an English comedian of the Charles Dickens era. Grimaldi, however, was never with a circus, but so great was the admiration for his genius as a wit, that clowns the world over are proud of the nickname, Joey.

There is no agreement among clowns as to the basic psychology of laughter. Wyatt Blassingame, in *The Family Circle,* quotes the opinion of George Mills, one of the top rodeo clowns of America, who claims that a clown who makes himself ridiculous enough in almost any situation will be funny. Pat Valdo, personnel director for R.B.B.&B. who was formerly a clown, thinks that the human impulse to destroy lies behind humor — allows the audience to get rid of impulses without doing anything themselves — a kind of "psychological therapy," as he calls this emotional reaction. Paul Jung, noted clown, agrees that people will laugh at destruction just as long as it is not gruesome — "keep these acts burlesque," is his advice.

There is one form of European gag which does not "go over" well in the United States — the kind of strip-tease in which the performer, for one reason or another, is forever losing his pants. Wyatt Blassingame, in *The Family Circle,* tells an interesting story about the well-known rodeo clown, George Mills, and his trial of this pants-losing gag. "Mills has perhaps the most dangerous clown act in the world. He travels with rodeos, working in the arena with wild bulls.

He is a matador without sword or cape to protect him. At one time or another he has had half the bones in his body broken. On this one occasion, he planned to allow the bull to pass so close that a horn would hook into his baggy clown trousers and rip them off, leaving Mills in long, red underwear. But the bull passed even closer than Mills had calculated, taking underwear as well as trousers. 'There wasn't anything to do,' Mills said, 'but just squat down where I was and wait for somebody to bring me a blanket." Fortunately, another clown attracted the bull's attention before it could turn and charge again.

"Making a nuisance of himself has always been one of the prerogatives of a clown," – and when this is done with that certain innocent technique, it is always good for a laugh. The court jester, the direct professional ancestor of our clowns of today, was always allowed special privileges. Blassingame also tells the story of Robert Sherwood, a star clown of fifty years ago, who was appearing in London before Queen Victoria. "All the performers had been warned to stay at least twenty feet away from the royal box, and to salute formally on entering and leaving the ring. Sherwood, remembering the liberties of his clowning ancestors, stopped directly in front of the royal box, went through a great pantomime of washing his hands and drying them on his costume. Then he climbed right into the box and shook hands with the queen."

This same Bob Sherwood, as Blassingame tells us, missed a command performance of the circus in London so that he could sing a sick child to sleep. All clowns are especially fond of children, and spend much of their spare time in children's hospitals and in entertaining underprivileged children. On a recent tour of R.B.B.&B. Circus, Paul Jung, star clown, spent part of every day he was in Fort Worth, Texas, visiting a child dying of leukemia. The complete adulation of a child for a clown brings out the best of the man that is in a clown.

And when the best of a man is given for the entertainment of sick children, then we know that his very soul is lifted.

Yes, clowns may be the "pegs on which to hang a circus," as Barnum called them, but they may also be called the international human spark plugs of the circus. Some are heroes, some are plain, quiet men, some have died to make you laugh. It is always, "Laugh, clown, laugh," — that all the world may laugh with you.

JOSEPH GRIMALDI
1778-1837

AT THE AGE OF THREE, young Joseph Grimaldi was forced to work, and was trained by harsh, even cruel methods.

When only fifteen, Joseph fell in love with Maria Hughes, and they were married in 1798 when he was nineteen. His child-bride died only one year later. A short time after her death, Joseph was badly burned in a fire at Drury Lane, and was nursed back to health by Miss Bristow, whom he married in 1804. In 1805 and 1806, Joseph reached the height of his fame at Covent Garden in "Mother Goose." To this day his name holds the acclaim of the world as the greatest pantomimist of all time, the "Michelangelo of Buffoonery." He was beloved by a whole nation.

It is believed that Joseph Grimaldi felt the depth of sorrow to such a degree that he forced a smile in order to block the descent of sorrow in the lives of others. His son, a clown of great hope, died from excessive use of alcohol. Later, Grimaldi had the misfortune of losing all his money. As has been said, although he was never a circus clown, so great was his fame and the admiration for his courage that circus clowns today are called "Joeys" in deference to him. Grimaldi introduced singing into his act, thus becoming the father of the singing clown. He could make love in a hundred different manners. His songs produced spontaneous and hilarious laughter. He "caricatured the ballerina and the juggler. His fun with oysters was proverbial," sympathizing and talking to them as he ate them. He possessed superpersonality, and "his power was such that, as soon as he showed himself on the stage and said, 'Well, how are you?' the whole house roared."

Joseph Grimaldi's farewell performance was given June 27, 1828. His path to fame was so sad and hard that his work may be referred to as "Comedy Born of Tragedy." He is one of the immortals of the entertainment world. No less a renowned author than Charles Dickens caught the light of a great spirit and held it aloft in his writings, *The Memoirs of Grimaldi*. Grimaldi, the most famous clown of all time, typified that set rule "Laugh, clown, laugh." Kings and queens and everyone thronged to see Grimaldi, the funniest clown of them all, and yet Grimaldi was known, by his intimates, to be one of the saddest people in the world, a truly melancholy soul.

At one time, a man, seemingly broken in body and spirit, consulted a doctor in London. After a thorough examination, the doctor, finding nothing wrong with the man physically, told him that what he needed was a few good laughs. "Go to see Grimaldi," he said, "London's merriest clown." The patient smiled grimly: "I am Grimaldi," he said, "London's merriest clown."

GEORGE L. FOX

GEORGE L. FOX was one of the truly great clowns. When he had reached a point of eminence, he was acclaimed, "The Grimaldi of America." He and Dan Rice were considered the top clowns of their day. Fox leaped to world fame in his "Humpty Dumpty" act, which ran for ten consecutive weeks at the Olympic Theater in New York. In that city alone, he appeared 1268 times.

It was an unkind fate that pulled the cord on that last curtain call for George Fox — he who had made so many laugh, made them genuinely happy and glad to be alive. His wit, his charm, his spontaneity, his ability, all had come naturally. He was last seen on the stage of the Booth Theater November 25, 1875, but that night he was the saddest, saddest clown that ever chalked his face. It seemed a stroke of fate, that he should again be appearing in his greatest success, "Humpty Dumpty." For some time friends and relatives had noticed evidence of mental affliction. So on that November night after the play it was thought best to take him to an asylum. He died two years later.

JULES TURNOUR

MR. AL RINGLING considered Jules Turnour the greatest of the talking clowns. Mr. Al acted as straight man for Jules in these conversational acts.

A well-known performance of Jules' was his horse-trading act, which always brought hilarious laughter from the audience. Jules had a wonderfully well-trained mule by the name of January. In the skit, the ringmaster enters the ring leading a horse. Jules follows immediately behind, leading his mule, January. Jules rushes up in front of the ringmaster, puts his mule through some extra good stunts and then banters the ringmaster to horse-trade, asking how much "to boot" will he give him for the mule. An argument follows, but Jules convinces the ringmaster that the mule really is worth much more money to the circus than the horse. The ringmaster pays Jules the substantial sum and Jules leads the horse on towards the exit of the tent. The minute Jules walks away, the mule sits down, and no amount of coaxing or pulling will budge January. By this time, the next act is waiting to come into the ring and these actors, becoming restless, get into an argument with the ringmaster, and to all appearances these actors become angered and are on the verge of quitting the show. In desperation, the ringmaster calls Jules to come and get his mule. Again Jules bargains and offers to move the mule for a nice sum of money. Completely outdone, the ringmaster pays him. Jules speaks to January, who immediately gets up and walks off with Jules, whereupon Jules unties the horse where he had left him near the exit, and looks back over his shoulder as he walks away leading both the mule and the horse, plus a handful of money which he waves at the audience.

Jules was born in a circus wagon in Galicia, Spain. His father was an acrobat and his mother a premier dancer. At the age of six, he was acting with his parents. He was apprenticed at ten years of age, and it was a hard school. The rigorous, and really vicious training, while so young, injured his body. During this training period, two grown people would hold him and bend the childish body backward until head and feet met, and subject him to excruciating positions while he cried in agony. He was to become a contortionist — he did, and was known as "The Human Baseball." Later in life, he grew very ill and was in a hospital for three years. When he came out, his body was stiff — at the age of twenty — so he decided to turn to clowning, in which capacity he became famous. Jules toured all over Europe, coming to the United States in 1899. He joined Ringling Brothers and later Barnum & Bailey, and remained when they consolidated, being with these shows for over thirty years. Altogether, he clowned for nearly sixty years.

Jules had been at home during a winter season when his son Frank was very young, and he and the little fellow had become pals. The first week out on tour Jules was in the wings, ready to go in the arena. In his act he carried a large doll baby. While waiting at the entrance for his cue, he was handed a telegram. It read, "Frank is dying." There he stood, holding the doll baby, and his own little son dying. He was too far from home to reach there in time, and at this very moment the ringmaster called "Jules! Jules! Where are you? Time for you." And Jules Turnour, carrying the doll, went in and made others laugh while tears streamed down his cheeks.

Jules was a very good friend of President Hoover, and one of his favorite performers. When the President was a boy in Iowa, he was sick on circus day, and the circus was playing on Dad Hoover's own lot. Jules, hearing of the little boy's illness, put on his clown costume, and went over to the Hoover home; while the little Herbert was lifted to the window, Jules did his best tricks. Many times during the following years Herbert Hoover visited with Jules on the circus lot.

Jules spoke six languages and often acted as guide for distinguished foreign visitors to the circus. As he grew old, he sold copies of the Circus Route Book and thus made extra money. He was also the circus postman, going to town twice each day for the mail. In this capacity he received no salary, but at the end of the year, a purse was made up for him. During his last few years, he had an assistant. Jules said being the postman was both a happy job and a sad one. Letters brought joy and laughter, or sorrow and tears, and many were the eager hopes that hung on his trips to town. Famous stars and roustabouts alike stood still in abject and silent thought when their names were not called.

Jules lived to be eighty. He held a unique place in the hearts of the circus performers. He realized the danger ever-present in their acts. He was forever walking up to famous stars and admonishing them to be careful. Although Jules always clowned to perfection while he gave this fatherly advice of caution, yet the actors all knew the heart beneath the painted smile — a heart full of love and consideration for every member of the circus.

FRANK "SLIVERS" OAKLEY

FRANK "SLIVERS" OAKLEY had magic! He had the unseen power of projecting the magic of his dynamic and intriguing personality on the spectators as a picture is projected on a screen. The audience seemed spellbound from the time he entered until his exit. People responded to the twinkle of his eyes, the waving of his hand. Just let him take one awkward step or stub his toe and to them it was comedy de luxe. His acts were hardy perennials. They were received with the same wild applause the last time as when first presented. After all, it was not the acts, it was Slivers, the one and only Slivers, whom they applauded so genuinely and heartily.

Wyatt Blassingame tells us that Slivers is usually given credit for having originated the female impersonator's bustle, as well as the big feet which are now almost standard equipment for clowns. He was best known for his baseball act, which became famous the world over. Those who had not actually seen it, had heard or read about it. He was such a hilarious hit in this act that he was given five minutes alone in the big top, where he kept 16,000 people in stitches. He would pantomime an entire baseball game, players, hits, runs, even an unseen umpire. And when he had his heated argument with the umpire, the house simply went wild. All of this he did entirely alone and without props. Everyone roared with laughter to the point of exhaustion, many fainted, and medical care was required. Such acting as that took magic — magic of a genius such as only the truly gifted and truly great possess.

Despite the adulation of the public and the love of his little daughter and wife, there came a time when Slivers was convinced he had outlived his art. "The world was no longer funny to Frank Oakley and so he left it — taking Slivers with him," the former custodian of the Hertzberg Circus Collection tells us. Yes, Slivers, who had become a demi-deity to children and parents — who had made the world laugh and forget its troubles — did not have a smile left in his soul. The verdict was suicide.

CLOWNS OF TODAY
EMMETT KELLY

IT IS GENERALLY ACKNOWLEDGED that there have been "Three Greats" in the past three eras of clowning: Grimaldi, Dan Rice, and Emmett Kelly. The adjective, "super-best," has been aptly applied to Emmett Kelly. He is a master of pathos. He has reached stardom and individuality in his art – the art of clowning – and he has perfected a technique all his own. He is a solo and at the same time a stellar performer in the world of clowndom. He and Slivers Oakley are the only clowns to achieve stardom with a circus since the famed Dan Rice. In 1950, Emmett Kelly was granted a leave from the circus for one year, that he might fulfill a Hollywood contract with David Selznick for a movie.

Lowell Thomas tells us interesting facts about Kelly and his rise to stardom. Years ago, Emmett Kelly created a character on paper in ink, and he gave chalk-talks using this character. Later he entered the circus, enacting this character in person – his Weary, Woeful Willie clown character. Emmett does not know whether "the character made him or he made the character."

It does not matter who made which. What does matter is that Emmett Kelly is the greatest of all pantomime circus clowns of the modern era and that he has made millions happy – made them laugh and keep on laughing as long as they watched him and long afterward, for his acting is never forgotten. He comes from Kansas City, Missouri – the state where you have to "show them." Emmett has done precisely that. He began his cartooning and chalk-talks when just a small boy. When not performing, he was busy over his drawing board. All of a sudden one day the idea of clowning his own tramp character hit him and he did so immediately. His was the star-overnight story. Within two years he was with Ringling Bros. and Barnum & Bailey Circus, and has been with them for more than twelve years.

Emmett Kelly is an all-time circus star. There is a touch of genius in his artistry. Never has his true greatness of facial expression been more unquestionably demonstrated than in the pitiful, lovelorn, dejected, yet appealing gaze which he literally fastens on some attractive girl or woman in the audience. Finally, in a last appeal for a mite of attention, he offers each a leaf of his cabbage, which he eats continuously as though it were a habit, so much so that one almost thinks of cabbage, along with abject pathos, as his trademark.

The story is told by Wyatt Blassingame about a child who had been watching him as he hungrily nibbled on the cabbage. The child began to cry very loudly, and begged her mother to buy the clown a sandwich. In order to pacify the child, the mother bought the sandwich. It evidently pacified Emmett too, for he sat right down by the child and ate it.

Considered by many to be Emmett Kelly's best act is his untiring attempt to sweep up a spotlight, which is thrown on the circus arena. Emmett sweeps from the outside of the circle of light inward, and due to ingenious manipulation by the electrician, the circle grows smaller and smaller as Kelly continues sweeping. Finally Emmett covers all but a flicker of circle light with sawdust. Then he takes a dustpan, sweeps this tiny residue of the circle of light into the pan (sometimes he sweeps it under an imaginary rug) and with seeming satisfaction over a job well done, starts off, broom over his shoulder, only to see, a very short distance in front of him, that same circle of light as large as it was in the beginning. With renewed interest he starts all over again. This excellent act is accomplished several times with the same perfect technique, and the same hilarious laughter from the audience as Emmett walks around the entire arena.

The privilege granted Kelly, by Ringling Bros. and Barnum & Bailey, of remaining in the arena during the entire circus and acting on his own, is unique in the modern world of clowns — a distinct honor. In 1943, when Emmett joined the Big Show, he was told to do the best he could and see how things worked. He decided to play to only a small section of the audience at a time, and he picked the spots. Many of his acts are remembered as top entertainment. During the war he became very patriotic and, as everyone was doing, planted a victory garden. He prepared his little plot of ground while the spectators wondered. Presently he commenced to plant the seed, at first with energetic speed. Gradually he slowed down. He was thinking of the delicious vegetables, and suddenly his hunger got the best of him and he ate the seed.

Another Kelly act which caused hilarious laughter, was that of the contractor. He would go up in the seat-stands, spread a tattered blueprint on the laps of two circus-goers. Then he would place a piece of wood between them on the seat, saw a few strokes, study his plans, saw a little more, when, all of a sudden he happened to glimpse a pretty girl passing, and leaving saw, plans, and plank, would rush to follow the vision of loveliness, only to return a few seconds later, gather up his plans, saw, and plank, with heartbroken expression and silent tears all but falling.

Ever so often during the circus performance, Emmett holds a dingy, small handkerchief under the tight wire performers, seeming to feel sure he could catch the group, and, in his melancholy way, fully expecting them to fall. We are reminded of his gag a few years ago, when he built a fire near the seal act, put his skillet on, and then vainly and dolefully tried to steal a fish from the seals.

Kelly's visible wearing apparel consists of a pair of very long, broken-down-at-the-heel shoes, a battered and torn derby hat, a greenish, bluish faded flannel shirt, a red striped tie, held in place by a clothespin, and ragged, baggy, faded pants several sizes too large for him, and a tuxedo coat so torn and tattered as to make one wonder how he manages to get into it. When he cannot tell heads or tails of this coat, he starts in "conditioning" another. He wets it, drags it in the mud, steps on it, pulls it in every direction, tearing rents and pulling sags in it. It is finally so unfit as to be fit enough for him to wear.

Kelly does not wear a wig; his own hair, permitted to grow long, is mussed until it looks for all the world like a wig. He is quiet, good-natured, and popular on the circus lot; the other clowns are not jealous of his success. Kelly studies his act; day and night he watches, thinks, plans. He told Lowell Thomas, "I do a lot of thinking about my other self, the little 'hobo.' I start feeling sorry for the poor little guy; seems more like he is somebody I know instead of just me working for a living. I'm really getting so I feel like two separate people — me and the little tramp. And, so help me, I'm beginning to like the little guy better than I like myself! And I kind of hope he feels the same about me . . ."

FELIX ADLER

FELIX ADLER is one of the best-known clowns with Ringling Bros. and Barnum & Bailey Circus. He is often referred to as "The King" of the clowns. He is featured extensively on magazine covers and in articles. Adler is also an author, having written several well-known books. He has an excellent radio voice and turns in a distinctive radio and television appearance. He is an "ad lib" artist in word and action.

At one time Felix was known as "The White House Clown." He was often invited into the presidential box during the Washington engagements of the circus. Those were the days of the Coolidge children, the Hoover grandchildren, and Sissie and Buzzie, the Roosevelt grandchildren.

Mr. John M. Kelley, lawyer for the Ringlings, tells us

that it was Adler's goose that created such turmoil that damage suits in many ciphers were lodged against the show. The case came to court and Kelley was defending. The incident was puzzling — women alleging indecent assault were in uproar. Several fainted.

At the time there was a fad in women's hosiery — clocks, sprays of flowers, or oats were embroidered on the side. Now the lady in question was wearing the oat pattern. The clowns were in the walkaround. All of a sudden this lady "let out" a scream. Evidently Adler's goose was an opportunist, and the oats looked good — or was it the oats?

Mr. Kelley had Mr. Charles Ringling assign detectives. The show moved on to Boston. At a later day the detectives spied said goose nipping the leg line of spectators from behind the reserved seats.

Mr. Kelley said, "How I loved that goose. In sealing her own doom, she freed the circus of charges on court records of obscene behavior of circus employees."

OTTO GRIEBLING

OTTO GRIEBLING is a very famous "tramp" clown, putty nose, battered hat and tattered clothing. Pantomime was an opportune medium for him. When Otto came to the United States he was only fifteen. Since he could not speak English, he decided to pretend that he was deaf and dumb. It worked. He got what he wanted by sign language of his own making, and facial expressions.

His pre-show routines have taken hold on the public fancy. He works while the audience is coming in and being ushered to their seats, thus he has time to build up and carry out an act. One of his best acts is that of a florist's delivery boy. He starts out as a very young boy, carrying a small pot plant, pushing his way around through the crowd, paging a Mrs. Shultz who has ordered this plant. Time passes. Otto keeps going around the ring at intervals. Each time around he becomes a little older and the pot plant has grown a little larger. At last he is an old, old man with a long beard, pushing a wheelbarrow in which is the one-time plant, now grown to a ten-foot tree. By this time, his sobs can be heard in between his weaker calls for Mrs. Schultz.

In another of Otto's acts, he is trying to deliver a block of ice to the same Mrs. Schultz. Each time around the arena the ice becomes smaller and smaller, until the last time around he is sobbing because he still cannot find Mrs. Schultz, and because he has no ice to deliver — he is all wet, with only the empty ice tongs hanging down his back. He is a true "Charlie" type, and is in a pitiful state of affairs all the time, which the audience thoroughly enjoys.

PAUL JUNG

"A HAPPY GOOF" is what Paul Jung calls himself, according to Wyatt Blassingame. His wife, Elsie, who has written several interesting articles, declares that being married to a circus clown, "is a circus in itself and just as much fun." When she and Paul first started going together, she had not paid such close attention to the clowns, and several looked like Paul to her. Here was a cue made to order for a clown. A clown, whom she thought was Paul, handed her a note reading, "Meet me in front of the arena tonight at six-fifteen." Later another clown, whom she thought was Paul, handed her a note. It read "Meet me in back of the arena tonight at seven." Later a third clown, whom she also thought was Paul, handed her a note bearing the message, "Meet me just outside the west entrance at seven-fifteen." By this time she was truly wondering why Paul couldn't make up his mind — or perhaps he was as goofy as the clown he portrayed. This joke almost boomeranged, because Paul was seen rushing from one designated meeting place to another. She solved the problem by not meeting him until he had taken off his make-up.

One of Paul's most popular stunts of his entire clowning career is his Adam Buster. He says the idea literally popped in his head. He was reading and thinking so much about the atom, when all of a sudden the idea of Adam Buster came to his mind. He immediately built a good-sized square box. The act was carefully planned and rehearsed. (It is still used.) At show time, this box was placed in the center ring of the circus. Above it, on a pulley, was hung a huge block resembling iron. At last, after much pleading and arguing, a clown is induced to enter the box. The door is closed and the huge iron block falls with an attendant explosion. The door of the box bursts open and four little midgets run out. The big clown, taking the part of Adam, of course, remains in the box unseen and is carried off with the box.

THE HANLONS

THIS FAMOUS Hanlon Brother team of clowns would be granted a diploma in any school of medicine as "Doctors of Mirth." They have put on clown steam and produced laughter for decades. (Hanlon has been a familiar name in circusdom since 1847.) Fred and Will Hanlon practice one hour each day in front of a mirror getting different effects of pantomime. "The mouth, nose, and the eyes are the cornerstones of pantomime" according to the Hanlons. In these mirror reflections they experiment with different and varied emotions — ways of expressing fear, doubt, sorrow, surprise, joy, anger, disappointments, enthusiasm, and many other physical reactions. We are indebted to Arthur Kanter for his fine article on the Hanlons.

76. EMMETT KELLY AND JACK LECLAIR

77. ERNIE BURCH

78. FELIX ADLER

79. GEORGE L. FOX

80. JOEY GRIMALDI

81. JULES TOUNOUR

82. FRANK "SLIVERS" OAKLEY

FRANK OAKLEY (SLIVERS).
America's Favorite Clown.
Oakley has revolutionized clowning and has made it an art.—*New York World*.

83. EMMETT KELLY

84. EMMETT KELLY, CIRCUS IMMORTAL

85. LOU JACOBS — "BELLS IN HIS BELFRY"

86. PAUL JUNG

87. FELIX ADLER
AND HIS GOOSE

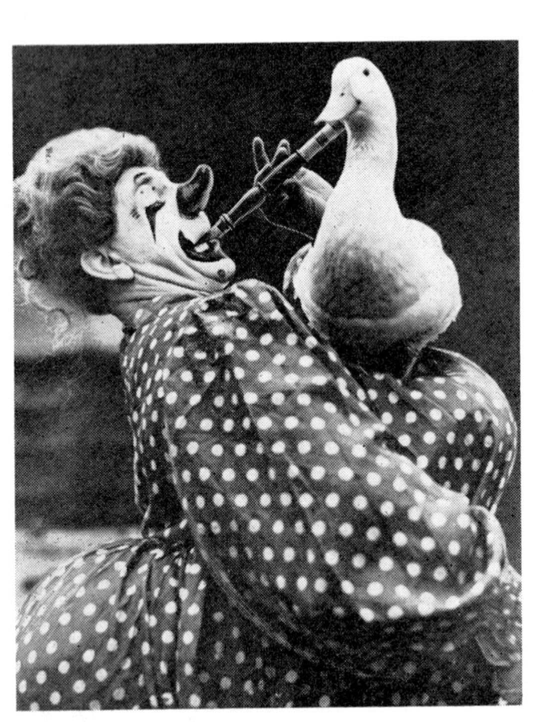

88. CHARLIE BELL AND PEANUTS

89. FRED AND WILL HANLON

90. PAUL JEROME AND HIS NEON NOSE

91. ARTHUR BEASON

CHARLIE BELL and PEANUTS

OR SHOULD PEANUTS be given a separate billing? This highly cooperative act is a sure-fire hit with the children, and it never loses its appeal to the oldsters. It is accomplished about four times in going around the arena. Charlie Bell has trained many dogs, but Peanuts seems to be his favorite. Peanuts, wearing huge rabbit ears, does some "tall" planning and fooling. On entering the arena, Peanuts manages to cut across and get quite a distance in front of Charlie Bell, who is stalking, gun in hand, looking for big game. All of a sudden, not very far in front of him, he spies a rabbit, sitting up straight. He shoots – his aim is good and Peanuts falls dead. Charlie prances up quite elated and proud of his kill, puts the rabbit (Peanuts) into his hunting bag, which is a large cloth sack, and patting himself on the chest, swings the large bag over his shoulder. The sack has a hole in the bottom. Peanuts drops out, and quickly sneaking a quarter of the way around the arena, again sits up, ears erect, and awaits the unsuspecting Charlie Bell, the successful big game hunter.

Charlie is elated when he sees another big rabbit. He shoots – Peanuts falls, and the whole clever act is repeated.

LOU JACOBS

HOW TRUE IT IS when the circus publicity man says, "When there are bigger grins in Clown Alley, Lou Jacobs will make them"; and he might predict that when bigger shoes are worn, Lou will wear them. Lou insists that he puts bells on his belfry to keep away the bats. Lou has been very successful through many years of buffoonery, and when it comes to getting up grotesque garbs, he possesses absolute genius.

One of Lou's most applauded stunts, puzzling to young and old alike, is when he gets out of his midget, or as he calls it, infant car. As the little car pulls up under its own power and halts in front of the grandstands, everyone is curious. Then as long, lean, lank Lou unfolds and steps out, Oh's! and Ah's! are heard throughout the audience. No sooner does someone remark, "How did he get out of there?" — when someone else asks, "Well, how in the wide world did he ever get in?" After a few worried antics as to the welfare of his car, as though wondering why it had stopped, Lou gets in and drives off very unconcerned, seemingly unaware that anyone has been watching him.

PAUL JEROME

PAUL JEROME, one of the top-flight fun-makers in the Clown Alley of R.B.B.&B. Circus, was, at one time, a burlesque comedian. This switch from stage to circus and from circus to stage is not unusual.

Paul Jerome is known to millions as the "neon clown." He wears an artificial nose which is connected with a battery; as he ambles and shuffles around the ring, he can light up his nose at will, as well as the neon heart which he wears outside his clothes just above his own big heart. Many young girls, old maids, and grandmothers have blushed with apparent ease when Paul would stop, beam and gleam with adoring eyes at them, and then, breathing audibly, light up his big red neon heart with love at first sight.

His huge collar and safety pin have become a trademark.

Paul Jerome has been with R.B.B.&B. Circus for twenty-seven years. Circus statisticians estimate that he has made 120 million people laugh.

BOBBY CLARK

BOBBY CLARK, well-known stage comedian, and his partner, the late Paul MacCullough, were circus clowns for many years. When they first joined the circus, Joe E. Brown was in a flying act called "The Casting Ashtons," and a pair named Wooley and Piers had an aerial bar act with a net underneath it. Clark says they left the net up at night and he slept in it. "The makeshift of my makeshift-beauty-rest made me look like a waffle and amused everyone, so perhaps my pattern for clowning was settled even then."

Clark says the best compliment to his and MacCullough's clowning came when they were ordered to stop working in front of the bandstand because their gags made the musicians laugh so hard that they couldn't play.

At the end of Clark's first year with Ringling Circus, he had sixteen pieces of luggage, though by contract, each clown was allowed only one 24-inch trunk. Mr. Al Ringling told Clark, "Bobby, you'll have to cut down on the luggage if you want to come back." Clark replied, "You're going to bill the show as 'bigger and better' aren't you, Mr. Ringling?" Ringling said he most assuredly was. "Well, how can you do that if you cut down on my luggage?" Mr. Al laughed and said, "All right, I'll see you next year."

Menagerie

WILD ANIMALS

GARGANTUA AND TOTO

THE GORILLA BABIES

SEA LIONS

ELEPHANT TRAINERS

SIDE SHOWS

HOUDINI

MIDGETS

VENTRILOQUISM

CHANG & ENG

CIRCUS TOWN U.S.A.

G.I. CIRCUSES

THE HARRY HERTZBERG CIRCUS COLLECTION

CECIL B. DeMILLE

The Greatest Show on Earth

and many, many others ☞

The Menagerie

The menagerie is far more interesting to the smaller children than are the circus acts; and the animals are remembered by them much longer. It is entertaining and educational for grownups, and to the adult mind the menagerie has a scientific and biological appeal. The menagerie joined hands with the circus when they were both in their cradle days, and they have advanced and grown simultaneously, sharing the same vicissitudes and the same triumphs.

GARGANTUA AND TOTO

JOHN NORTH, Roland Butler, and Frank Braden have become known as the "Ringling News Geyser" on account of their terriffic wire barrages, news coverage, and picture displays which encircle the globe. All of this experience and talent was used with the bang of dynamite when Gargantua the Great, the mighty gorilla, "The Earth's Most Terrifying Living Creature," walked upon the scene. The stories of Gargantua, and later, of Toto, are the greatest circus features the world has ever known.

According to the following biographical sketches of these gorillas given by J. Bryan III, the pre-circus lives of each bear striking similarities.

Gargantua weighed but thirty-five pounds when the master of a freighter bought him from a missionary in late 1932. Buddy was his name, and he soon became the ship's pet. Just before docking, the master went to find Buddy, so they might have their daily romp. He was sitting in a corner whimpering. A disgruntled sailor had thrown acid on him; his face and chest were burned raw, his eyes were swollen, and he was almost blind. The master of the ship had paid $400 for him in Africa and had hoped to get $3000 for him in New York, since he was such a fine specimen. The acid ruined these hopes. He sold Buddy, a sick gorilla, and six chimpanzees for $2500.

Buddy's new owner was a Mrs. Gertrude Lintz of Brooklyn, New York. She had been successful in raising other animals, so she decided to try a gorilla. She secured the aid of a young German, Richard Kroener, as Buddy's keeper.

Mittens were fastened on Buddy's hands so he could not scratch his deeply-burned face, chest, and eyes. Although he was given every care and medical attention, it was six months before the burns were healed, but scars were left — a long one on the left side of his chest; and facial scars which drew his lips into a sneer. He was friendly with Mrs. Lintz and Kroener, seeming to realize that they were helping him. His self-respect was developed when she had him wear overalls during his school hours, or training. As long as she held his hand, he would, very happily, walk upright, but not one step otherwise. She decided on some training strategy. She filled his hands with peanuts and placed a banana under each armpit, then she walked across the room and called him. He stood a minute, and she could tell he was definitely thinking just what would be the best course to pursue. He decided it would be wiser to walk erect than drop the food he liked so well. He seemed to comprehend exactly what was expected of him. From that time on, whenever he was dressed, he walked erect. Certainly this behavior showed a composite pattern of thought; he realized the food was definitely connected with his walking upright, and the clothes completed the whole idea in his mind. It was evident that he was very proud of himself. In order to increase this feeling of superiority, Mrs. Lintz had some shoes made for him with metal taps on them so he could hear himself walk. Now this really did develop his ego.

By the end of the year, Buddy readily understood a number of Mrs. Lintz's commands: "Put on your clothes"; "Get your kiddie car"; "Bring me a banana." Mrs. Lintz accidentally fell upon a unique way of securing obedience. All she had to do was point a Chinese mask at him and say, "Look out! It's the bogey man!" and Buddy obeyed immediately. Later she obtained the same results by using a doll head and someone suggested that perhaps he noted a resemblance between the red and white face of the doll and the African bat, also with red and white face, which is greatly feared by all animals.

Buddy was ill-fated. In 1936, Mrs. Lintz had carried him to Florida for the winter. A house boy, whom she had discharged, gave him a glass half filled with sugar syrup and half with disinfectant. The effect on Buddy was the same as acute poisoning. For five weeks he could not retain a meal, and he lost eight pounds in weight.

Although Buddy had reached the weight of 400 pounds,

Mrs. Lintz did not realize the danger until one day she saw him stroke his pet kitten on the head, crushing its brains in the process. There seemed no alternative; he was put in a cage. He resented this confinement. He seemed puzzled, dazed, not understanding why he should be punished.

One night a terrific thunderstorm came and Mrs. Lintz was awakened by the lightning and thunder. She heard the knob on her door turn, quietly — easily, and then the pad of bare feet. Buddy was there by her bed. His rough fingers were laid on her shoulder. He was seeking, in his fright, that friendly, trusting, leading hand. She called, "Buddy, let's go get a banana." She slipped out of bed, held his hand, and they walked downstairs. He whimpered and shivered whenever the lightning flashed or thunder pealed. Someone had carelessly failed to snap the padlock on his gate, and so he found his way out easily when he became frightened. She coaxed him into his cage with a bowl of fruit.

By morning Mrs. Lintz had decided the time had come when she must part with Buddy, as much as she hated to give him up. She told Kroener her decision and they discussed the matter. Kroener suggested that she wire John Ringling North. North came at once, and in a short time had closed a deal, paying Mrs. Lintz $10,000 for Buddy and two chimpanzees, and Mr. Kroener agreed to go with North as Buddy's keeper. The sale was an excellent stroke of business luck for both parties.

North immediately gave Buddy a more impressive, awe-inspiring name — Gargantua — so named after a giant, a character in a book by Francois Rabelais. To John North, Gargantua was worth his weight in silver, if not in gold. He made exciting news each day, and with the Ringling Circus publicity so precision-geared, it was channeled so that the whole world listened. Gargantua reacted to all this conversation and publicity about him by having less to say than a clam on a windy day.

After a few years of exhibition and sizzling news wires, North bought a prospective mate for him, the tantalizing Toto. She was quite a bit smaller, and was quiet in manner, and had a better disposition than Gargantua. Then came a master stroke of showmanship — the world-famous wedding of Toto and Gargantua at Sarasota, Florida. The bride and groom pictures appeared in magazines and papers around the globe.

No expense had been spared in the building of Gargantua's air-conditioned castle-on-wheels; and now a duplicate was ordered for Toto, each costing $20,000. Pictures of the bride's and groom's castles created endless comment and publicity.

Toto's life had been very much like Gargantua's — she had twice escaped death by accident — she was also the pet of a rich woman who had no children. And, when North bought her, the same provision was included, namely, that her keeper go with her. Toto's life story begins in 1932, when Mr. and Mrs. Kenneth Hoyt were hunting big game in the Belgian Congo. Mr. Hoyt shot a very large male gorilla. Immediately five leaderless and frightened females were speared by the natives for food. They were skinning the last of these when they took an infant, clinging to her fur. The baby was too skinny to eat; and so they said to Mr. Hoyt, *"Memsehib, hapa ntoto."* (Mistress, here is a youngster.) Mrs. Hoyt felt sorry for the little one, so she kept it. She called the baby "Toto," or youngster, in the native tongue. The Hoyts were told that the New York winters were too severe, that the baby could not survive. By this time they had become so attached to the good-natured little one, that they moved to the warmer climate of Havana, Cuba, buying a beautiful estate there.

As Toto grew, they built for her a house with bedroom, living room and all conveniences; a keeper, Jose Tomas, was hired from Cuba. Toto's is truly a Cinderella story. It is impossible to imagine the money lavished upon her. Mrs.

Hoyt had a microphone installed in Toto's house so she could listen in to make sure of every little sound or grunt of lucky little Toto.

One afternoon in 1940, Mrs. Hoyt was playing with Toto in the garden when a friend, whom Toto did not know, came in. Toto intended to protect Mrs. Hoyt, but in pushing her to safety, or away from the visitor, she used such force that both of Mrs. Hoyt's wrists were broken. This was serious, so Mrs. Hoyt decided she must make some arrangement as to Toto's future. Again Mr. North was called and he immediately bought Toto. The price was not disclosed.

Gargantua had become more unhappy and vicious and the circus folks thought he was lonely. Surely now, with Toto there, he would calm down into settled married life and bliss.

In February, after the world-famous wedding, the two cages, Gargantua's and Toto's, were shoved end to end. Reporters and photographers had gathered. The steel doors were slid back, leaving only two iron bars between them. As a surprise to all, Gargantua made the first friendly gesture. He picked up a stalk of celery and poked it over the bar to Toto. Toto had always obeyed her keeper, so he called to her, *"Da Gargy un 'besito' ."* (Throw Gargy a kiss.) Toto did not obey. She, who had always been quiet and timid, surprised all by going into a fit of anger — she screamed, jumped up and down, pulled on the bars, gibbered, and spat. Gargantua was completely taken aback. He could not understand such a hostile reaction to his companionable move.

So the whole courtship was called off and never tried again for fear one might injure the other. Gargantua's pride was hurt — he had been lonely and wanted company. Now, having been spurned, he would shrink away to the corner of his castle, and for days at a time he seemed to brood.

However, Gargantua continued his usual way of life. Each morning he washed his face and under his arms. This was the only routine of his early training which he manifested. He never did walk erect after coming with the circus.

Dr. J. Y. Henderson, who was the circus veterinarian, gives some interesting stories in his fine book, *The Circus Doctor,* about how he and Gargantua's keeper doctored Gargantua on several occasions. Once when he was thought to have pneumonia, the vet put sulfa in his milk and cured him. On another occasion, when he was ill, the vet showed him a snake. He rushed into the small compartment of his "castle" and closed the door. The vet poked a bottle of soda water through the bars. Just as Gargantua was about to take the drink, the vet jerked it away. This he did three times. Gargantua became very angry, and then the vet switched bottles, giving him one-half full of soda water and half filled with castor oil. Gargantua gulped it down greedily and immediately realized he had been fooled. He screamed! He grabbed his large rubber tire, his favorite toy, and threw it against the wall of his cage. He jerked the bars until the vet feared he might escape.

Finally, one morning in Miami, Florida, the last show date of 1949 before the circus was due to go into winter quarters, Gargantua was found huddled in the corner of his cage, his chin relaxed on his chest, his legs stretched out in front of him, his huge arms hanging limp and his facial expression set. He drank little of the liquids offered him and he would not eat. For several days prior to this his keeper and the vet had noticed that he was not acting normally. They had watched him very closely. Before going to bed each night Gargantua was given a thick cotton blanket. As was his custom, he would spread this on the floor, and if necessary, spend a whole hour getting it smooth. He would not lie down on it if there was a single wrinkle in it. The last few days he had been careless about the wrinkles, but according to his regular morning custom, he still tore the blanket into shreds, his own original way of making up his bed. Of course, he was always given a new blanket each night.

The vet and Gargantua's keeper tried every remedy and medicine which they could, in safety, administer, but to no avail. However, good trouper that he was, he held out until after the last show of the season, and during the night death came.

Upon thorough examination, it was found that Gargantua died of lobar pneumonia, a kidney disorder, and four bad wisdom teeth, which had kept him from eating, thus contributing to his run-down condition.

Although Gargantua and Toto had lived alone, in separate cages, yet they could watch each other as their palatial cages were always stationed side by side. Now Toto grieved. Her loneliness was evident. For days she sat as though puzzled, lost in a strange world, and lonely.

THE GORILLA BABIES
Gargantua II and Mlle. Toto

JOHN RINGLING NORTH had always hoped that Gargantua and Toto would have some little babies of their own, but since that was out of the question, he decided that they should have some foster babies. It was a strange coincidence that, at the very time Gargantua was dying, two baby gorillas were on their way from their "Congo Cradle" to the Greatest Show on Earth. They were friendly, happy little ones. They were christened Gargantua II and Mlle. Toto. Gargantua II was eighteen months old when purchased, and Mlle. Toto less than a year of age.

The skilled anthropologist, Martha Hunter, was engaged

to care for the babies. If animals do react to being reared as children, with all the comforts of civilization and devoted mother-love — for Mrs. Hunter truly loves these babies — the world should learn much from this venture.

Mrs. Hunter says that if you spank a chimpanzee he will obey, but not a gorilla — he is an obstinate animal and must be controlled by affection. She explains that all monkey babies cling to their mother's fur when she jumps from limb to limb, so it is quite necessary to give them something to which they may cling, something which they can hold tightly in their hands. So the first thing she did, when taking over the care of Gargantua and Mlle. Toto, was to give each a blanket and pillow.

Mrs. Hunter was very strict about their food, both as to formula and schedule. She was successful in teaching these babies cute stunts, although their dispositions are so very different. Whenever Mrs. Hunter clapped her hands together and called to Mlle. Toto to "patty-cake," the little one did so immediately, and if there was a crowd around her cage and they laughed, Mlle. Toto obligingly did it several times. Gargantua never failed to grow jealous, getting behind his blanket and pouting. But after many tries and unlimited patience, she taught him stunts which she called upon him to do at the very minute Mlle. Toto patty-caked. Thus there was much laughter when both performed. When he realized that he too was receiving attention, he was quite happy. He would swing in a low rope swing. She would tell him to, "Stand up. Show the people what a big boy you are." He would stand up and stretch with arms above his head, to the applause of the onlookers. He would not mimic Mlle. Toto, yet she mimicked him all day. He nipped at her and she never fussed; but if she nipped him once, he whined and felt terribly mistreated. He would not let her have his toys, but he took hers. One day Gargantua fell flat and the crowd around the cage roared with laughter. He was "plenty" smart and took the cue, and after that he would fall in the same manner every time a crowd gathered.

Mrs. Hunter taught them to sit at separate little tables for their meals. Mlle. Toto's manners were always good, but the minute Mrs. Hunter's glance was turned, Gargantua took the palm of his little hand and literally pushed in all the banana his small mouth would hold. Unless they wiped their mouths with their napkins, Mrs. Hunter would not let them kiss her. They were so affectionate that they gladly cleaned their little hands and faces. She always let Gargantua kiss her first because he was jealous and she had to be very careful not to let that jealousy develop. Anyway, Mlle. Toto had such a sweet disposition that she did not mind being second. Mrs. Hunter managed to love her when Gargantua wasn't looking.

These little gorillas were so very much like children, in their manner of playing, and in their likes and dislikes. In pulling their little tin wagon, they always put something in it so there would be a rattle and racket. They, like children, were much more interested in watching children than in watching grownups. They were energetic, intelligent, lovable, and most interesting. There was always a large crowd of people around their palace-cage.

Since they were on their way over to America when Gargantua died, his keeper had his cage thoroughly fumigated and freshened and all ready for the gorilla babies on their arrival. They certainly proved a stellar attraction.

MABEL STARK

MABEL STARK, considered the greatest woman cat trainer, and one of the greatest trainers of all time, must have lived so closely and intimately with the big cats that she has gained their vantage point of nine lives—or at least she has warded off nine deaths. She admits that she owes her life, at least one time, to the habit-pattern in a cat's life. She was handling the cats at the Jungle Compound, and relates, "Once I had to give a show after a heavy rain and the floor of the arena was covered with straw to give the cats a better footing. I was trying to make a young tigress take her seat when I slipped and fell. Sheik, a big Bengal, grabbed me by the thigh. His teeth sliced through the flesh and I could feel them grate on the bone. I knew my leg must be nearly severed. Then my thoughtful cage boy rattled the chute door. That's the signal for the cats to leave the arena. Sheik promptly dropped me and ran for the exit. Then he remembered me and turned back. But by that time I was on my feet again and could handle him."

Many trainers contend that the smell of blood makes a cat vicious. This belief was discredited by an incident in Mabel's life. During her early circus days, she was on a high platform when the supports gave way and the platform collapsed. In falling, Miss Stark was hit in the head and rendered unconscious. When she came to, the lion she was training was standing beside her licking the blood from her cuts.

Mabel Stark is small of stature, five feet, two inches, a blonde. She was only seventeen years of age when she started training cats, and she was considered by many old-timers as, "The Child Wonder." She played the feature role in the filming of her autobiography, the name of the picture being, "Hold That Tiger."

Through all of her training years she has insisted that kindness and patience are the greatest requisites in the successful training, not only of cats, but of all animals, wild or tame.

We eagerly await the biography of Mabel Stark. Training cats is her occupation. She loves the work, and her tigers and her circus public love her in return, and have granted her an honored niche in the annals of circusdom.

ALFRED COURT

ALFRED COURT is acclaimed as the world's greatest wild animal trainer of all time. He was born in Marseille, France.

After several circus ventures, he risked all in the world he had on wild animals. In 1924, his Zoo Circus had the greatest zoological collection in France. He soon gained wide-spread fame as a trainer of wild animals and he also trained men who wanted to make a profession of training wild animals. Alfred Court never used any of the tricks of showmanship which are sometimes used by trainers to impress the audience. He proved that kindness in manner and voice soothe an animal and that patience can accomplish wonders.

Court contended that a jungle-born animal could be trained in much less time than a cage-bred animal. This is because the wild animal never loses his fear of man, while the one in the cage has become accustomed to man, almost contemptuous of him. Once in a while, a cat will take pleasure in mastering many tricks. Court declared that such rareties are truly, "Jungle Geniuses." Young lions will imitate their elders when allowed to watch them perform. When a lion growls or snarls he may be in a very good humor, but when he puts his ears back and seems to pout, then he is dangerous. Cats are especially restless in rainy weather — they detest mud.

Alfred Court was very particular and exacting as to the food his actors received. He was always sure there was not a speck of sawdust or trash on the feeding floor. Cats are easy prey to indigestion.

Court was most renowned for his mixed animal acts — the most difficult and dangerous of all. For his master act, he put three polar bears, two black bears, eight lions, two leopards, two tigers, a jaguar, two wolves, and two dogs together in the same cage. This was the greatest wild animal act of all time. Although all performers were natural enemies, all performed tricks. This was "super" in the realm of animal training.

DAMOO DHOTRE

DAMOO DHOTRE learned a great deal about animals from the famed Alfred Court. He is a good showman and an excellent trainer himself. He agrees with others that training a wild animal is one thing but taming it is another — that there is no such thing as a wild animal tamer. A man in a cage is there by the kind permission of the animal. Damoo never strikes an animal nor uses a gun. His theory is that animals soon learn to respect a man, and they must never fear him. He says that if Sheba, one of the leopards in his act, "snarls a sneer," he does not mind her snarl since he considers it a "fair challenge to battle, but when I spot her smirking, I know that I must get ready for a sneak attack." Damoo explains that a trainer learns the facial expressions of his animals and what these expressions mean. He insists that wild animals demand, and deserve, a certain amount of respect, since they are themselves intelligent and dignified.

Damoo Dhotre has a beautiful spotted leopard named Sonya. When his circus act is finished all the animals are turned back into their animal cages except Sonya. Damoo throws down his little training quirt-like whip and spreads out his arms to Sonya. She steps down from her pedestal, stands erect on her hind feet in front of Damoo, puts her forearms around his neck, her chin on his shoulder, and together they make a friendly exit.

He often carries Sonya draped around his shoulders as a fur neckpiece. Another of his famous cats, Negus, a 170-pound black jaguar, warms his neck and shoulders in this manner.

Tom O. Inabinette, well-known trainer, always insists, "Lions can be trained, not tamed."

SEA LIONS

SEA LIONS, in circus language, are "Sugar Babies," not because they eat sugar but because they can always be counted upon to do their best, and also, to keep their eyes on the fish payoffs. Mr. F. Beverly Kelley tells us many things about these sleek, intelligent creatures who work on the reward system. They are very shy, and if scolded severely, they may refuse to perform for a week. Trainers realize their prima donna temperaments, and are very gentle and loving with them.

Sea lions are agile, and though by nature they are "Wonder Equilibrists," they require a long process of patient training before they balance the large colored ball with such ease. When playing the wind instruments, a sea lion seems to strain every muscle that he may get the precision of the note.

Roland Tiebor, with R.B.B.&B. Circus, who has one of the greatest sea lion acts ever seen under the Big Top, explains that you must talk to a seal, that he not only understands words but entire sentences. He explains that they are trained for twenty minutes at a time twice a day – if trained longer, they become irritable, and bite. (Since it requires three weeks to train one not to bite, certainly care should be taken not to irritate one into biting.)

Three years of patient training are required to teach a seal to do the handstand on one flipper. When the sea lion applauds himself, it looks as though it were spontaneous but it has taken months of training to perfect this self-encore stunt. F. Beverly Kelley points out that sea lions *roark;* they do not roar. And when one roarks in anger, fast talk and faster footwork is required to avoid that bite.

The salt water in the circus seal tank is kept at 65°. Once in a while, seals are allowed a dip in fresh water. On one occasion, Mr. Kelley tells us, Tiebor allowed his seals to go for a frolic in a nearby swimming pool. They went immediately to the deep end of the pool, sank to the bottom, and stayed there, one or two at a time surfacing for air. Time came to return to the circus, and Tiebor tried every known entreaty to coax them from the pool. Finally, in desperation, he started back to the show. All of a sudden he heard excited roarking, and there were his seals bouncing along after him, afraid he was leaving them.

Roland Tiebor terms Frisco his "glamor girl." She is a seal clown and seems thoroughly to enjoy "gumming up the works." As soon as musical seal Dolly has played an orthodox rendition of "America," Frisco gallops up and saucily does it in swing-time. She applauds herself on every turn, applauds for the others, and really smiles while she is clapping.

The most interesting of all Tiebor's lions was Sparky, who literally "knew his way around." Tiebor had only to show him the passages and stairs in theaters one time, and after that Sparky could lead the troupe without ever making a false turn. Sparky was a rope-walking sea lion and, as he was growing old, Tiebor had trained another seal to take his place. However, when the moment came for Sparky's act, he would quickly "shoulder the understudy" aside and do his own rope-walking act. These feats – the rope-walking, his eagerness to do his own act, and his accurate sense of direction in finding his way around, were all the more interesting and truly amazing to those who knew Sparky, because, says Mr. Kelley, Sparky was stone-blind!

ALBERT RIX AND HIS "BRAINY BRUINS"

PERHAPS NO OTHER MAN is better acquainted with the "bear necessities" of life than Albert Rix, and Daniel P. Mannix has explored his career thoroughly in his *White Tops* article. Rix has spent more than twenty years in the "schoolroom with his furry pupils." He says that all depends on the mentality of the individual bear. As to his ability to learn – some never learn, some are patient pupils and learn some things, while others grasp an idea immediately. Most bears seem to have the same type of memory as is accredited an elephant – they never forget. They have a high rating as to animal intelligence. Once a bear learns his act, he seems to enjoy his work thoroughly.

The head-stand seems the easiest stunt for a bear to learn. To teach one to walk upright is the hardest task of all, requiring about three months' training. The 500-pound brown bear, Tommy, gives the most intellectual and impressive performance of all the Rix group. He walks upright – very erect – continuously from the beginning to the end of the act, at all times towering over seven feet in height, and does indeed give the impression that he is the director of the entire act, and that Rix is there only to carry out his orders. He wears a most agreeable smile all the time he is in the ring. He claps his paws in the most appreciative manner whenever an act is completed. This seems to be his own idea of boosting his teammates, as well as, in a most affable manner, reminding the audience that applause is justly due. Every so often during the act, he goes to Rix and seems to whisper in his ear just what the next stunt will be, kissing and licking Rix's ear affectionately at the same time. Rix admits that this insistent kissing habit of Tommy's is, at times, a little upsetting. There is always the possibility that Tommy may become too amorous and bite off an ear.

Rix uses many gallons of fish oil during the year keeping his bears' fur glossy and in excellent condition. He is gentle, kind, and most patient with them. He works on the reward system – 160 lumps of sugar are required at each performance to "sweeten their bearish dispositions." During training, the bear is rewarded with his favorite foods: sugar, grapes, bananas, apples, lettuce and milk. The first trick a bear usually learns is to drink milk from a bottle.

The bear is, by far, the most difficult of all wild animals to train. (The black leopard is thought by many to be an equally difficult pupil.) The bear is not quick-tempered, but when he is aroused to anger or hatred, his aim is death. The disposition of a bear cannot be trusted. He gives no warning. Once a bear sets his teeth in a victim it is impossible to prize lose or unwedge his jaws, as he is equipped with mortised teeth.

ELEPHANT TRAINERS

A LIST of the well-known elephant trainers would be far too long to be given here, for there have been many famous ones: George (Papa) Denman, probably the best-known of all; Cheerful Gardner; Walter McClain; Larry Davis; Arthur Huff; Baptist Schrieber, and many others.

One of the best-known elephants of all circusdom was Old John. He was the favorite of George Denman all during the years that Denman was with the circus. Old John was almost human, so great was his wisdom, intelligence, and reasoning ability. A flaw was never found in his disposition — he seemed always eager to please, self-sacrificing, and patient. In his youth, Old John was called John L. Sullivan on account of a boxing act in which the old elephant became famous. He wore a glove on his trunk and kept his clown opponent very busy defending himself. It was a superb clown act. Old John died in 1931 at the age of seventy, in Sarasota, Florida — a sudden and natural death. Many stories are told of the unusual and devoted friendship which existed between Denman and Old John. George Denman and Old John have become a legendary pair.

Another well-known trainer was the late Cheerful Gardner; articles on his success in handling elephants have appeared in national magazines. The act which all children, and grownups as well, seemed to enjoy most was Cheerful's plank-walking elephant. Each end of a narrow plank, not as wide as the elephant's foot, was placed on a stool. The elephant would walk across, turn on the stool, then walk halfway back, stop, turn completely around on this narrow plank, and return to the stool. At the time of Gardner's death in Los Angeles, in 1952, Cheerful was Dean of the Elephant Trainers, according to well-known circus writer, Harry Quillen. He was sixty-eight years of age. As is the old custom, "sawdust was sprinkled in his grave; and his military suit, brownie belt, and red-ribboned cap were buried with him."

Walter McClain, another capable elephant trainer, always seemed to be partial to baby elephants. Larry Davis was especially interested in the pigmy elephants. Arthur Huff and Yasso were star performers, Yasso being the elephant in whose mouth Huff placed his head, allowing Yasso to carry him, pendulum-like, around the ring. Huff's great love for Yasso was similar to that of Papa Denman for Old John.

It is said that Wallace Beery, an elephant trainer and later a movie star, started the "Tail-up," trunk-to-tail formation of elephants. Each elephant holds the tail of the elephant in front of him with his trunk – this helps to keep them in line and also keeps their trunks out of mischief.

(See story on Tillie, considered by many as the best elephant actor of all time – page 21.)

MASCOTS
NEGRESS

A BOOK ON THE CIRCUS would not be complete without saying something about the mascots and pets carried by the circus folks. Special emphasis is given by the management of all circuses to the family life of the personnel. The North brothers, with 1400 members of their "big traveling family," R.B.B.&B. Circus, make every effort to attain domestic happiness and home atmosphere. However, the mascot accompaniment of the Greatest Show on Earth was reaching such an unwieldy size — several hundred, and growing — that this "mascot-home-touch" had to be curtailed. One can imagine the extra rail accommodations required for transportation, to say nothing of the extra amount of food, and the attending confusion. Tiny Mr. Bigety, toy terrier, was forever picking a fuss with Lop Ear, a mongrel, just as much beloved by his owner; or the parrot, Busybody, who had learned the names of many of the actors, would call them, delaying them when they were in a hurry.

But Negress, the dog guard, was needed. He has always been a most popular mascot, yet he is different. He is a worker. Three hundred men who work with the animals or around the R.B.B.&B. menagerie tent and at the animal house in Sarasota, claim Negress as their mascot. Mr. Blackie Barlow, the assistant animal superintendent, claimed that Negress should have the animal spotlight, as it is the duty of Negress to guard all the animals. And he does not stay off duty night or day. He rushes to the cookhouse, gets his packaged supper, and comes back immediately, eating while on the job.

One day, according to Mr. Barlow, Negress stood very still and quiet for a long time, watching the elephants pull the ropes which hoisted the Big Top. Then, all of a sudden, he rushed over like a streak of lightning, grabbed the end of a rope and started pulling. He has been helping to raise the Big Top at every stop since that day.

Negress has crossed the United States several times, and has visited in every city of importance. He is the perfect watchdog, making the rounds of all the cages and animals at intervals, and reporting quickly if all is not well. He is a medium-sized fox terrier, but a bundle of nerve and courage. He ignores small dogs — merely gives barking orders to dogs of his size — but "goes for" any large dog found meddling around his animals.

SIDE SHOWS

PRACTICALLY ALL side show managers are talented talkers. They are usually prepossessing in appearance, sonorous of voice, and employ humorously dramatic and alliterative delivery in its most highly effective forms. They are, as a rule, called professors or doctors. They are also known as orators, barkers, spielers, grinders — most any name which denotes talking.

The side show ticket-seller keeps up a continual chatter to attract attention. The larger side show, as a rule, has a band which is brought out at intervals, making what is called "an opening." Drums beat, all hands shout and beckon, and the ballyhoo is "on." At the proper time, silence descends, and the orator starts his discourse on the wonders inside the tent, which are depicted on the "bannerline" — the canvas or paper advertisements, usually placed overhead.

A turnaway crowd from the big show is an ideal setup for the side show and the outside stands. Usually, under these promising conditions, the "openings" are short, for there are many people on the midway eager to spend money. The slogan of Old Yankee Robinson, great showman, "Get 'em in, and get 'em out," has become a byword among circus people, and they work hard and unceasingly to carry it out.

When there are small, indifferent crowds, the spieler is more enthusiastic, the band plays longer, some of the freaks are brought outside for a sample exhibit. On occasions when the band starts playing immediately after the orator finishes, a half-dozen or so "cappers" (people connected with the show — stooges, as it were, to lure in the patrons) push forward and purchase tickets, in an effort to start the crowd going inside, but this procedure is not needed with first-class attractions, as a rule.

The side show bands soon took on the minstrel idea, and once inside the tent the musicians doubled as minstrel performers. Many of these shows were excellent, and moved on to become vaudeville minstrels.

The four old favorite side show performances — Punch, Magic, Ventriloquism, and Marionettes, still hold their own in the side shows, but their timing is faster and they are modernized. The astounding and sometimes frightening performances of sword swallowers continue to be a platform standby. Mentalists and fortunetellers have been, and still are, of great variety and interest. Fire acts continue to draw crowds. These acts consist of a routine of placing fire and hot irons in contact with the flesh and in the mouth, and blowing vapors which are ignited. Bizarre appearance is usually regarded as a part of these acts.

James P. O'Connell was about the first tattooed exhibit, as far back as 1835 on the old "Lion Circus." The most famous tattooed person was the Greek, George Costenteus of the Barnum Show. The lecturer had a rare story about this man, of the torture inflicted by savages doing the work of tattooing.

From the time the early museums started, when the large snakes were imported to this country, there have been many snake charmers with the side shows — Hindus with trained cobras, beautiful ladies with twenty-foot pythons, which they allow to coil about them; Indians handling rattlesnakes. Showmanship plays a great part in a snake charmer's success.

Sword-ladder walkers are an unusual side show attraction — walking on broken glass, sharp nails, etc. There have been many legitimate exhibits of genuine wild people — genuine natives of wild tribes. The Impalement Exhibitions are with almost every show today. A woman stands before a wooden-frame background, and a man, a number of yards away, throws knives which finally surround her body, sometimes so close as to impale her clothing.

The trained birds and animal acts were formerly more numerous in side shows than today. Strong man acts have always been a drawing card — weight-lifting, bending iron bars and horseshoes, expanding chests and breaking chains, having rocks broken on their heads, and many other such feats of strength. Glass-blowing is almost a lost art. In bygone days, it was a most popular side show attraction. The changing times have erased the once-popular glass ship on the mantlepiece. Dancing and music remain a "good bet" to "draw." Oriental dancers, also Egyptian, Persian, Hindu, and Hawaiians with their hulas, have all been, and still are, popular.

Other side show attractions are varied; harpoon exhibition and lectures on whaling; needle eating; human ostriches who swallow almost anything; bird and animal imitators; trick top spinners; jugglers; wrestlers; jig and clog dancers; illusion and black top acts; in fact, almost every form of entertainment has found its way into the side show.

Very seldom is a repulsive act shown. All the side show managers require their freaks to give an act such as singing, dancing, or an exhibition of other talents, if it is at all possible, which adds greatly to their "draw."

In the Spence-Bradna book, *The Big Top,* an interesting story is told about Roland Butler, publicity whirlwind with R.B.B.&B. — how he drew nation-wide attention to the two mopheads, "Iko and Eko, the Men from Mars." There was a convention in progress in New York — the "National Convention of Hairdressers," at the Hotel Astor. Butler "equipped his prodigies with big hats and sat them in the front row of the convention hall. He then rushed away to summon press photographers. As the convention president rapped his gavel to start the day's proceedings, Eko and Iko removed their hats and allowed their monstrous hair to be photographed against a background of well-groomed stylists." (Good advertising for all concerned.)

Almost all of the freaks are conscious of their deformities, and do not go out much. They "pal" among themselves. An added reason is the fact that they do not want the public to see them free. They eat before the other personnel of the circus, since they start their show long before the main circus begins. They work as often as the crowd warrants.

And so the side show is still with us today, and we hear the barker's cacophony — "Hurry! Hurry! Hurry!"

HOUDINI

THE GREAT HOUDINI, the best-known and most famous of all magicians, was born in 1874. His real name was Enrich Weiss, but he took the name Harry Houdini, after the French magician, Houdin. He was honest as to his work and he went out of his way to expose fraudulent mediums. He had published several most interesting books: *Handcuff Secrets, Unmasking Robert Houdin,* and *A Magician among the Spirits.* He lived in Appleton, Wisconsin, where his father was a rabbi.

Houdini was known as the "Handcuff King," so successful was he in freeing himself of all types of handcuffs securely locked. He invented the water torture act — the magician must escape from a water-filled and sealed box before his breath gives out. From this most difficult feat, he became known as "The Escape Artist." He gave public demonstrations of escape from strait jackets, iron safes, jails, all kinds of handcuffs, from sealed boxes dropped in the river, a grave, — though not his own. (He and his wife had worked out a plan whereby, should one die, the other could contact the deceased. It is said that she complied with his wish for many years, following every detail of procedure — but it never worked.)

Houdini had developed the muscles of his abdomen to such a degree of expansion, hardness, and strength, that a person could hit him as hard as he wished without effect. One morning a man came up to Houdini and asked, "Is it true that a man may hit you as hard as he can and it will not faze you?" The two words, "It is," had barely escaped Houdini's lips when the man hit him suddenly and viciously, not giving Houdini a chance to expand, or tense, his muscles. Houdini said he had no idea the man was going to hit him.

That same evening in 1926, Houdini performed one of his most famous tricks — allowed himself to be put in a casket filled with water, lid nailed on, and then a steel band placed around the casket, and dropped to the bottom of the river. He had done this many, many times before, and had always surfaced in just a few minutes, hale, healthy, and smiling. This day he did not come up. When the casket was drawn to the top of the water, he was dead. An autopsy revealed the location on his body of the dreadful bruise which the man had inflicted on him without warning. His appendix had been burst from the ferocious blow early that day.

MIDGETS

"PETS OF THE CIRCUS," and "Dolls of the Sawdust," are names which literally belong to the midgets. They are general favorites, privileged characters, and usually are very mild-tempered and affable. These diminutive little people are, as a rule, very immaculate as to personal appearance and dress.

The most famous midget of all time is General Tom Thumb. (See page 49.)

Hattie Angeres, three feet, one inch, was one of the famous Singer midgets. She was born in Alszburg, Austria.

Lya Graf (Margaret Furthman) measured one foot, nine inches, at maturity. Lucia Zarate, Mexican midget, was known as the smallest of all female midgets. At the age of thirty-five, she measured a scant twenty inches in height. Fatma also measured about twenty inches.

The smallest male midget recorded is Great Peter the Small, whose height is given as nineteen inches at the age of seventeen years; he weighed six pounds and fitted into a top hat.

The best-known of all the present-day midgets are the Doll Family. They traveled with R.B.B.&B. Circus for many years, billed as early as 1933. They have retired and are now living in their lovely little house in Sarasota, Florida.

The Versatile Cucciola! This little gentleman is just that. Not only is he most interesting and entertaining as a midget, but he is an experienced actor with R.B.B.&B. Circus. He rides exceedingly well; is a good acrobat; and clowns to perfection.

The Del Rio family of midgets are an attractive trio. Chiquita, The Doll Lady, was the direct cause of a bitter court fight because she married a man with another show and went with him. She was with the Colonel Bostock Show. He lost his suit because marriage altered her contract with him.

JACK EARLE AND MAJOR MITE

JACK EARLE, whose real name was Jacob Earlich, was born in Denver, Colorado, but spent most of his life in El Paso, Texas, where his parents still reside. He weighed 385 pounds and reached a height of eight feet and seven inches, and wore size eighteen shoes. He drove from the back seat of his car—had the steering wheel built up. He was well-proportioned, extremely likable, possessed a pleasing personality and remarkable intelligence. He was very fond of midgets. He was with R.B.B.&B. Circus for a number of years.

Earle was forty-six years of age at the time of his death, 1951 or 1952. Few giants attain such an age.

Major Mite (whose real name is Clarence Chesterfield Howerton) was born in Salem, Oregon, in 1909. At twenty-five years of age he was two feet, two inches in height. He appeared with Jack Earle in the Greatest Show on Earth. He is a happy, mischievous little person and is known for "The Major Mite Grin" – from ear to ear.

THE KENTUCKY GIANTS

THE LATE Captain Martin Van Buren Bates of Lechter County, Kentucky, was one of the early circus giants. Others may have weighed more, but Captain Bates was a magnificent specimen of brawn, power, and muscle, tipping the scales at 525 pounds. His large head, perfectly proportioned, was filled with intelligence and common sense. His features were strong and clear, his eyes kind, and his heart was understanding. He possessed a photographic mind. He taught in the mountain schools before the outbreak of the War Between the States.

When war came, Martin volunteered immediately as a Confederate soldier, and served under Captain E. A. Webb. He became known as "The Kentucky Giant" and performed his duties on the field of battle so well that he was soon commissioned as a captain.

When the war was over, Kentucky was not the same. Capt. Van Buren decided that the circus offered the best for him in financial gain. After being with several small circuses, he joined the Robinson Circus at $400 per month. Later big money came. Travel, cash, new scenes, new faces, good meals, good clothes—all of these things for which he had longed when a youth in the mountains were now his, and he enjoyed life thoroughly.

The Robinson Show toured Nova Scotia. Here Bates met his mate, Anna Shannon Swan, a beautiful, well-proportioned woman, eight feet in height, one inch taller than the giant. Although John Robinson engaged Miss Swan for his circus, she and the giant were not married until later when they both had joined Barnum & Bailey Circus for a European tour. They were married in London, England.

In the meantime, Queen Victoria had met them and, impressed by their size and gentle dispositions, had presented each with a watch, with attached gold chain, costing $1000. The captain's was as large as a small pie.

These two young giants stole the show. They became renowned in every nation in which they visited. They amassed a considerable fortune and retired. Captain Bates built a beautiful house in proportion to their size—fourteen rooms, with huge doors and windows to the floor; extra tall, 14-foot ceilings. He had furniture made—a bed ten feet long and with proportionate width, and twice as high as an ordinary bed; also a dressing table for Mrs. Bates with a mirror the size of an ordinary room; and enormous chairs. These comforts made life a pleasure. Their carriage was drawn by six strong horses, and the wheels of the carriage reached almost to the second story of an ordinary house.

The Bates' had two children, Babe, weighing eighteen pounds at birth, and Sister, twenty-four pounds at birth. Both died in infancy. Captain and Mrs. Bates were people of refinement, quiet and temperate in manner, and were beloved by their townsmen.

When Mrs. Bates died, there was a three-day delay in order that a casket might be made. The captain desired to avert this delay at his death, so he had his casket made, which was "on display" long before he died. He had a carved granite statue of his wife placed above her grave. It stood twenty feet above the ground. When Captain Bates died, there was placed at the foot of his grave the Civil War Star with the number "61-65." (The photograph of Captain and Mrs. Bates, in Section IV, and a great deal of the information contained in this chapter, is reproduced through the courtesy of G. E. Ratliff, author of the column, "Big Sandy — Past and Present," which appears in the Ashland [Kentucky] *Daily Independent.*)

VENTRILOQUISM

VENTRILOQUISM is the art of producing sounds and words without any motion of the mouth, so that the sound seems to come from some other source than the person speaking. This art, or trick, does not depend on any peculiar structure of the organs of voice, but upon dexterity. The name came from the supposition that the voice comes from the stomach.

CHANG AND ENG

THE ORIGINAL and most famous Siamese twins were named Chang and Eng, or Right and Left. They were born in 1811 in Siam (now Thailand) near Bangkok.

When Chang and Eng came to America, they took the name Bunker. Later they married sisters, daughters of a farmer-preacher in North Carolina, and had twenty-two children. Their descendants have included such distinguished citizens as the president of the Union Pacific Railroad, and a major general in the U. S. Air Force, and many other highly respected citizens and taxpayers — all, without a known exception, owning their own land. They are a healthy, strong tribe — brunettes with dark eyes, heavy, black eyebrows and lashes, and frank, open countenances.

Mr. Archie Robertson has made quite a study of this

most interesting family, and has published his observations in *Life* and *Reader's Digest.* He has seen the double-sized chairs on which the original twins sat before the fires in the evenings, and the double-length gold watch chain which they wore.

Chang and Eng cut the logs and built the church where some of their descendants still worship. In chopping wood, they did not have to shift their axes; one chopped with a left slant and the other with a right. They were A-1 shots and sporting hunters, shooting only on the wing.

Mr. Robertson tells about their getting on a railroad train with only one ticket. They wore large loose coats which concealed the connecting band which was at the lower part of their chests, or breastbone. The conductor asked for their tickets, first accosting Eng; when told he didn't have a ticket, the conductor told him to get off. When Eng got up to go, of course Chang arose too. Chang protested that he had a ticket and if the railroad didn't let him ride he'd sue the railroad.

Sometimes they quarreled with each other, but let an outsider even look angry at one and he had them both to fight. On a very hot day they were on top of a wagonload of hay — started fussing — and were soon wrestling. Chang called out to Eng, "If you don't let go, I'll throw you off this wagon."

The mother of Chang and Eng (when they were quite young, before they could realize they were different) taught them to swim, run, play games and frolic, so that they would be as normal as possible, for which they were eternally grateful to her.

The twins' first job, or rather occupation, was selling preserved duck eggs which they prepared themselves, and it was a long tedious process. When they were fourteen, they gave a command appearance before the King, Roma III. He was favorably impressed with them and they also visited his seven hundred wives, from whom they received many presents. A few years later the king sent them, as a good will gesture, with an embassy to Indochina.

Later the twins traveled as an exhibition. They aroused a great deal of scientific interest. Doctors examined and studied them, especially in England, all agreeing that their nervous systems were separate, their dreams different, and that the connecting band was, in reality, a common navel. The twins were more comfortable when standing with their arms around each other, yet they could lie back to back, swim in perfect rhythm, jump, ride horseback, and enter into most activities.

They were pleasing in manner, friendly and smiling, possessing charm and gentle natures. They were very witty. Mr. Robertson tells that they always refunded half the admission price to all one-eyed people, saying such people saw only half as much, and that they offered cigars and money to people with only one arm or leg, because (they would say) they were so fortunate in having four of each.

Chang and Eng did not like the life of being considered freaks. They were businessmen, husbands and fathers, and be it said to their lasting glory that they made for themselves a respected and useful place in their community. Their father was Chinese and their mother Chinese and Siamese. They did not fit the popular conception of Orientals, but they were distinctive and individual. It was pleasing to be with them, and they were excellent conversationalists. In 1872, Chang, who had always been the more independent and progressive of the two, suffered a slight stroke. Then Eng took the initiative. They had always maintained two separate houses, so that their wives might each feel mistress in her very own home. They stayed three days and nights at one house, and then stayed exactly the same time in the other home. They never allowed anything to disrupt these set rules.

Chang's health gradually failed. He became quite deaf, was restless and melancholy. He wanted to stay up late and play games and Eng wanted to go to bed. On one particular night, Chang was feeling unusually miserable, as though he was taking pneumonia. The hour came for them to go for their three days at Eng's house, and although Eng begged Chang to stay on there in his own home and not risk getting out, Chang would not hear to such. That night Chang said he couldn't breathe, and they sat up very, very late. Finally they went to bed. Eng awakened with a most peculiar feeling. He called one of his sons and told him something was wrong. After a second, the son said, "Uncle Chang is dead." Eng called all his family and told them that he would go soon. They hurriedly summoned the doctor, that he might perform that long-desired operation which would separate them and make them free, an operation which all doctors had advised against — but now it was different. In just a few minutes Eng called out in a low voice, "May God have mercy on my soul" and was gone before the doctor arrived. A post-mortem showed that the operation, if performed, could not have been successful, for their livers were connected or associated in some way.

Chang and Eng had never been free, yet each had dreamed of freedom — physical and mental freedom, so each could live as an individual. After the death of these twins, their will was found to include a strange yet very beautiful and impressive paragraph. Part of the money of their estate was to be devoted to "Freedom." No particular object or plan was stipulated, except that "Freedom" must form a part of it. And so — the money was spent for something that has meant freedom to millions of people and will continue to guide millions more to freedom, for, with the bequest of Chang and Eng Bunker of Mount Airy, North Carolina, work was begun on the base of the Statue of Liberty, New York Harbor, United States of America.

There was an inherent greatness in these two men. The spiritual and physical adjustment which they had to make, one with the other, must have required mountains of manhood and spiritual strength. They came to a strange country, and by sheer strength of mind and soul, became a part of their beloved, adopted country — good will ambassadors from their native land.

There have been many other famous Siamese twins who have been with circuses or shows and on vaudeville tours. Best known among these are the Hilton Sisters, and the Gibb Sisters.

CIRCUS TOWN U.S.A.

GAINESVILLE IS A SMALL CITY in Texas that goes about its normal life the same as any other city. Part of the year it is just plain Gainesville, Texas, and along about April — through September — it becomes Circus Town, U.S.A. The Gainesville Circus is a professional performance put on by amateurs — just plain townspeople: the preacher, the lawyer, butcher, doctor, grocer, housewife, high school students, and younger children. This is the only organization of its kind in the world.

The Gainesville Circus came into being in the depression year of 1930, when many businesses were closing. And it was because the Gainesville Little Theater was about to close, that the Gainesville Circus was born. Mr. Morton Smith, a newspaperman, suggested holding a community circus. The idea clicked. Everyone contracted "sawdust fever." The profits in a year ran well into five figures, all of which went back into new equipment. No performer ever made one penny. They advertise, "We get our pay when the children laugh."

Starting on a shoestring with only $300, the circus grew, owning its big top, which seated several thousand, its own calliopes, performing animals, and a square block of buildings for winter quarters.

By 1953, the show had been filmed fourteen times for newsreels, had been televised, and 127 magazine articles had appeared about it.

In 1950, the State Department's Voice of America broadcast a fifteen-minute program about the circus to the Iron Curtain nations, citing it as an example of American community life. Mail has been received by the circus from many foreign countries. This circus has become world-famous.

SCHOOL CIRCUSES

EACH YEAR, the High School of Sarasota, Florida, presents the well-known "Sailor Circus." To Bill Putman, Director of Physical Education for the high school, goes the credit for the idea. Since its inception in 1950, it has grown to a position of national prominence, acclaimed both for excellency of performance and educational value. The project furnishes not only opportunity for development of highly specialized skills, but a common interest for cooperation of many departments of the school not associated directly with physical education. More than 200 students take part in the actual circus, and well over 400 participate in preparations, including advertising, publicity, art work, costumes, make-up, and properties. It has been successfully filmed.

The above is true of "Flying High," the name of the circus given annually by the Florida State University.

G. I. CIRCUSES

ALFRED S. BENDALL, JR., lieutenant colonel in the army reserves, organized four G. I. Circuses in Europe after World War II. This was done to boost morale.

Performers and acts were recruited from France, Belgium, Holland, and Germany.

All performers who were asked were eager to do their bit, asking only that their half-starved, war-rationed, performing animals would be well-fed again and restored to health.

The large, portable, Air Force hangers became the Big Tops, seating several thousand appreciative young men and boys. Some of the boys built makeshift calliopes. Pink lemonade was served free. The whole undertaking was a huge success, and time was turned backward as once more weary and homesick G.I.'s caught the happy spirit of the circus.

THE W. P. A. CIRCUS

IN 1938, there was a W.P.A. Circus which employed 375 unemployed performers.

The salary was low, only $23.86 per week, and only one person in a family could draw that, but often whole families put on an act. Many of these actors were great stars who had commanded big salaries. Yet these people, with so little recompense, these people of big hearts, gave many, many free shows for hospitals, and for crippled and underprivileged children.

Melvin Hildreth, well-known Washington, D. C. attorney, and one-time president of the C.F.A., was influential in getting the circus included in the federal theater program.

The W.P.A. three-ring circus is the only circus known to have played New York City for a period in excess of sixteen consecutive weeks. They are still going strong — after 114 weeks!

92. COLONEL NILE — SAY "AH!"

93. FAMOUS WORLD WAR II "V FOR VICTORY" POSE

94. JOE BARBETTI AND CLIFF CHAPMAN WITH BIG RUTH

95. FRANKIE SALUTO AND PRINCE PAUL

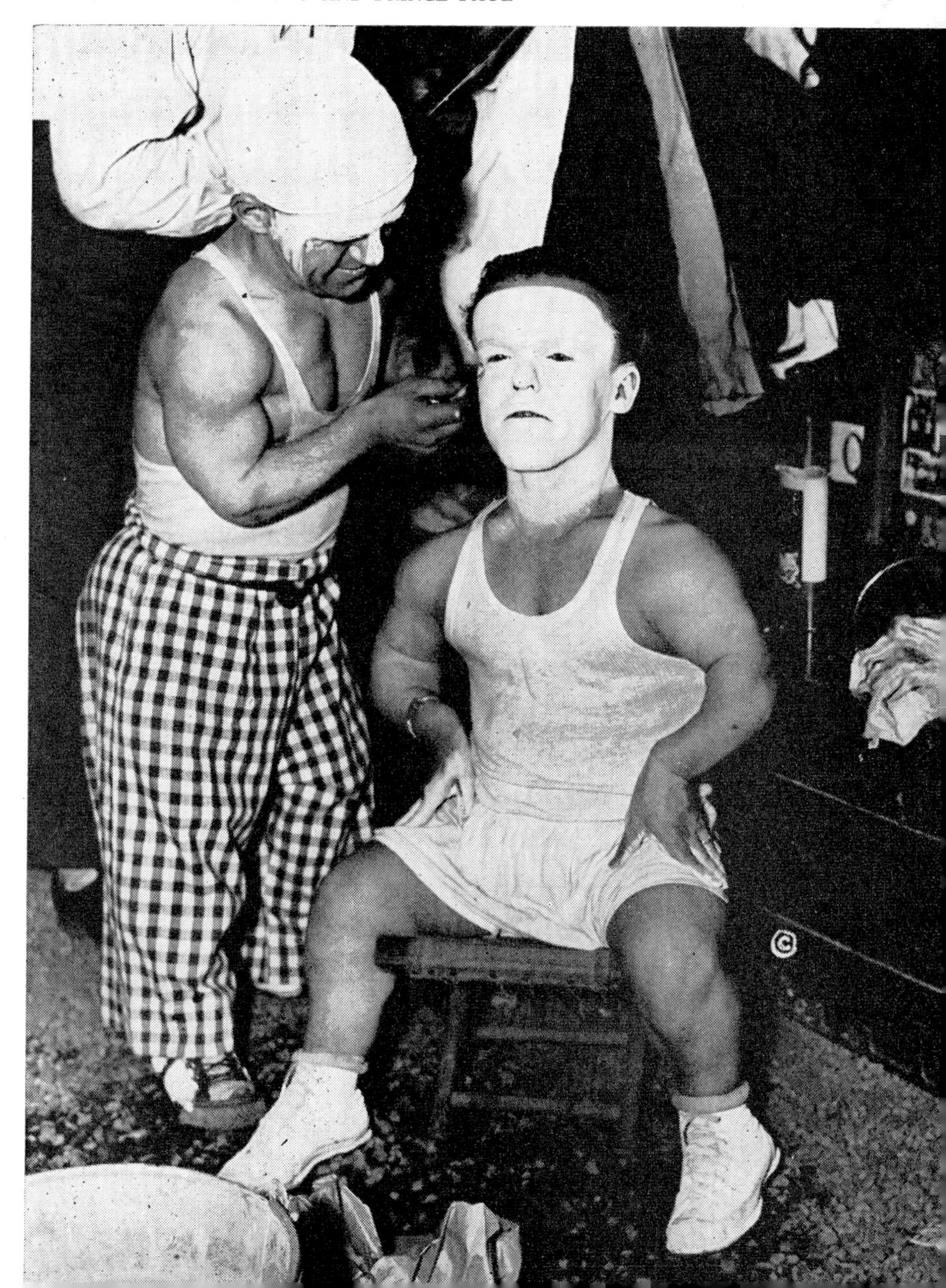

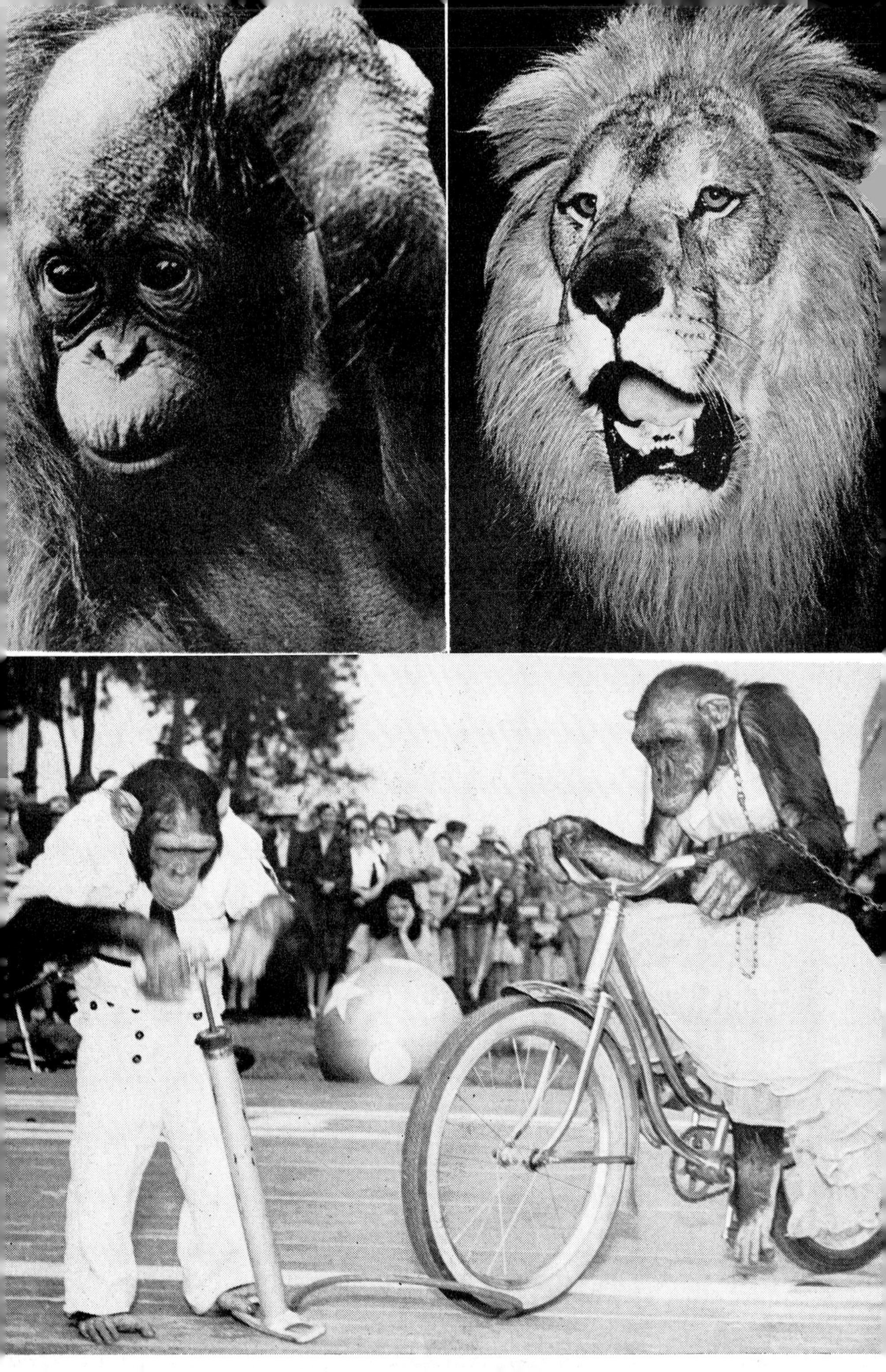

96. ADAM THE ORANGUTAN

97. PORTRAIT STUDY OF JOE

98. FIXING A FLAT

99. ROPE-WALKING TIGER

100. BIG RUTH

101. EMIR THE LEOPARD

102. PORTRAIT STUDY OF TOTO

103. MLLE. TOTO AND GARGANTUA II

104. PORTRAIT STUDY OF GARGANTUA

105. MABEL STARK AND HER FAMOUS ROPE-WALKING TIGER

106. ROLAND TIEBOR AND FRISCO

107. ALFRED COURT AND SATAN

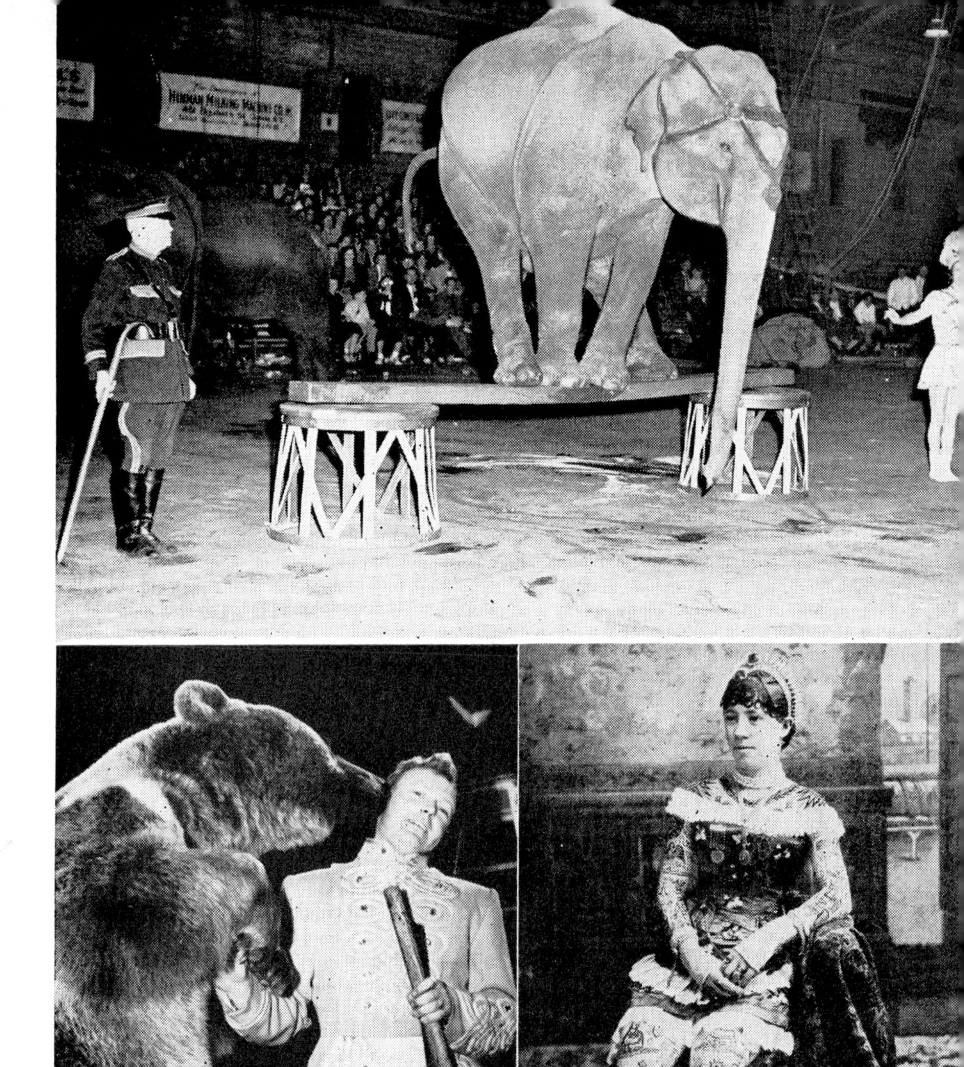

108. CHEERFUL GARDNER AND HIS PLANK-WALKING ELEPHANT

109. ALBERT RIX AND TOMMY

110. IRENE WOODWARD, WORLD'S MOST TATTOOED LADY

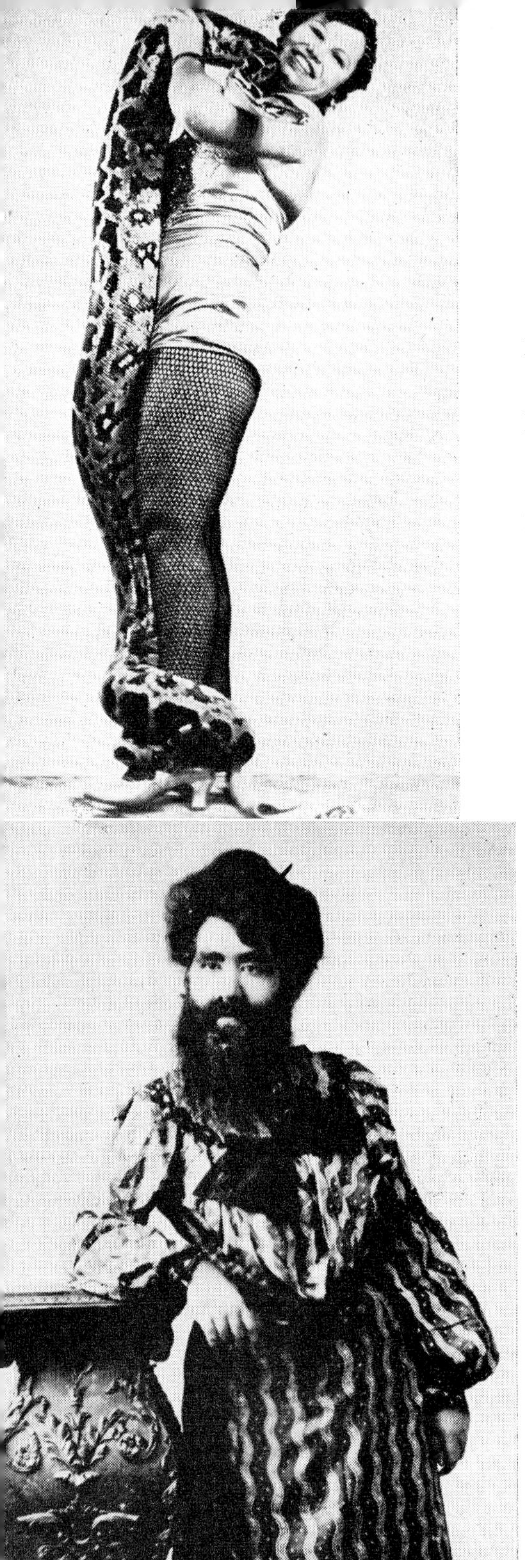

111. ADA MAE SALO

112. GRACE GILBERT,
THE BEARDED LADY

113. BABY RUTH (RUTH PONTICO)
THE FAT LADY — 815 LBS.

114. "GIRAFFE-NECK" WOMEN

115. UBANGI WOMEN

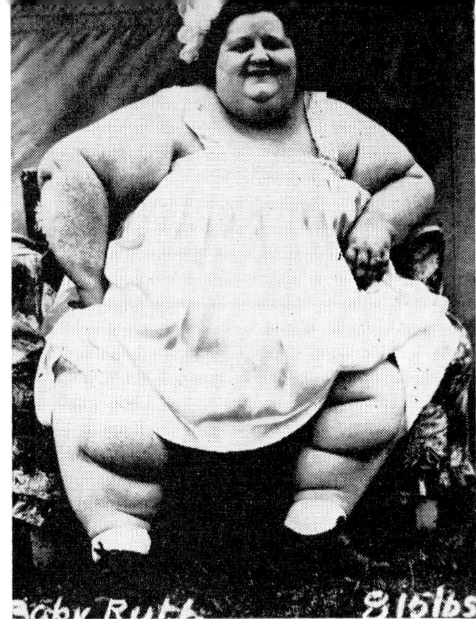
Baby Ruth
815 lbs

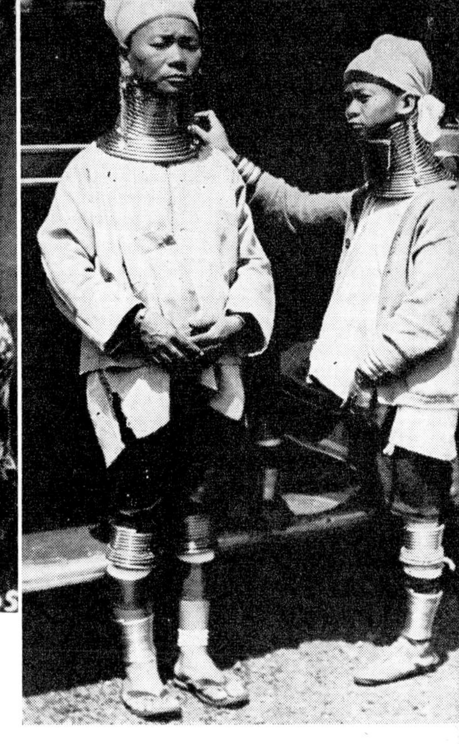

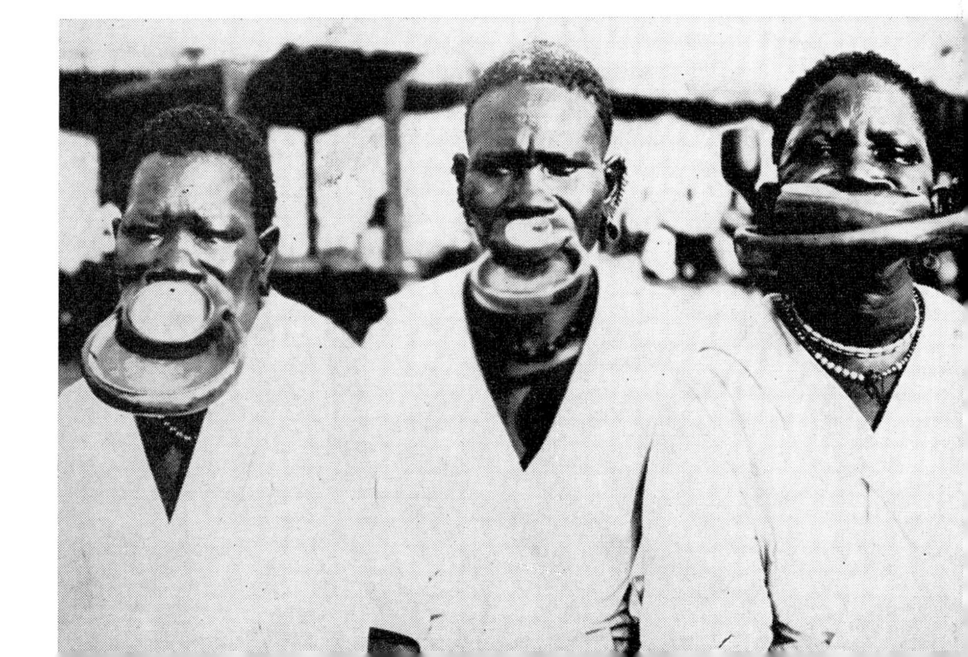

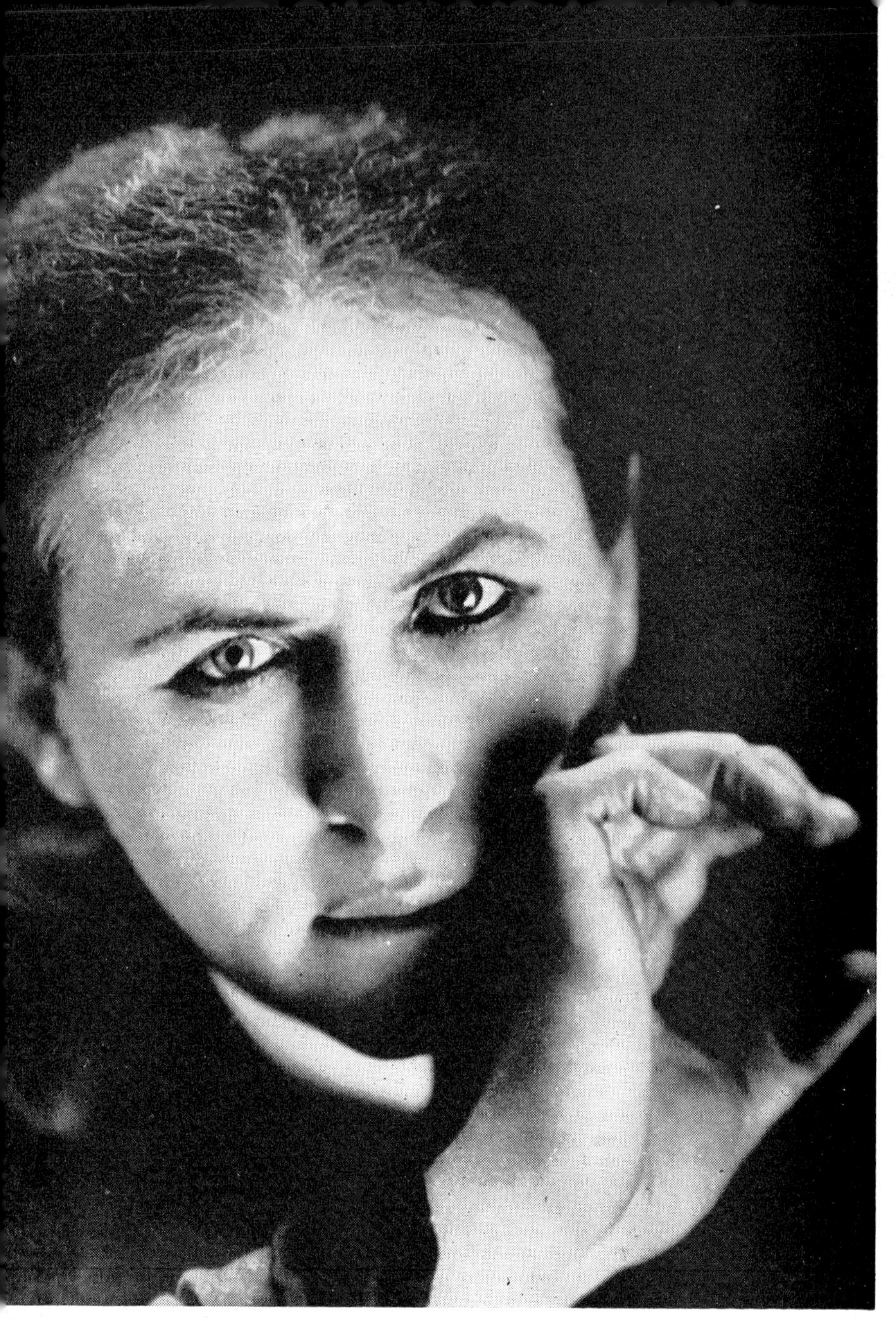

116. HARRY HOUDINI

117. CUCCIOLA, THE MIDGET, WITH ZOPPE, FAMOUS BAREBACK RIDER

118. THE DOLL FAMILY, HARRY, TINY, GRACIE, AND DAISIE

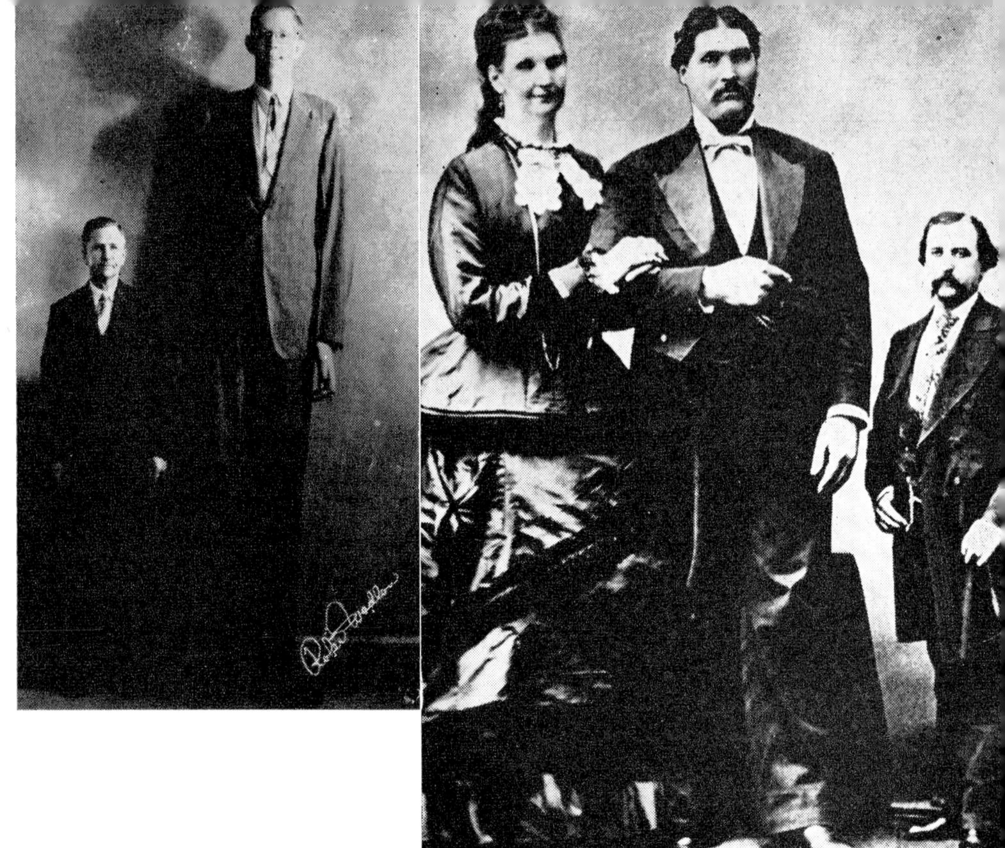

119. ROBERT WADLOW, THE TALLEST MAN WHO EVER LIVED (8 FT. 9 INCHES), WITH HIS FATHER

120. CAPTAIN AND MRS. MARTIN VAN BUREN BATES, THE KENTUCKY GIANTS

121. JACK EARLE AND MAJOR MITE

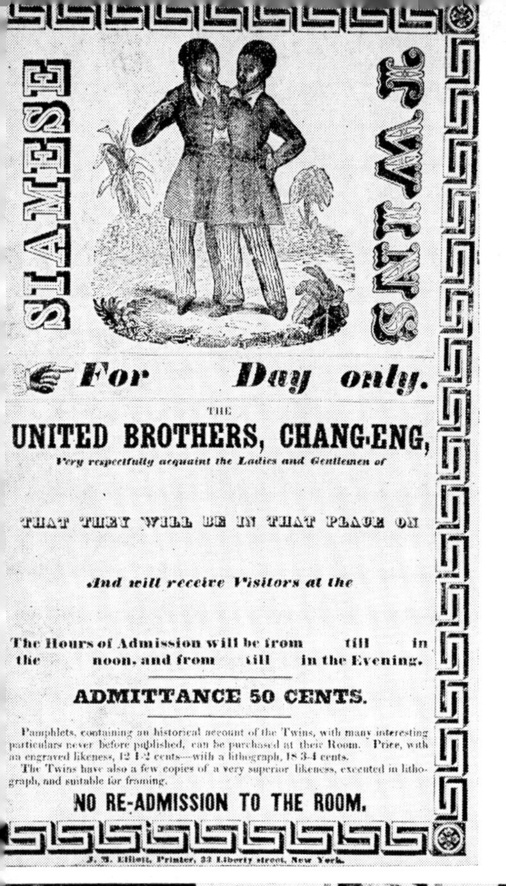

SIAMESE TWINS

For Day only.

THE

UNITED BROTHERS, CHANG-ENG,

Very respectfully acquaint the Ladies and Gentlemen of

THAT THEY WILL BE IN THAT PLACE ON

And will receive Visitors at the

The Hours of Admission will be from till in the noon, and from till in the Evening.

ADMITTANCE 50 CENTS.

Pamphlets, containing an historical account of the Twins, with many interesting particulars never before published, can be purchased at their Room. Price, with an engraved likeness, 12 1-2 cents—with a lithograph, 18 3-4 cents.

The Twins have also a few copies of a very superior likeness, executed in lithograph, and suitable for framing.

NO RE-ADMISSION TO THE ROOM.

J. M. Elliott, Printer, 33 Liberty street, New York.

122. FAMOUS HANDBILL, ADVERTISING THE UNITED BROTHERS, CHANG AND ENG

123. KARL KAE KNECHT, ORGANIZER, CIRCUS FANS OF AMERICA, AND FOUNDER OF WHITE TOPS

124. CECIL B. DE MILLE AND PAUL HOROMPO ON SET OF "THE GREATEST SHOW ON EARTH"

125. THAT'S ALL, FOLKS

THE C.F.A.
CIRCUS FANS' ASSOCIATION OF AMERICA
and
KARL KAE KNECHT

WHEN THE RINGLING BROS. and Barnum & Bailey Circus was in Evansville, Indiana, the newspaperman Karl Knecht was out early doing the whole lot. This date was August 27, 1924. Stanley Dawson, who sold reserved seat tickets from one of the boxes inside The Big Top, called Knecht and told him that there were two circus fans down East, men who loved the circus just like — well, maybe not as much as Knecht — anyway, they were forming an organization of circus fans. Dawson said he was helping them by telling all the real fans whom he chanced to meet, to write to them, and he gave Knecht their names: Mr. Marshall L. King of Alexandria, Virginia, and Mr. Robert P. Johnson, Concord, N. H. Dawson also suggested that Knecht, who was both cartoonist and reporter, design a letterhead to be used in writing to circus-minded folks everywhere. Knecht responded.

Interest was aroused and names continued to pour in. John and Charles Ringling expressed themselves as highly in favor of such an organization. The first general meeting was May, 1926, and all attending were allowed to become charter members, bringing the total to 106. The Circus Fans' Association has continued to grow in activity and membership, numbering, in 1954, well over 1000 members. Karl and his cooperative wife, Jannie, keeping up their hard and consistent work for the organization, have endeared themselves to all the members of the C.F.A.

The members of the C.F.A. represent leaders in all branches of public life — doctors, letter-carriers, bankers, artists, ministers, realtors, salesmen and others, as well as nationally-known characters: Cecil B. DeMille, Joseph Cotton, Joe E. Brown, Jimmy Durante, Sir Cedric Hardwicke, and many others. Fans now gather for the C.F.A. conventions from forty-six states, Washington, D.C., Canada, Cuba, and South America. There are active C.F.A. organizations in England, France, Italy and Holland.

In the United States, each state has a subsidiary organization known as a "Top" and there are local branches in the cities known as "Tents." These are named for men and women who have become famous in the circus. (Circus personnel are not eligible for membership in the C.F.A. organization.)

The purposes of the C.F.A. of America are expressed in the preamble of its constitution:

"We who love the circus, and being ever mindful of the increasing problems with which the circus is confronted, and which tend to impede its operation and continuance, bind ourselves together in the hope of forming fast friendships, and an organized effort to create an enthusiasm for, and an interest in, the circus as an institution, and thus preserve for future generations this beloved American institution known as the circus."

The *White Tops* is the official, bi-monthly publication of the organization. In 1927, Karl Kae Knecht, then secretary-treasurer of the C.F.A., issued a four-page sheet called *Chatter from Around the White Tops,* and it is still going strong, better and bigger than ever, a full-fledged slick magazine with only one slight change and that in name. In 1932, it became *The White Tops.*

Karl Kae Knecht, founder of *The White Tops,* had been its editor for eight years when he resigned. He brought to this publication his wealth of experience and knowledge as a newspaperman, able cartoonist, and syndicated columnist. Successful as *The White Tops* has been, the C.F.A. owes most to Knecht for his untiring energy and vibrant personality, to his dynamic drive, given impetus by his inborn love of the circus, in making the C.F.A. what it is today, a great and most unusual organization.

Dr. Knecht's sister, Klara Knecht, did circus educational and press work for many years for R.B.B.&B. Circus, also for Clyde Beatty Circus; Brookfield Zoo; and Decca Records. Her work has won recognition by a multitude of nationally-known authorities, including the late Robert Ripley.

COLONEL C. G. STURTEVANT, CIRCUS HISTORIAN and CIRCUS ORGANIZATIONS

COLONEL C. G. STURTEVANT was called to the Big Lot on December 26, 1952. By his death, the entire circus world lost one of its most powerful and stalwart friends. So steeped was he in the life and lore of the circus that there were no international boundary lines. He was a true scholar, a research genius. Of all the stories he has written and which have been published over many years of prolific writing, the accuracy of one of them has never been questioned. It was said, on many occasions, that he knew more dates correctly than any other living man. He had what F. Beverly Kelley called the "Kipling quality for meticulous research." His style was clear, concise, and positive.

The Circus Historical Society was founded in 1939, with ten charter members. In order to belong to this organization, one must have a creditable collection of circusana. The purpose of this club is eventually to place the highlights of all collections in an accredited museum, where they may be enjoyed by all circus fans.

The Circus Historical Society issues a magazine called *The Band Wagon,* which gives information on all the old-time circuses and circus history, as well as recording facts and incidents of the present-day circuses and circus life, showing the tremendous "tie-in" of circus history with state and national history.

There was a group of New York City circus fans, (C.F.A.), who met weekly at luncheon at Sardi's restaurant, where a room was fitted out tent-style with circus pictures and posters. In late 1929, they withdrew from the Circus Fans Association and organized an association named "Circus Saints & Sinners Club of America, Inc." A number of other cities have formed similar clubs. One thousand usually attend the meetings in New York City.

Other circus-minded organizations of America are the Circus Clown Club of America, Gag Writers, and Circus Model Builders. The Circus Clown Club has chosen as its slogan "Fools of the World Unite." The aim of this organization is to perpetuate a better understanding among the clowns of the world, as well as to stimulate interest in the circus and the clown activities.

THE HARRY HERTZBERG CIRCUS COLLECTION

HARRY HERTZBERG coined the slogan "We Fight Anything that Fights the Circus." This has become a motto among the members of the Circus Fans' Association of America.

At his death in August, 1940, Harry Hertzberg left his famous circus collection to the San Antonio, Texas, Public

Library, and also money enough to pay all expenses. His collection ranks second to the Museum of the American Circus, Sarasota, Florida.

The Hertzberg collection includes over 2,500 items. It is best known for its Tom Thumb material.

The San Antonio Library, with this Hertzberg collection, has become a mecca for circus-minded people. Mr. Leonard Farley, the present curator, has worked tirelessly to make this trove of circusana available to San Antonio — and the world.

THE SOUL OF THE CIRCUS
By Cecil B. DeMille

"The soul of the circus? . . . who can say . . .

"But not all the drama of The Greatest Show on Earth is played in the Big Top's three rings. For the curtain is always up in the Backyard and Clown Alley . . . here is a world in miniature . . . independent, self-contained, self-sufficient . . . here are some of the strongest bodies . . . some of the best minds in the world . . . . . . courage and cowardice . . . tragedy and comedy walk the same wire . . . life and death swing through the air with the greatest of ease.

"For the circus is a magnet drawing its people from far-flung lands . . . and their languages are as varied as the tongues of Babel. To some it is a home . . . to others it is fame and excitement . . . to many it is fortune."

CECIL B. DeMILLE'S
Motion Picture
THE GREATEST SHOW ON EARTH

THE FAMOUS motion picture producer, Cecil B. DeMille, had always had the desire to do a "stream of civilization" story. He had looked for this story in mammoth railroad stations as the drama of life passed by; looked in the lobbies of large hotels, hotels housing several thousand people; looked on the passageways and in the buildings of fairgrounds; on Broadway in New York, where the four corners of the world rub shoulders. Always the element was missing and the stream of civilization, as he wanted to express it, was not there.

At last Cecil DeMille found it — in the circus. Not only were these people "banded together for a common cause, sharing sorrows and sufferings, enjoying common successes and feeling the independence and liberty which come from individual effort," but he found the circus to be a unifying force, a kind of United Nations of its own — for people from twenty-eight nations were working together under the Big Top.

Cecil DeMille observed the circus audiences. There was no age limit of enjoyment — "boys were seven to seventy." A sea of fascinated faces was held by the magic of spangleland — wonders from all over the world — clowns, jugglers, aerialists high in the air; horses, elephants, wild beasts, band music — shimmering, scintillating beauty everywhere.

Yes, here indeed was "the stream of civilization."

DeMille's long quest was over — "the creative heart of the circus — a one-scene definition of this perfect community under the Big Top." There were hates and jealousies, heartaches and sorrows, but a common fundamental, a unity of purpose, was adhered to by all. Perhaps this unity is best summed up in the phrase, "THE SHOW MUST GO ON."

A lifetime in dreaming, a lifetime in planning, and three years in making, and Cecil DeMille gave to the world a masterpiece in the motion picture field, "The Greatest Show on Earth."

It seems that nature, "in prophetic strain, dropped into the bloodstream of Cecil DeMille" the lure, the desire, and the power which would ordain a fulfillment of a promise, for now the glamor, the art, the music of the circus — the tinsel of the sawdust ring and the glitter of its spangle-land in glorious technicolor, may go into the four corners of the world, into remote places where it is impossible for the circus to travel.

Cecil DeMille performed a great service to humanity, filming in color the extravaganzas — the genius of man and the perfection of art — holding aloft the very soul of the circus, caught in its greatest era of glamor and glory, thus leaving to posterity the brightest star ever to shine in the firmament of the entertainment world.

Bibliography

Allen, Fred — R.B.B.&B. Program.
Armstrong, O. K. — *Reader's Digest.*

Babcock, Harlan — *White Tops.*
Banks, G. Lineaus — *Blondin — His Life and Performances.*
Barnum Museum, Bridgeport, Connecticut.
Barnum, P. T. — *Struggles and Triumphs of Forty Years — Recollections of P. T. Barnum.*
Bartlett, Tommy
Barton, Billy — *White Tops.*
Beatty, Clyde
Blassingame, Wyatt — *Family Circle.*
Bogart, Reggie
Bowman, Harry P. — *As Told on a Sunday Run.*
Braathen, Suerre O. — *White Tops.*
Braden, Frank — R.B.B.&B. Circus Press.
Bradna, Fred — *The Big Top,* (as told to Hartzell Spence), Simon and Schuster.
Brandt & Brandt, Literary Agents for Courtney Ryley Cooper and J. Bryan, III.
Bria, George — *White Tops.*
Bridgeport Public Library, Bridgeport, Connecticut.
Brooks, James — *The Diners Club News.*
Bryan, J., III — *The Strange Stories of Gargantua and Toto — Life; Colliers.*

Bump, Mr. and Mrs. Benjamin J. — "The History of Mr. and Mrs. Tom Thumb."
Butler, Roland — R.B.B.&B. Circus Publicity Manager.

Calkins, Herbert A. — *Troy Record,* Troy, N. Y., *White Tops.*
Canon City *Daily Record.*
Canon City Museum, Canon City, Colorado.
Carlisle, John M. — Clyde Beatty Circus Program.
Carpenter, Russell — Circus Clowns Club of America.
Chindahl, George L. — *White Tops.*
Chipman, Bill — *New York Daily News;* R. B. B.&B. Program

Circusana – Publication by Hertzberg Circus Collection.
Circus Collection, Princeton University.
Clark, Bobby – R.B.B.&B. Circus Program.
Clark, Mabel
Coffin, Patricia – *Look* and *Promenade.*
Cole, Harry W. – *White Tops.*
Concello, Antoinette
Concello, Arthur
Conklin, George S.
Conover, Richard C. – *Bandwagon.*
Cooke, James Francis – *Etude Magazine.*
Cooper, Courtney Ryley – *Circus Day,* Rinehart.
Cosmopolite – *White Tops.*
Coxe, Anthony D. Hippisley – *White Tops.*
Crosby, Bing – R.B.B.&B. Circus Program.

Danenburg, Elsie N., Book on Bridgeport, Connecticut.
Dallas News, The
Davis, Jean
Davis, Larry
Delarue, Allison – *Hobbies.*
DeMille, Cecil B., R.B.B.&B. Program.
Denman, George (Papa)
Duble, Charles E. – *Bandwagon.*
Dunshee, Ken – *Philadelphia Record; News from Home.*

Elkhart Truth, Elkhart, Indiana.

Family Circle
Farley, Leonard V. – Museum Librarian, Hertzberg Circus Collection, San Antonio, Texas.
Fields, William – R.B.B.&B. Circus Program.
Fox, C. P. – *Bandwagon.*

Galt, Floree – *White Tops.*
Gardner, Mr. and Mrs. Cheerful
Gaudreau, Leo – *White Tops.*
Gibbs, Blevens Miller (Mrs. Jim)
Gorrow, M. G. – *White Tops.*
Graves, Edward – *World's Fair* (Showman's paper).
Greenhaw, Capt. Anthony – *White Tops.*
Griffin, J. R. – R.B.B.&B. Circus Office.
Gumpertz, Samuel, R.B.B.&B. Program.

Head, Bernie
Henderson, Dr. J. Y. — *Circus Doctor,* Little, Brown and Company.
Henry A. B. Bishop Historical Room, Bridgeport Public Library, Bridgeport, Connecticut.
Hertzberg Circus Collection, San Antonio, Texas.
Hildreth, Melvin D. — *White Tops;* R.B.B.&B. Circus Program.
History of Animals — Booklet, P. T. Barnum and London Shows Combined.
Hohenadel, W. H. — *White Tops.*
Holling, Joe
Howe, Edward — Cole Bros. Circus Program.
Hoyt, Dr. Chester — Museum of The American Circus, Sarasota, Florida.
Huff, Mr. & Mrs. Arthur

Inabinette, Tom — *White Tops.*

James, Harry — R.B.B.&B. Circus Program.
Johnson, Van — R.B.B.&B. Circus Program.
Jung, Elsie and Paul

Kantor, Arthur — R.B.B.&B. Circus Program.
Kelley, James W. — *Bandwagon;* R.B.B.&B. Program.
Kelley, F. Beverly — R.B.B.&B. Circus Press; *Liberty.*
Kelly, Emmett — R.B.B.&B. Circus Program.
Kelly, Marge V.
Kennedy, John B. — Commentator; R.B.B.&B. Circus Program.
Kessler, F. C. — Curator, Canon City Museum, Canon City, Colorado.
King, Marshall L. — *White Tops.*
Knecht, Dr. & Mrs. Karl Kae — *White Tops.*
Kobler, John — *Life.*
Kunzog, John C. — *Bandwagon.*

Leonard, Bette — Circus Historical Society.
Lester, Allen J. — R.B.B.&B. Circus Press.

Mannix, Daniel P. — *White Tops.*
Mars, Vivienne — Curator, Hertzberg Circus Collection.
McCarthy, Clem — R.B.B.&B. Circus Program.
McClain, Walter
McGarrity, Richard J.
McKendrick, Bill
McLemore, Henry — *White Tops.*
McNeill, Don — R.B.B.&B. Circus Program.

Miller, Mr. & Mrs. Dick
Milwaukee Journal
Montague, Bill – *White Tops.*
Morris, Steve – *Louisville Times; White Tops.*
Morrisey, Frank – R.B.B.&B. Circus Program.
Museum of the American Circus, Sarasota, Florida.

Nelson, Mrs. William
Nemes, Sylvester – *White Tops.*
New York Mercury
New York Times, The
Noble, Clyde V. – *White Tops.*
North, Henry Ringling
North, John Ringling

Perigo, C. E.
Phelps, William Lyon – *Billboard.*
Phillips, Fred H. – *White Tops.*
Posey, Jake

Quillen, Harry – *White Tops.*

Ratliff, G. C. – column, "Big Sandy – Past and Present," *Daily Independent,* Ashland, Kentucky.
Reader's Digest
Richardson, Vivian – *Dallas News.*
Rick, Herman L.
Riley, James Whitcomb – *Rhymes of Childhood,* Bobbs-Merrill, Inc.
Robertson, Archie – *Life; Reader's Digest.*
Roselli, Rex de – *The Studebaker Wheel; White Tops.*
Rosenfield, John – *Dallas News.*
Rowell, Dr. Hugh Grant – R.B.B.&B. Circus Program.
Russell, Eugene – *Bandwagon; Elkhart Truth.*

San Francisco Chronicle, The
Sarasota Herald Tribune, Sarasota, Florida.
Sawdust for Memory
Scaperlanda, M. S.
Sharpe, R. L. – *A Bag of Tools, MASTERPIECES OF RELIGIOUS VERSE,* Harper and Brothers, Inc.
Shettel, James W. – *White Tops.*
Siegrist, Joe – *White Tops.*
Smith, A. Morton
Smith, Dorothy L. – *Life.*

Spence, Hartzell – *The Big Top,* Simon and Schuster.
Stafford, Fred – *White Tops.*
Stark, Mabel
Steele, Goldie – Assistant Curator, Hertzberg Circus Collection, San Antonio, Texas.
Sterling, Janet – *White Tops.*
Stern, Bill – Commentator, R.B.B.&B. Circus Program.
Strook, James – *The Diner's Club News.*
Studebaker Wheel
Sturtevant, Col. C. G. – Circus Historian, *White Tops.*
Sullivan, Ed. – Columnist, *New York Sunday Times.*
Sullivan, John L. – Curator, Museum of the American Circus.
Swann, John W. – *The Language of the Circus Lot.*

Thomas, Lowell – Commentator.
Thompson, Fred Bailey – *Bandwagon.*
Tiebor, Roland
Tomlinson, James B. – R.B.B.&B. Circus Program.
Tom Thumb Museum, Lakesville, Massachusetts.
Tufts College (Museum), Medford, Massachusetts.

Uleland, A.

Waco News-Tribune
Wagner, Jacob A. – *White Tops.*
Williams, Mack – *Fort Worth Star-Telegram.*
Winchell, Walter – Commentator.
Wirth, Charles – *Billboard.*
Wixom, Clyde – *White Tops.*
Wolfe, Fred de
Wolfe, Bertha de

PHOTOGRAPHERS

Atwell, Harry A.
Baldwin, Helen
Bogart, Reggie
Burnell, W. Earl
Butler, Dick
Chestor Photo Service
Davis, Jean
Good, Robert D.

Hawkins, Richard
Kobel, Bernard Lyle
Mass Foto Service
McKendrick, Bill
Miller, Dick
Mueller, Thomas O.
Nielsen, Vittus
Nethersole, Louis (Bertram W. Mills' Circus, London, England.)
Okerbloom, Carl
Rasmussen, Carl
Ratliff, G. C.
Rick, Herman L.
Star Photo Service (Bill Matteson, Head)
Quillen, Harry
Varney, Earl W.

CIRCUS TERMINOLOGY

"Lot Lingo"

ACE: A dollar (paper or silver).

AFTER SHOW: Concert, formerly a musical, later a wild West exhibition, wrestling, etc. – an added attraction, at extra cost, which takes place immediately following the main performance.

ALDERMAN: Office stooge.

ALFALFA: Paper money.

ALL OUT AND OVER: Entire performance is concluded.

ANNIE OAKLEY: A free pass or complimentary ticket. Annie Oakley, an expert shot with Buffalo Bill's Wild West Show, could puncture pasteboards with precision. Theater or circus tickets were punctured, as if by bullets, to show they had been properly purchased.

AT LIBERTY: Out of work, or an act.

AUGUSTE: A slapstick clown who performs in whiteface.

BABIES: Pumas.

BACK DOOR: Also performers' entrance. A large opening in the main tent connecting with the back yard used by most acts for entrance and exit.

BACK YARD: Space between the big top entrance and dressing rooms, and where properties, used during performance, wardrobes, and wagons are kept.

BAGGAGE STOCK: Heavy draft or work horses.

BALE RING: A solid, round, heavy steel ring, put around every center pole, to which is hooked the open sections of tents, before being pulled up.

BALLY: A ballyhoo or spiel in front of side show.

BALLYHOO: To attract attention.

BALLYHOOERS: Girls who ballyhoo in front of side show to draw attention.

BANNER LINE: A series of canvas or paper pictures stretched in front of a side show.

BANNERS: Huge canvas affairs with paintings on them describing the curiosities and wonders within, which are lined up along fronts of side shows. Also cloth signs or advertisements used by the advance men, tacked on buildings, signboards, etc.

BARKER: The man who talks the people into buying tickets for the side show. (See *Opener.*)

BEEF: A complaint; to bellow over a real or an imaginary wrong.

BEETLE: A female.

BIBLE: The magazine-programme of a show.

BIBLE-BACKS: The floorboards for the grandstand section.

BIG CAGE: The collapsible cage used for exhibiting wild animals in the ring.

BIG ONE: The Ringling Bros. and Barnum & Bailey Circus.

BIG TOP: The big tent used for the main show.

BIG TOP GANG: Canvasmen and utility men who work on the main tent equipment.

BIG TURK: Ostrich.

BIRD DOG: Local helper who does the leg work for an advance agent.

BLADDERS: Toy balloons.

BLOCK (or turnip) : A watch.

BLOCKS (or "block boys"): Small 6x6 square pine blocks, 1 inch thick, which are always put on ground for footing legs of seat jacks to keep same solid, and from slipping. Boys who handle and pick up same when seats are taken down after show are "block boys."

BLOOMER: Poor stand, where town fails to come to show.

BLOW DOWN: Heavy storm that levels tents.

BLOW-OFF: The end of a show, climax, also special performance. A behind-the-curtain show that caters mostly to morons.

BLOW THE STAND (also BLOW THE SHOW): Cancelling a town selected or billed. To leave the show.

BLUES: Plain board or cheap seats usually painted blue; also called "general admission" seats, generally around the ends of the big top.

BOOSTER: Confederate of gamblers; or a "capper"; or a "sure thing" man.

BOOSTER-HANDLER: One who stands behind the shill to relieve him, the booster, of money as fast as he picks it up. (Almost passed out of existence – shows are honest and cleaner now.)

BOSS BUTCHER (or CANDY BOSS): Head of refreshment stands and workers.
BOSS ELEPHANT MAN: Head of the elephant department, and generally the trainer, solely responsible for elephants.
BOSS HOSTLER: Man who has charge of and is responsible for horses on show.
BOSS OF PROPS: Head of properties, or "props" used in big show-rigging, staging, and handling all articles used by performers in acts.
BOSS OF RING STOCK: Man who is responsible for performing horses and ponies used in performance.
B.R.: A roll of currency – a bankroll.
BROADS: Tickets.
BROAD-TOSSER: A three-card monte dealer.
BUGS: Chameleons sold on the ground.
BUG-MEN: Chameleon vendors.
BULL: Any elephant of either sex.
BULL ACT: Performing elephants.
BULL HOOKS: Elephant goads or hooks used in managing elephants.
BULL MEN: Men who handle elephants, or elephants keepers.
BUM STEER: To send on a wild-goose chase, or to give wrong information.
BURN UP: To exploit with grift (dishonest practice) a route, territory, or circus name to the extent of making it unprofitable.
BUSTER: An accident.
BUTCHERS: Candy or lemonade peddlers – purveyors of refreshments.

CAKE CUTTER or CUT THE STRAWBERRY CAKE: A short-change artist.
CALLIOPE: A steam piano on wheels. Pronounced *kally'-ope* by circus personnel.
CAMEL PUNK: A boy who attends camels.
CANVAS MEN: Men who work on the tents.
CAPPERS: Personnel of side show, who, when crowds are reluctant to buy tickets, rush up and buy entrance tickets in hopes a crowd will follow. (See *Booster.*) One hired to win.
CAPTAIN, MAJOR, or COLONEL: Circus and midway troupers who carry military titles, get their commissions from their help.
CARRY THE BANNER: To sleep in a park or stay up all night because of not having a bed.

CAT: Lion, tiger, leopard, panther — a member of any feline family.

CAT ACT: Any performance of trained cats or felines.

CATCHER: The member of an aerial act who catches the flyer after he leaves the trapeze or hands of another catcher.

CATCH TRAP: The trapeze used by a catcher in an aerial act.

CAT RACK QUEEN: A female agent on a ball-throwing concession.

CATS: Rebel-yelling, troublesome hillbillies.

CATTLE GUARDS: Sets of low seats placed in front of "blues" (end seats — see *Blues*) for overflow crowd.

CENTER POLE: One of the large perpendicular poles which hold up the tent at the peak. Similar poles used at the outer perimeter are known as quarter poles.

CHAIN TO RAILS: To prevent the show from moving by legal interference.

CHAMBERMAIDS' FROLIC: An all-girl aerial ladder act.

CHARACTERS: Titles for people not connected with the show.

CHARLEY: Wastepaper can on the bill-car.

CHARLIE: A blackface clown who wears a derby hat, tattered clothes, and works through pathos.

CHERRY PIE: Extra work.

CHIEF: An executive title.

CHIVE: A dagger or knife.

CHOKERS: Men who handle wagon wheel blocks on the flatcars.

CHUMP: Mark, sap, rum luken, or sucker.

CLEM: A fight. Town hoodlums attack shows and meet resistance. A free-for-all.

CLICK: To succeed, to accomplish.

CLINK: Jail.

CLOSS or GRAVEDIGGERS or ZEKES: Hyenas.

CLOWN ALLEY: The dressing tent reserved for the clowns' use in making up, also the corps of clowns.

CLOWN STOP: Brief appearance of clowns while props are changed.

COLD DECK: One who cheats at anything.

COLONEL or MAIN GUY: Manager.

COME IN: The interval between the gate opening and the grand entry.

COME-ONS: Suckers, boobs.

COMMITTEEMAN: Head of an organization or auspices who

can get a show anything it needs but seldom obliges.

CONCERT: (See *After Show*) Extra show after the big show performance. A short program of an unusual or specially advertised feature.

CONNECTION: Area-way between menagerie and circus main tent of "big top," or between any two tents.

CONVICTS: Zebras.

COOKHOUSE: Dining tent.

COOKHOUSE GANG: Employees in cookhouse who erect and take down the cookhouse, ranges, steam tables, other tables, dish washing and drying machines, and other equipment.

CRAZY ACT: Any clown routine.

CROAK: To kill.

CROAKER: A murderer.

CRUMB: Circus bee.

CRUMB CASTLES: Dining room tents.

CUT THE STRAWBERRY CAKE or CUT CAKE: Shortchange.

DAMPER: The front door cash register.

DAUBS: Spaces other than regular billboards, for posting paper (circus posters) – sides of barns, sheds, fences.

DAY AND DATE: Simultaneous date and town of show with an opposition, or other show.

DEAD MAN: A wooden block, made secure by stakes to which the rigging for aerial and high wire acts is fastened. It is so-called because it lies flat on the ground, is dead weight, and is very difficult to budge.

DEEMER: A dime.

DENS: Animal cages

DENTIST FRIEND: Anything sweet to eat.

DICK: Private detective or police carried by the show.

DOG: Hippopotamus.

DOG AND PONY SHOW: A term applied to small shows. (Sometimes used derisively.)

DONAGHER or DONAKER: Rest room.

DOORS: A call, meaning they are about to open and allow public to come in.

DOWN YONDER: The southern tier of states.

DUCKET GRABBER: Door tender or ticket taker.

DUCKETS or SKULLS: Circus tickets.

DUKE HIM IN: Steering a victim.

DUKE: Hand.

DUKE NIGHTLY: To pay off each night after the show is over.
DUKER: A meal ticket.
DUKIE: A handout put up for workmen. (A lunch handed out at the cook tent.)
DUKIE BOOK: A pad of detachable tickets to be exchanged for meals.
DUKE 'EM: To hand a child or young woman a confection, balloon, or novelty, and by means of this insinuation, force the parent or escort to buy. Also to hold back a coin in the palm of the hand after change has been counted out to the patron. (Count it out in palm up and turn palm down in handing it to patron, by which means the part held in palm is hidden from view of patron.)

ELOPE: To marry and leave the show without notice.
EQUESTRIAN DIRECTOR: The performance manager; "The man who blows the whistle." Often confused by the layman with RINGMASTER (which see).
EXTRAS or DOUBLE-STAKING: Putting extra or two stakes in ground with which to hold ropes, especially in very threatening or windy weather.

FAKES: Tickets.
FALL GUY: Anyone to blame for anything wrong – one responsible. One on whom to lay the blame, real or imaginary.
FAN: An enthusiast; to search hastily.
FINISH: The last "trick"; the show is over; or concluding number by a performer or rider. Riders call it "style."
FINK: A broken novelty; a torn balloon.
FIRST OF MAY GUY: One who has just joined the circus and is greenest; a novice; greenhorn; simpleton.
FISHPLATE: Metal connecting bridge between two flatcars – enables circus to unload lengthwise of the car.
FIXER or MENDER: Diplomatic agent who pays licenses, fees or adjusts; legal adjuster of damages, accidents, claims, or "raw deals" (unfair claims) on the circus. Often a former attorney. Also called "squarer" and "adjuster."
FLAG: The signal raised over the cookhouse when a meal is begin served.
FLAG'S UP: A message that is called out by different ones over the circus lot when they chance to see the flag has been run up. (The full-of-pep modern boy calls out in his home, "Come and get it.") On the R.B.B.&B. Circus, in times past,

they called out "Joe Blow," because the man whose duty it was to run up the dinner or meal-message flag was named "Joe Blow."

FLASH: Generally meaning the appearance and prosperous look.

FLAT JOINT: A game operated by control.

FLATS: Flat cars of the show train.

FLOOKUM or FLUKEM: A powder containing synthetic flavor and color used in soft drinks.

FLUNKEYS: Waiters in the cookhouse.

FLYER: A member of an aerial act who leaves his trapeze to fly through the air.

FLYING RETURN: The return trip by a flyer from the catcher's hands by way of the trapeze, to the pedestal from which he originally took off.

FLYING SQUADRON: First section of the circus train to reach the lot.

FORK JUMP: A leap from the ground to the back of a horse, alighting astraddle.

FRAMING A SHOW: Planning to start a show.

FRIEND OF SHOW: One who enjoys special privileges around the show – a member of the Circus Fans' Association, or other kindred organizations, or one looking for a favor, being a member of fan or hobby clubs.

FRONT: A good appearance, but more usually a reference to the front of the side show – or lineup of the banners, platforms, etc.

FRONT DOOR: The entrance to the circus tent used by the patrons – also for an attache, stationed at or near the front door for running errands, etc.

FUZZ: Police officer.

GAFFER: The circus manager.

GAFFS ON THE JOINT: The novelty spindle is working crooked.

GARBAGE STAND: Novelty booth.

GARTER: Tape held for a performer to leap over.

GAWKS or LOT LOAFERS: Townspeople watching unloading of trains, or who throng the show lots.

GAZOONIE: A man who works cheap or for nothing.

GEEK: Snake eater.

GENTLING: The process of subduing wild animals and teaching them to perform tricks or take parts in group acts.

GETAWAY DAY: Last day of engagement.

GET WITH IT: To get busy; to hurry; to work harder; to step lively.

GIG SHOW: Minstrel show.

GILLS: Country men, farmers, outsiders, etc.

GILLY or GILLY WAGON: The large wagon or truck that makes final trip to and from the lot and circus train. To carry, by a small wagon or by hand, lighter pieces of equipment around the lots. Small one- and two-car shows use a "knock-down" wagon, and carry everything to and from train this way. With a big outfit, to "gilly" is to use wagon or a means of carrying that is different from that usually used – an extra wagon or cart, often smaller.

GILLY SHOW: Small carnival that is loaded in boxcars and carries very little.

GLOOMER: A geek (snake-eater).

GOLD BRICK: A pass.

GONE SUNDAY SCHOOL: Said of a circus that has abolished the grift (see *Grift*). (Most all circuses have done this, especially the large ones.)

GONE TO THE CHARLEY: Throw in the wasterpaper can that is carried on bill car. (See *Charley*.)

GONK: Paste on the bill car. TO SERVE UP THE GONK: Fill the paste bucket.

GOOBERS: Peanuts.

GORGE: Food.

GRAB JOINT: Centrally located eating stand that sells pink lemonade, sandwiches, etc.

GRAFTERS: Gamblers or "shortchangers" who traveled with, or who "trailed," some of the early-day (and a few of today's) shows, and plied their practices upon gullible or greedy "towners" – also known as "slickers" and "Luck Boys." They more often trailed along the same route, so as to "work" the big crowds, and had no connection with the show proper. But very few circuses of today allow such. (The C.F.A. hopes to see the day when none will permit it.)

GREASE JOINT: Hot dog, or hamburger stand.

GREEK: Snake-eating wild man, mostly featured on carnivals which use live chickens instead of snakes.

GRIFT: Dishonest practices or "graft"; unlawful and dishonest concession joints, etc.

GRIND SHOW: (For "all-day grind") A side show or small show that performs continuously.

GROUCH BAG: A money bag suspended by a string, carried

inside the clothing.

GUY OUT: Drunk.

GUYS: Heavy ropes or cables that "guy" up the big center poles.

HAMMER GANG: The men who drive the stakes. A "stake-driver" is a machine on the lot, never a man.

HARD MONEY: Silver money.

HARD TICKETS: General admission tickets. (Hard seats, not upholstered.)

HAUL: The distance from railroad to the circus lot.

HEADS UP: Meaning "look out"; a warning, often used to notify people to prevent being hit by approaching workmen, carrying paraphernalia, approaching wagons, horses, elephants, etc.

HEEL BOX: The last ticket stand inside the big top.

HEFTY: Performer who does an old-fashioned "strong man" act.

HEP: Road-smart, traveled lots.

HEY, RUBE: A fight. A rallying cry, or cry for help in a fight — expression was common only to old-time circuses of a shady character, and limited to a general fight or rumpus between circus workers and quarrelsome townspeople, or town roughs, but which is happily almost unknown since the 'seventies and early 'eighties — "Picking on" the smaller circus troupes was once a popular sport in some of the more turbulent towns years ago, and the town "roughs" and "smarties" generally got "what they were looking for," since the trained workmen invariably worsted the "towners." A show's security and success depends upon its moving every day (as a rule), and they cannot afford to be the aggressors, even if tempted. Called the "Battle Cry" of the circus.

HIGH-SCHOOL HORSE: A horse trained to execute all the standard steps of the Spanish riding school.

HIGH SEATING: Inducing patrons to crowd up to the topmost tiers of "blues" or general admission (cheaper) seats, so that latecomers could be more easily seated.

HIP or HIPPO: A hippopotamus.

HIP-KICK: Back trouser pocket.

HIPPODROME TRACK: The cinder track all the way around the arena just in front of the patrons' seats.

H. O.: Holdout.

HOGGER: A greedy showman.

HOME GUARD: A native of the town where circus is playing.

HOME SWEET HOME: Generally referred to as the concluding date or performance of the season. A curious custom of billposters is to post one stand (the advertisements of a show's date of arrival) of paper, generally the last one of the year, upside down.

HOME RUN: The trip from the show's last performance to winter quarters.

HOOK ROPES: Stout ropes with hooks on ends, to be hooked into rings on wagon sides, and used to hitch extra teams on, to aid in mud and soft ground.

HOOK-UP TEAMS: Teams that are used in loading and unloading wagons at the trains. Also called "pull-up teams" or "pull-over teams."

HORSE: One thousand dollars.

HORSE FEED: Poor business or attendance. "Didn't get horse feed," means a very poor or losing stand.

HORSE OPERY: Jocular for any circus.

HOTSCOTCH: The grease joint (which see) at the greatest distance from the circus lot.

HOWDY: An elephant howdah; also a chair carried by camels.

HUMPS: Camels.

IN DONIKER: Bad location, lot, or wrong side of town.

IRONS: Iron stakes used on hard lots.

JACKPOTS: Tall tales of big dough the easy way.

JACOBS LADDER: A cheap flophouse that has no elevator.

JAM or SQUEEZE: A difficulty, an uncomfortable fix, or condition.

JANE: The most uncomplimentary noun used for a woman, short of obscenity.

JOCKEY ACT: Horseback acrobatics, usually by several people on a single mount.

JOE HEPP: An imaginary person or character. BILL HEPP: "Joe's" brother.

JOEYS: Clowns. So named after the famous "Grimaldi" of early English days – Joseph Grimaldi, who was the most famous, successful, and beloved "Joey" of his time.

JOHNNY COME LATELY: One who is in his second year with the circus and thinks he knows all the answers. (One a bit cocky or too sure of himself.)

JOHNNY TIN PLATE or TIN PLATE: A small town constable or marshal.

JOHN ORDERLY: Hurry it up; get going.

JOHN ROBINSON or QUICK SHOW: A show cut to the barest essentials in order to get the crowd out ahead of a storm.

JOINT: Any concession stand or novelty spindle. (See *Spindle.*)

JONAH'S BAD LUCK: Wallowing in bad weather, or unusual mud.

JUICE: Lemonade and drinks.

JUICE JOINT: Lemonade stand.

JUMP: The distance between points of showing.

JUMP STAND: An extra stand near the front door, from which tickets are sold when there is a big rush.

JUNGLE BUGGY: House trailer.

KEISTER: Traveling bag, grip, or suitcase.

KICKING SAWDUST: Following a circus, being part of it.

KID MONEY: Admission collected at front door, for children "under age."

KID SHOW: Side show.

KID WORKERS: Bosses who direct extra boys of towns, when short of help – who aid in getting the show ready upon late arrivals – or show movements. (And what kid hasn't "worked his way in" some time in his life?)

KIESTER (Keester): Trunk or wardrobe box.

KIFE: To swindle the suckers.

KINKER: Almost any performer, but originally applied to acrobats. Once called "Spangles."

KIP: Bed.

KUSH, KALE, JACK: Money.

LACING: Small rope loops by which sections of the big tent or "middle-pieces" of same are securely tied together, making one whole-appearing top. "Bust the lacings" is a command to untie or separate the lacings when dismantling tents.

LAG: Leak.

LAM: Depart swiftly, run.

LARRY: A punctured balloon or broken novelty, broken merchandise, or bad date.

LAUNDRY QUEENS: Girl dancers.

LAYOUT MAN: One of the first men on lot who measures off and directs placing of iron pins to designate stakes for tents.

LEAD STOCK: Zebras, yaks, camels, ring stock, etc.

LEAPER: A tumbler who performs acrobatic jumps by using

a ramp and leaping board.

LEAPS: Leaping over each other and tumbling.

LIBERTY ACT: A group of horses which performs without riders, executing maneuvers on the command or signal of a trainer who stands in the ring. A liberty horse is one that works in such an act.

LIGHT WAGON: The electric power unit; a symbol in that it is the last wagon loaded on the circus train. "The light wagon's on" means "We're ready to go."

LIMBER JIM: A contortionist.

LITHOGRAPHER: A man who sticks circus bills on show windows.

LONG: A pass with a reserve seat coupon.

LONG SIDE: The side of the cookhouse in which the workmen eat.

LOT: Always meaning the shows' exhibition grounds.

LOT LICE: Townspeople who hang around the lot looking on while the circus is being set up, and stay late without spending any money.

LUCKY BOYS: Gamblers, those connected with gambling privileges.

LUMBER: Loads of seats, poles, etc.

MAIN GUY: A guy rope that holds up the center pole in the big top.

MAKE AN OPENING: To make the first spiel in front of a show.

MANEGE (Pronounced MÁNAGE): To ride a high-school horse so that it shows off properly all its steps. "To ride a high-school horse" means "to work a manége act."

MARCH: The street parade (alas — no more).

MARK: A victim.

MARQUEE: Main and canopied entrance to big show.

MECHANIC: An apparatus consisting of a waist belt to which is attached a rope which is suspended from a pole. It is used to prevent beginners from falling off a horse, or flyers from falling during practice.

MENDER: Legal adjuster.

MIDWAY BONUS: Mostly used on carnivals. A big promise, usually a promise on last year's sweepstakes.

MIDWAY SNITCH: Carnival press agent who reports the news — sometimes writes up bad weeks as good weeks.

MILKY WAY: Frozen custard machine stand.

MIMI: Early Roman clown.

MITT JOINT: A fortuneteller's tent.
MITT READER: Fortuneteller of either sex – mostly old women.
MONDAY MAN: A man who had the exclusive right to steal from village clotheslines, once a circus concession (no longer exists).
MORGUE: A dead town.
MOUTHPIECE: A local legal representative.
MUD SHOW: One traveling by wagons, trucks, or autos. Sometimes called an "overland trick." Usually shows in small towns or suburbs of larger cities. As a rule, this show remains on one location longer than the larger shows.
MUG JOINT: A while-you-wait photographer's tent.
MULE SKINNER: Tractor driver.
MUSH: Umbrella.
NIGGER BOARDS: Platform sections spread on ground in older days, to be used as floor for the concert acts, dancers, etc., before days of common use of the stages, now used universally.
NUT or BURR: Expense of operating. "The Nut" meaning the operating expenses of any show. "What's the nut?" always means "What are your real expenses for running the 'opry'?" (See end of Circus Terminology for further explanation.)

OFFICE: Show's business headquarters. Sometimes called "The Complaint Room" or "A Sign of Understanding" – "Giving him the office" means "Tipping him off"; flashing certain intelligence, often with a look or wink.
OLD FOLKS: The monkeys.
OLD MAN: Owner or director of the show.
OLD RAG: Big top tent.
OLD STAR BACKS: Reserve seats (had stars painted on backs).
OLIVER or OLLIE: An officer.
ON THE SHOW: Performers and all connected with the show. Term, "with the show" is never heard – always "on."
ON THE STRAW or STRAWING THEM: Seating people on straw strewn on the ground in front of other seats, when all regular seats are taken.
OPENER or TALKER: The man who talks the people into buying tickets. Laymen, but not circus people, often call him "Barker" or "Spieler."
OPENING: Initial lecture or spiel in front of side show.

OPERY: The circus.

P. A.: Press agent.
PACIFIC WATER DOG: Seal.
PACKED TO THE RING CURB: Said of a crowded performance.
PAD ROOM: Dressing room — so-called owing to the trappings and "pads" for horses being kept and placed therein. In former and early days, the riders in the ring rode on large pads, fastened to the backs of their prancing steeds. "Bareback" riders are comparatively recent.
PAINTED PONIES: Zebras.
PALEFACE: A clown.
PAPER: Circus posters.
PAPER HOUSE: An audience composed largely of people admitted on passes.
PAPER SECTION: The section in which spectators bearing passes are placed.
PATCH: Legal adjuster.
PAYOFF: Pay day.
PEARL DIVER: Dishwasher. This term is likewise common in the navy, and elsewhere.
PERCH ACT: A balancing act performed on a circus stage. Sometimes referred to as "The pole balancers' performance."
PETE JENKINS or A PETE JENKINS ACT: Generally performed by a riding clown, dressed in rags, feigning intoxication, who clowns awhile, discards rags, and becomes a most daring bareback rider.
PHYSIC MAN: Medicine pitchman.
PICTURE GALLERY: The tattooed man or woman.
PIGGIE BANK: A fat girl's stocking.
PINCH: An arrest.
PINHEAD: One who is dull. Some freaks are known as such.
PIP: An exceptionally good thing.
PIPE: A letter.
PIRATE: To appropriate, or take over, another performer's routine, costume, or props, without his consent.
PIROUETTE: To whirl completely about in rapid manner. On horseback, it is performed on the toes, or by an upward leap and spiral. In the air it is a quick turn or spin in space after the flyer leaves the catcher and just before he grasps his trapeze. A most difficult maneuver.
PITCHMEN or RACKETEERS: Balloon, whips, or concession salesmen, a live-wire glitter agent.

PLANGE: To throw the body completely over one arm with the assistance of a swivel. (The plange was the great Lillian Leitzel's feat of endurance.)

PLASTER: Mortgage on the show.

PLING: To ask for donations for help, to mooch or beg.

POKE: A purse or pocketbook.

POLE: A wagon tongue. Tent poles are qualified as center pole, quarter pole, and so on.

POLERS: Men who handle wagon poles in loading and unloading at the runs.

POLLAR: Man who steers wagons.

POSSUM-BELLY: A compartment under railway cars providing extra storage space.

PRATT OUT: To push a knocker out of any tip or play by shoving him with one's buttock.

PRETTY BOYS: The circus bouncers; strong-arm men, who, in a way, "take care of situations," keep order.

PRIVILEGE CAR: A restaurant, or lunch car on the circus train, for use of, and heavily patronized by, all show members—after night performances, the "workingman's club."

PRIVILEGES: Refreshments or articles sold around the show.

PUDDING WAGON: Frozen custard truck.

PUNK ROUSTER or PUSHER: Worker on show who chases under-age children from in front of gambling concessions while games are going on.

PUNKS: Children, babies, or young animals or colts.

PUT ON THE BEE: To ask for a touch; in the summertime, it is considered a loan—in the winter, it is a donation.

PUTTING UP PAPER FOR YOURSELF: Bragging.

QUACK: A pretender.

QUAD RAT: One lower than another.

QUAGGA: A zebra.

QUARTER POLE: See *Center Pole.*

QUARTERS: Winter quarters where all shows rest and refit for the coming season.

QUICK SHOW: See *John Robinson.*

RACKETEERS: See PITCHMEN.

RAG: Tent

RAZORBACKS: Men who load and unload the cars, and not to be confused with *Roustabouts.* The term, razorback, came from command of the boss, to the men who stooped under the heavy track runs from car ends to the ground, and raised the runs into place; "Raise-yer-backs."

READER: The town, country, or state license.
READ THE LOT: To look for tent stakes, or articles of equipment after the show is "down" at night.
REAL ESTATE: Concession space.
RED LIGHTING: To eject a person from a train, or leaving one behind.
RED ONE: A good stand, a winner, named from red numbers or winners on grind-store charts.
RED WAGON or THE TICKET OFFICE: So-called because it was formerly painted red.
RED WAGON MUSIC: Circus music, marches, fast gallops.
REHASHING TICKETS: Resell, an act of becoming a partner in a show without an investment.
RIB: To taunt; to tease.
RIDGE ROPE: Strong rope, or cable stretched length of tents at tops of center poles – forming the top ridge of the structure, as in a house.
RIDING RUBBER: Going in an automobile.
RIGGERS: Those who put up aerial rigging.
RINGBANKS or RING CURBS: Circular dirt mound thrown up in making the rings, in older days, but in recent days all big shows use wooden curbing, which is in sections.
RING BARN: Building housing a regulation-sized circus ring where riders and other acts learn and practice their acts while in "winter quarters."
RINGMASTER: The man in the ring with a whip, who keeps the horses under control during an equestrian act. Not to be confused with Equestrian Director (which see).
RING STOCK: All performing horses, ponies, etc. Sometimes known as "Lead Stock," as such animals are led to and from cars, by attendants, and never do any of the heavy hauling.
RIOT PANIC: Great applause.
RISLEY ACT: Any performance, in which one person, lying flat on his back, balances and juggles with his feet, usually juggling humans. (Another definition given of this act is – an act in which three acrobats lie on their backs and toss a fourth from one to the other.) A Mr. Risley was said to be the first man to perform this act.
ROPER: A cowboy.
ROSINBACKS: Horses used by the riders in the rings – their broad backs being sprinkled with fine rosin before entering the ring (especially in damp or wet weather) – to make

for a surer footing by their daring masters.
ROUGHNECK: A working man.
ROUND: To turn without attracting attention.
ROUST: To chase or run away.
ROUSTABOUTS: Men used for common labor around a circus (sometimes called "roughnecks"). Men working on tents are called "canvasmen."
RUBBER MAN: A balloon vendor.
RUBBER VAGS: People who live in house trailers.
RUNS: Where the trains are located — unloaded and loaded.
RUNT: A dwarf.

SAP: A cane. Also applied to a "Gawk" or "Know-nothing."
SCHILL: A come-on man; to win easily at gambling games; to entice suckers.
SCOFFINS: Food, in cookhouse, same as "gorge" and "chuck."
SCRAM: Beat it; get away.
SEAL: Any sea lion, especially one trained to perform.
SEAT BOSS or PLANKMAN: Superintendent of erection and taking down of all seats.
SEAT MAN: A schill (which see).
SECOND COUNT: A shortchanger's method.
SHAKE or SHAKEDOWN: Extortion, or frameup for added or put-up job, payment — a boosted price. A raid by officers after a fix has been paid; double-cross by officers.
SHAMUS: Police officer.
SHANTY or CHANDELIER: Man or men who operate or superintend the lights or illumination — more prevalently used in the days of torches, gasoline lamps, gas lights, etc.
SHECKLES: Money in any form.
SHEETING or SHEETING 'EM UP: Posting bills — terms used by all circus bill-posters.
SHELF: An upper birth in sleeping car or truck.
SHILL: To pass in free; one who is purposely passed by the door — to "shill in," is to walk right by the doorkeeper with a nod.
SHINER: A diamond.
SHORT: A pass without a reserved seat coupon.
SHORT CAKE: To outcount a person in money.
SHORTING: Shortchanging, stealing, or holding out money (See *Grifters*).
SHORT SIDE: The section of the cookhouse in which the staff and performers eat.
SHRINE CIRCUS: Any circus performance put on by a Shrine

Temple. This type of circus entertainment is growing rapidly.

SHYLOCK: Office secretary.

SIDEWALLS: The loose canvas flaps or walls from the perimeter of the tent top to the ground.

SILVER WAGON: The owner's or manager's administrative wagon, so-called because it is usually painted with silver gilt.

SKINNER: Circus teamster.

SKIN ODDITY: Freaks with skins like that of an alligator.

SKULLS: Circus free tickets.

SLEEPER: Money overlooked.

SLOUGH: To tear down preparatory to moving; to close a show or concession.

SMOKE WAGON: Two small, strong wheels mounted on axle like an auto trailer, with which the heaviest poles are moved to and from place, and the pole wagons.

SNIPER: A bill-poster who sneaks up at night to place his paper.

SOFT LOT: Wet or spongy ground.

SOFT PAPER: Advertising poster on which is printed dates, handbills, etc.

SOFT SPOT: Unusually good or favorable show town.

SOUP DEALER: Carnival knife rack operator.

SPEC or SPECTACLE or TOURNAMENT: A parade of all the performers, human and animal, around the hippodrome track early in the performance; the grand opening pageant; also ENTRY.

SPIELER: See *Opener.*

SPINDLE: A novelty gambling wheel.

SPINDLE MAN: One who operates the above.

SPOT: A location on the lot, or placing circus wagons.

SPRING: To release, or to go in one's kick for more money.

SPRUNG: To be released by the show's mender or adjuster.

SQUADRON: The first section of the circus train.

SQUASH: A kiss.

SQUARE A BEEF: To refund money, or to pay back an amount shortchanged.

SQUAWK: Complaint.

STAKE AND CHAIN: A wagon that is used solely to transport rigging, stakes, chains, bale-rings, flag halyards, hammers, etc. — generally the wagon where canvasmen hang around while the show is going on — the "headquarters" for workingmen, on off-duty hours; a "club" or "loafing place," if there are many such moments to "loaf."

STALL: To wait, to divert; kill time; or to hold off.

STAND: Any town that is played.

STAR BACKS: Reserved or more expensive seats (in older times, these seats had a star painted on each) — the opposite of "blues" or cheap seats.

STAUBS: Stakes driven into the ground to which are tied ropes for holding down or "guying" out tents.

STEER: To direct.

STICKS: Outside support.

STIFF: Legal attachment or writ.

STILL DATE: When the show is not billed.

STORES: Gambling games in the olden times — crooked outfit.

STRAWHOUSE: An overflowing house. Got its name from the habit of laying straw in front of the regular seats when a circus was sold out. Thus additional customers could be accommodated. (This practice was discontinued after a horse, racing around the arena in a Ben Hur spectacle, threw a shoe and injured a small boy, resulting in lawsuit. Fred Bailey Thompson recalls that the boy collected $25,000.)

STRAWING: Seating patrons on ground strewn with straw, when all seats are taken.

STRIPES: Tigers.

SUCKERS: Circus-goers; dumb ones; those who are gullible; unsophisticated persons.

SUNDAY RUN: A long distance.

SUNDAY SCHOOL SHOWS: Shows on which gambling games for the public have been prohibited; and "cleaned-up" or "clean" show as compared to grift (see *Grift*) shows.

SUPER: Extra person in act.

SWEEP ROPES: Ropes sewed into canvas tops, elliptical shape, or following the upper contours of entire tops, to hold it together better, and make it stronger.

SWEETENED AIR: Cotton candy.

SWELL PIPES: A good voice.

SWINDLE SHEET: Expense account.

TAG: Banner or streamer on front of top.

TAIL UP: Command to elephant to grab, with his trunk, the tail of the elephant in front of him in a parade or march.

TAKE A POWDER: To leave without giving notice; to slip away.

TAP: Price of admission.
THE ADVANCE: Contracting and billing agents who go a-head, some weeks in advance, contracting and advertising.
THE BIG ONE: The Ringling Bros. and Barnum & Bailey Circus, in contrast to all other circuses.
THE MARCH: Parade on streets.
THE TRICK: The entire show.
THE WAGON: Main ticket or bookkeeping wagon, where all accounts are kept. The main office wagon.
THREESHEET or THREESHEETING; Boasting or bragging.
THUMPER: A drummer.
TIP: A crowd.
TO HEEL: Leave without paying debt.
TOOK THE FENCE: To blow or leave with the receipts of a show or concession.
TOOTH TINKER: A dentist.
TOOT UP: To attract attention by means of a calliope.
TOP: Any tent. It is *BIG TOP* (main tent); *MENAGERIE TOP; KID TOP* (side show); *COOK TOP* (dining tent), etc.
TOP MOUNTER: In a human pyramid, the person on top.
TO SAP: To strike one with a cane, or club, even with fists.
TO SIDE WALL: To sneak in under the tent, which is known as the side wall.
TOSSING A BONE: Giving a buck to a down-and-outer.
TO SWING WITH: To take without owner's permission or consent.
TO THREE SHEET: To pose as a big show operator or what one is not.
TOURIST: A lazy workman; one joining the show for first time, to see all.
TOURNAMENT: See *Spectacle*.
TOWNERS: Those who are not connected with the show in any way; people residing in places where the show visits.
TRAINER: An animal handler or trainer of animals.
TRAP: Any trapeze.
TRAPPER: Groom for horses.
TRICK: An organization.
TURKEY: Losing, or a bad show.
TURNAWAY: Crowds turned away from performance, due to lack of room.
TURNING THE DUKE: To shortchange a person.

TWENTY-FOUR HOUR MAN: Agent or representative who travels one day ahead of the show to make sure that all arrangements are concluded, seeing that the feedman, bread and milk men, and all other supplymen will be on hand — and this is especially important in the event that storms or other causes require a change in "lots," unloading places, etc. — for "tomorrow" is too short a time to make changes, and TIME is the big factor in moving a huge enterprise like the modern large circus.

TWO DUKIE RUN: A long trip, or skip between towns, where cook would have to hand out two meals ready-fixed. (One dukie run, one meal.) See *Duke* or *Dukie*.

WAIT BROTHERS SHOW: Ringling Bros. and Barnum & Bailey combined Circuses. "Wait for the Big Show!" is the wording used on their posters.

WALK-AROUND: Clown routines in which the clowns walk completely around the hippodrome track, each performing his stunt a half-dozen times en route.

WALK AWAY: A person who forgets his change.

WARDROBE: All dressing or costumes for performers, elephant blankets for parade, etc.

WASHOUT: A failure.

WAXIE: A circus harnessmaker.

WEB SITTER: Ground man for aerialist.

WEDGED: Stranded, no funds.

WEED: To hand another person money.

WHISTLE TOOTER: Equestrian director or a ringmaster.

WHITE FACE: A clown.

WHITE WAGON: The main office on the circus lot.

WINDJAMMER: A hornplayer in the band, sometimes used in a general way for a musician in the band.

WING-DING BROAD: A girl or woman who faints in front of a geek (snake-eater) to draw customers into the tent.

WINTER QUARTERS: The permanent home of the circus, used when the show is not on the road.

WIRE WALKER: Telegraph delivery boy.

WITH IT: A trouper whose heart is with the show and his work — loyalty, attachment.

WORK: To stage a performance with animals.

WORK LIONS: A lion trainer.

X: An exclusive concession bought from the management.

ZULUS: Negroes who participate in "spec."
ZULU TICKETS: Credit slips given Negro workmen in "spec."

EXPLANATION OF THE WORD "NUT"

NUT: Total cost or expense of a show.

"We're off the nut" means that expenses have been cleared at the box office and the show is now "on velvet," in profit or in black ink.

"We've cracked our nut" means the same as above, but nut is used in a distorted sense. (A circus nut does not grow on a tree, but is a bolt off a wheel axle.)

"We made the nut" – we made expenses.

"We got our nut back and then some" – made expenses and some profit.

"We got our nut back" is probably the purest use of this idiom.

Samuel Gumpertz, who once bossed the Ringling Show, explained the use of the word "NUT" as:

"In the 1820's, the wagon shows moved through upper New York State as a sort of parade. The lead wagon was an elaborately decorated wagon or truck with huge wheels.

"To make sure that the circus paid its bills for food and feed, in every town the sheriff seized a nut off the axle of the lead wagon. If the sheriff thought the bill would be high, he would sequester all four nuts of the lead wagon and then nuts off other wagons. If bills were settled, he would return the nuts. They would be screwed on. The wagons could then travel to the next town."

On being asked why the show didn't carry several spare nuts and still clear out without paying bills, Gumpertz replied, "There were no standard machine-made wagons. Everything was hand-wrought. A nut on one of the big wagons cost about fifty dollars.

"Usually all the nuts were seized. If a circus had sufficient money to carry duplicate nuts, its credit would have been so good that no nuts would have been held. But there were no shows in those days with that kind of money."

Index

C

About Esse Forrester O'Brien

Esse Forrester O'Brien, a lifetime citizen of Waco, Texas, is the author of an imposing galaxy of books, among them, *Art and Artists of Texas, Elephant Tales* (dubbed one of the fifty "books of the year" by the Dallas Public Library and the American Institute of Graphic Arts), *Animal Tots,* which rated first place honors in the 1956 contest of the Texas Women's Press Association; and *Clowns of the Forest,* acclaimed by the Yellowstone Park Authorities. Her *Cinders to Sawdust* is the result of seven years spent in culling the annals of circusdom, both here and abroad. Much of her time was spent in Copenhagen, studying the Schumann Circus, reputed to be the oldest still-performing circus in the world.

An avid clubwoman, Mrs. O'Brien moves in many circles. She holds membership in the T.W.P.A., the N.W.P.A., the Texas Folklore Society, and the Texas Poetry Society. Readers can readily understand the esteem in which she is held by her associates in the Circus Fans' Association of America.

She is married to John L. O'Brien of Waco, and is justly proud of their son and their two fine grandchildren. In her leisure time, Mrs. O'Brien devotes hours to hunting, fishing, and bridge. She enjoys lecturing, especially in the field of Art, and has appeared before assemblies at some of the nation's leading universities.